IN THE SHADOW OF INVISIBILITY

Standing portrait of Ralph Ellison. Rockefeller Foundation. Photographs, Series 100. Courtesy of Rockefeller Archive Center.

IN THE SHADOW OF
INVISIBILITY

RALPH ELLISON AND THE PROMISE
OF AMERICAN DEMOCRACY

Sterling Lecater Bland Jr.

Louisiana State University Press   Baton Rouge

Published with the assistance of the V. Ray Cardozier Fund

Published by Louisiana State University Press
lsupress.org

Manufactured in the United States of America
First printing

Designer: Barbara Neely Bourgoyne
Typeface: Sina Nova
Printer and binder: Sheridan Books

Jacket illustration: *Seated portrait of Ralph Ellison*. Rockefeller Foundation.
Photographs, Series 100. Courtesy of Rockefeller Archive Center.

Library of Congress Cataloging-in-Publication Data
Names: Bland, Sterling Lecater, Jr., author.
Title: In the shadow of invisibility : Ralph Ellison and the promise
    of American democracy / Sterling Lecater Bland Jr.
Description: Baton Rouge : Louisiana State University Press, [2023] |
    Includes bibliographical references and index.
Identifiers: LCCN 2022017757 (print) | LCCN 2022017758 (ebook) |
    ISBN 978-0-8071-7850-8 (cloth) | ISBN 978-0-8071-7922-2 (pdf) |
    ISBN 978-0-8071-7921-5 (epub)
Subjects: LCSH: Ellison, Ralph—Criticism and interpretation. | Ellison, Ralph—
    Political and social views. | Politics and literature—United States—History—
    20th century. | United States—Race relations—History—20th century.
Classification: LCC PS3555.L625 Z593 2023 (print) | LCC PS3555.L625 (ebook) |
    DDC 818/.5409—dc23/eng/20220802
LC record available at https://lccn.loc.gov/2022017757
LC ebook record available at https://lccn.loc.gov/2022017758

For Wendy

[N]ot infrequently books speak of books:
It is as if they spoke among themselves.

UMBERTO ECO, *The Name of the Rose*

CONTENTS

List of Illustrations xi

Preface and Acknowledgments:
Going Where We Have Been, with a Difference xiii

Introduction: A Story Often Told, Seldom Heard 1

1. Invisible to Whom? The Uncreated Consciousness of the Race 31

2. The Golden Age, Time Past 85

3. Personal Vision, Living Culture: Translating Politics into Art 125

4. In the Shadow of Democracy 165

5. Negro-Americanizing the Novel 199

Notes 237

Bibliography 251

Index 265

ILLUSTRATIONS

Standing Portrait of Ralph Ellison frontispiece

Invisible Man: A Memorial to Ralph Ellison xxii

Communist Party demonstration in Union Square, May Day 193? 34

First graduating class of African American pilots in US Army Air Corps 41

Booker T. Washington 54

Gunnar and Alva Myrdal 57

Richard Wright in his study 65

Charlie Parker, Miles Davis, Tommy Potter, and Max Roach 92

Louis Armstrong 94

Duke Ellington at the Aquarium, New York 106

Frederick Douglass with facsimile signature 116

Dr. W. E. B. Du Bois 120

Ralph Waldo Emerson 167

Lifting the Veil of Ignorance 180

House in Washington, DC, where Lincoln died 201

African American demonstrators outside the White House 207

Boys in front of the Lincoln Memorial 216

PREFACE AND ACKNOWLEDGMENTS
Going Where We Have Been, with a Difference

We shall not cease from exploration
And the end of all our exploring
Will be to arrive where we started
And know the place for the first time.

    T. S. ELIOT, "Little Gidding," *Four Quartets*

OUR MASKS AND OUR SHIELDS

We must learn to wear our names within all the noise and confusion in which we find ourselves. . . . They must become our masks and our shields and the containers of all those values and traditions which we learn and/or imagine as being the meaning of our familial past.

    RALPH ELLISON, "Hidden Name and Complex Fate"

Books are written to be in conversation with the world in which they are composed. Eventually, they take on a life of their own. That is most certainly the case with this book, which I began writing without entirely knowing that I was doing so. Ellison's writing—*Invisible Man,* the essays, the long-anticipated second novel—has been in my life for as long as I can remember. I first encountered *Invisible Man* as a teenager and subsequently as an undergraduate and graduate student. I thought, as I struggled to untangle the novel's allusions, that Ellison had managed to do what no other novel at that point in my life had been able to do: reflect my experience in a novel about various rites of passage and rebirth while simultaneously connecting that experience to something far greater and more significant.

The novel is dated in some important ways, but it nevertheless led me to Ellison's essays and voluminous correspondence. At each stage of my life, as a reader, a teacher, and a writer, Ellison's writing has meant different things to me. In each instance, I felt—like his invisible narrator—as if I understood the writing, truly knew its meaning, for the first time. Or, as Senator Adam Sunraider in *Three Days before the Shooting…* says during a speech from the floor of the senate: "Where we shall go is where we have been; where we have been is where we shall go—but with a difference."[1]

Ellison worked in a cultural environment that unfolded far more quickly than his own thoughts about art and racial progress. We live in a time in which authors are regularly reconsidered in contemporary contexts. Readers hold them accountable for their responses to the questions and pressing debates of their time that we may now be able to see more clearly in the fullness of our time and perspective. Ellison, now as much as ever, deserves a reexamination of his work that acknowledges his achievements and recognizes his weaknesses. There is a great deal that is at stake in the effort to understand Ellison's ideas in this way. Ellison was a complicated figure. He clearly saw the need for the nation to end segregation. But he also offered little public support for the leaders of the movement for civil rights and seemed torn in his support of their objectives. He saw the need for racial justice though his vision of what that justice should look like remained ambiguous.

Ellison often remarked that the act of writing was about presenting a clarity of vision. But his writing, particularly the novel he left unfinished at the time of his death, reveals an ambiguity that even he found impossible to clarify and bring to fruition. His weaknesses were certainly not the source of his strength, but those weaknesses—real and perceived—are contained in every aspect of his intellectual and literary strengths. Ellison's personal, political, and artistic characteristics are the precise reason that readers need to continue to engage with his work. His literary and artistic achievements, as well as his shortcomings, reflect the complicated intersections of race, history, class, economics, politics, and art that have defined the nation and that continue to shape us all.

Ellison, in his life and legacy, has certainly been no stranger to criticism directed at him from a variety of corners. The grievances leveled against Ellison by biographers and critics alike accuse him of a comprehensive list of questionable behaviors and opinions. He has been characterized as being aloof. He was accused of being a Black intellectual overly enamored with his engagement with and relevance to white writers and intellectuals. Some saw him as being unsupportive of emerging Black writers and academics who were influenced by him and who often sought his approval. He was highly critical of Black nationalism and the art it produced and dismissive of most of the jazz (and the musicians who produced it) that emerged after the swing-era music to which he so often returned.

He was uninterested in feminism and the experiences of Black people who lived outside of the United States. He has been accused of being unwilling to acknowledge the Marxist radicalism from which he emerged to the point that he actively blurred the depth of his engagement with the Left. He has been questioned for being obsessive enough about myth, symbol, allusion, and writing that he attempted to write a novel more epic than the novel that won him the National Book Award. He privileged art and culture over political ideology. To the disapproval of some, he elevated aesthetic concerns over political concerns. He steadfastly dismissed the idea of acknowledging a "Black aesthetic" over a universal artistic aesthetic to which writers of all races and ethnicities were bound by their craft. His writing could contain sharp appraisal critique bordering on dismissal. It has been implied that his inability to complete work on his second novel was caused in some part by the distance he created between himself and Black America.

But for all the ways in which he has been critiqued, Ellison was a Black writer for whom the experiences of Black Americans enrich the nation and humanity. His writing reflected a lifelong inclination to recognize the consequential influences of Black culture in general and of Oklahoma and Oklahoma City in particular. In his essay "The World and the Jug," Ellison emphatically makes that very point: "[W]ho wills to be a Negro? *I* do! [*emphasis in original*]."[2] Ellison never tired of emphasizing Black humanity and its cultural production, even when that culture was produced under the weight of slavery. Black American culture was undeniably Black. But it was, at its very core, American. This was the self-evident truth, echoed in the Preamble to the Declaration of Independence, onto which the nation held. Black culture and American culture emanated from the same source. Louis Armstrong and T. S. Eliot, working at the same time from opposite ends of the Mississippi River, reflected for him that shared cultural source. It is hardly an exaggeration to say that *Invisible Man* and *Three Days before the Shooting...* speak to this invisible truth. Perhaps it is because Ellison was so insistent on being an American writer that he looked to models outside of Black culture and bristled at the idea that race should either limit or define his work. Richard Wright had been an early literary sponsor, but Ellison far more often cites Walt Whitman, Mark Twain, Stephen Crane, and Ernest Hemingway as his literary lineage.

In a well-known letter, John Keats writes of what he sees as Shakespeare's "Negative Capability." It was the achievement of being able to exist in a literary state of uncertainty in which truth and beauty can be rendered and appreciated from mystery and without the burden of reason.[3] That, for Keats, was the nature of true creative work. That was also the nature of Ellison's work. For Keats, true creative genius "has no self—it is everything and nothing—it has no character and enjoys light and shade; it lives in gusto, be it foul or fair, high or low, rich or poor, mean or elevated—it has as much delight in conceiving an Iago as an Imogen. What shocks the virtuous philosopher delights the camelion Poet [sic]."[4] The true artist embraced the artistic exercise of negative capability and personal principle without letting one overtake the other.

Although he spent a great deal of his writing life instructing readers on how to read his work (particularly *Invisible Man*), Ellison claimed to be disinterested in that every exercise. Ellison focused on imagination, the influence of the vernacular on Black American experience, a willingness to live in contradiction, and a tragicomic vision of the world. In lectures, interviews, and essays, Ellison regularly described the world he saw around him as being defined by "chaos" and "complexity" in which he saw his responsibility as a writer to exist in that "complexity" and distill form and meaning from the "chaos." The world may not necessarily be what it appears to be, and its meaning is certainly not absolute and unambiguous.

In setting out to write this book, I hoped in revisiting Ellison's literary and intellectual contributions to explore what Ellison's ideas tell us about race and America and what examining his work through the lens of our nation's history and often-invisible past tell us about Ralph Ellison. In the current environment of racial assessment, Ralph Ellison's work is as compelling as it has always been and is equally ready for serious reassessment. The democratic principle is a central element for Ellison. Its aspirations have grown increasingly urgent in the nation's ongoing conversation about race. Ellison's writing insightfully reveals the national ethos of race. His writing also reveals the disturbing qualities contained in that ethos.

Ellison could not escape race. Neither can we. The nation's response to race has too often been cruel and violent. What we think of Ralph Ellison and his writing tells us a great deal about what we think of ourselves and about how we reconcile our relationship to the ongoing confrontations of race, nation, and the past. Ellison's ideas are challenging and invigorating in the most Ellisonian of ways. This book is an act of literary explication. But the explication also contains an attempt to participate in the process of illuminating Ellison himself. Ellison's work is unambiguously tied to the sweep of American history yet, at its best, firmly rooted in the American present. Being American—particularly being Black in America—is complicated. He recognizes the complexity contained in the circumstances and experiences of being American that so many of his readers thought they already understood.

*   *   *

This book has been long in the making. Toni Morrison said that "if there's a book that you want to read, but it hasn't been written yet, then you must write it." This is my attempt to do just that. It is a pleasure to be able to acknowledge in these pages the love and generous support I received from so many, including some who are no longer here to be thanked. My concern in these words of thanks is a fear of omission. Much of this book came about with the help of family, friends, and colleagues who, knowingly or not, steered me away from bad ideas and toward good ones. Simply put, the completion of this book is the result of the contributions of a large, disparate community. I was also guided by an unknown number of silent cherubs. I gratefully recognize and acknowledge the influence of all.

This book is intended to be in conversation with recent texts that focus on Ralph Ellison and his work. This book is fortunate to be able to participate in this community of scholarship in its attempt to break new ground in its contribution to the growing body of Ellison scholarship and to make a case for Ellison's contributions to American intellectual thought. This time is an important and fruitful moment in the production of scholarship examining Ellison. This book is situated in this scholarship and provides new readings of the discussions about Ellison that occur at national and international conferences. I am particularly indebted to the attention that Adam Bradley, Marc C. Conner, Barbara Foley, Lawrence Jackson, Arnold Rampersad, and Timothy

Parrish have given to Ellison's work. I gratefully acknowledge the contributions that Barbara Bourgoyne, Catherine Kadair, and James Long at Louisiana State University Press as well as copyeditor Stan Ivester and indexer Jessica Freeman made to bring this volume from manuscript to fruition. Thanks also to the anonymous reviewer from the press. The suggestions I received were thoughtful, insightful, and certainly improved this book in ways big and small. It goes without saying that any remaining errors are mine alone.

I have been fortunate to have had the opportunity to share my work at the conferences of numerous organizations, including the American Studies Association, the Modern Language Association, Multiethnic Literature of the United States, Northeast Modern Language Association, and the Ralph Ellison Society.

My research was greatly facilitated by the support I received as Fulbright Visiting Research Chair in American Literature at McGill University, Faculty of Arts, Department of English, in Montreal. I am particularly grateful to the collegiality of Trevor Ponech and Allan Hepburn.

I gratefully acknowledge my colleagues at Rutgers University–Newark in the Department of English, the graduate program in American Studies, and the Department of African American and African Studies for their collegial encouragement and support. I am particularly thankful to Fran Bartkowski, Barbara Foley, Gabriel Miller, Clement Price, and Robert Snyder. Elizabeth Surles, an archivist at the Institute of Jazz Studies at Rutgers University, and Renee Pappous, an archivist at the Rockefeller Archive Center, provided invaluable assistance locating images. I gratefully acknowledge the help of reference librarians at Rutgers University, McGill University, Princeton University, and Seton Hall University. I especially welcome this opportunity to thank the many students with whom I have discussed these (and other) ideas. It is particularly gratifying for me to recognize that this book is the result of a mutually supportive conversation between teaching and scholarship.

The unwavering support of friends and family—immediate family and extended family—have helped propel this project forward and have provided welcome encouragement and diversion. Everyone should have the benefit of the same kind of love and support. My thanks go to you all. I am particularly grateful for the love of my parents, Sterling Bland Sr. and Ula Bland, and my maternal grandmother, Freddie Belk, for the depth of their love. I am sorry that they are not here to accept my heartfelt gratitude and acknowledgment of all that they continue to mean to me.

Wendy Donat has lived with this book for almost as long as I. My deepest thanks are reserved for her love and support.

IN THE SHADOW OF INVISIBILITY

Invisible Man: A Memorial to Ralph Ellison. Sculptor Elizabeth Catlett, 2003. Riverside Park at 150th Street, New York City. Bronze and granite. Photograph by author.

INTRODUCTION

A STORY OFTEN TOLD, SELDOM HEARD

Well, there is one thing that you have to admit. And that is, dealing with Ralph Ellison is no easy matter. It is no easy task to fully characterize the nature of Ellison's life and work.

    LARRY NEAL, "Ellison's Zoot Suit"

THE WAY IT IS: AN INITIATION RITE

[W]e don't solve problems of history by running away from them.

    RALPH ELLISON, "A Very Stern Discipline"

Who has better wrestled with the question of how race is at the foundation of the American experiment and how American democracy is inexorably connected to a meaningful engagement with race than Ralph Waldo Ellison? How does Ellison's work consider the ways national culture gets formed? Scholarship on Ellison often seems to take this basic question for granted. Ellison's multi-voiced strategies for addressing this question anticipate the central theme of the chapters that follow. The question of how Ellison situates the democratic impulse in the larger fabric of American culture is essential to this consideration of national culture, its formation, and its implications. There is simply no way to define and isolate American experience that does not acknowledge the cultural appropriation that pluralizes and de-essentializes American experience in the first place.

    The question that Ellison posed for the thinkers with whom his work engaged during his time, as well as those who consider his work now, is why has Ellison seemed so detached from other influential Black thinkers, particularly when weighed in relation to contemporaries like Frantz Fanon and James Baldwin, whose work, broadly speaking, considered many of the same kinds of ideas? Ellison's work does not reflect the socially oriented styles of writers like James Baldwin, Richard Wright, or Langston Hughes. As chapter 3 discusses, Larry Neal, a founding voice of the Black Arts movement, initially dismissed Ellison for ignoring race and instead focusing on integration rather than separation in American politics. But Neal eventually backtracked and recognized the significance of Ellison's insistence on Black vernacular. For Ellison, Black nationalism reductively pitted race against politics in ways that separated Black people from the crucial role of participating in the pluralistic realities of the democratic process. The national experience was already blackened by a presence that had been assimilated into the nation long before white people even recognized either its origins or its implications. Conversely, why have so many white readers been reluctant to consider the influence of Black experiences in America on Ellison's thinking and work? Simply put, why is Ellison's position in American thought as conspicuously singular as it is? This book reconsiders Ellison's relevance in these terms.

This book looks at these ideas through the lenses of the leftist political ideologies that Ellison encountered in the 1930s and 1960s, sociology, the cultural contributions of Black vernacular culture, Ralph Waldo Emerson, and Ellison's circuitous attempts to tackle the subject in his unfinished second novel. To be clear, the focus on what seems to be Ellison's trajectory through these ideas is through the framework that Ellison himself laid out in his fiction, his essays, his interviews, and his correspondence. Ellison was certainly not only in conversation with himself. But he far too often remains invisible to everyone but the scholars who continue to study his work and the implications of his thought. Understanding Ellison through the lens of how national culture is formed matters a great deal in reconciling how we see Ellison as an influential, albeit anomalous and often isolated, thinker of and about the nation. Thinking about Ellison in these ways has profound implications for considering how the nation's primary questions recirculate in ways that cannot be reduced beyond their blackest elements.

Ellison has so often been misunderstood because readers have failed to consider the corrective effects of considering him in the fullness of race, nation, and culture contained in the published work that sits on our shelves and that is regularly taught and discussed and the novel that remained unpublished at the time of his death. If *Invisible Man* can be seen as summing up the tensions of Jim Crow America, the second novel explicitly addresses the question of how to reconcile what came before the end of Jim Crow with that which has come after. The symmetry should not be lost: Ellison's view of the contemporary nation returns us to its beginning.

This book is an attempt to recover and reconstruct the lineage of Ellison's intellectual process of deracializing the nation's culture and to argue for the importance of its radical pluralism as a fundamental component of the nation's cultural currency. Universalism, certainly the kind that appears at the conclusion of the epilogue to *Invisible Man,* has for much of the nation's history been the sole providence of white men. One consequence for this book is to reconsider the insistence of some readers that all Black artistic production is, by its very definition, political. This was a central entanglement of Ellison's career.

This is why Ellison matters: What Ellison produced in *Invisible Man* and his other writing was nothing less than a dynamic embodiment of the intersection of race and culture in the formation of America's national culture. Existing literature on Ellison often coalesces around the reading of *Invisible Man,* but the construction of Ellison's thought is far more expansive. His writing and intellectual approach reflected a tragicomic symbol and style that became something far greater than the sum of its parts. In the appreciation entitled "The Achievement of Ralph Ellison," published soon after Ellison died, James Tuttleton offers the opinion that Ellison's combination of aesthetic concerns and thematic richness engaged and extended many of the ideas contained in writers broadly associated with the New Negro movement like Jessie Redmon Fauset, Nella Larsen, Jean Toomer, Walter White, and Zora Neale Hurston. When read in relation to the work of his contemporaries in the 1930s and 1940s like Richard Wright and William Attaway, Tuttleton sees in Ellison's work a depth of intellectualism and aesthetic experimentalism that was unmatched in the ways he reflected the experiences and advocated for the cultural contributions Black Americans made to the nation. In *Invisible Man,* Ellison produced a novel that largely eclipsed much of the writing of Black contemporaries like James Baldwin, Amiri Baraka, and John A. Williams. But these examples of Ellison's ability to engage Black American experiences in the formation of national culture should not consign him to the literary segregation that so many Black writers suffered. Tuttleton had developed a working relationship with Ellison when Tuttleton chaired the Department of English at New York University during the time of Ellison's Schweitzer Professorship.[1] What he leaves unsaid in his assessment is that

Ellison became a writer in mid-twentieth-century America when race emphatically determined the limitations that Black writers experienced in terms of subject and audience. But even with this constraint, Ellison's work, in its aspiration, reception, and influence, also outshone for Tuttleton the writing of Ellison's white contemporaries.

Ellison grew up in Oklahoma City in the first third of the twentieth century at a time when the former territories represented a crossroads of racial and cultural elements. His apprenticeship as a writer in mid-twentieth-century America was shaped by his attempts to shape himself and his writing against the influences of poverty, racism, radical ideology, Black nationalism, and the demands of his audience. Much of this may seem self-evident. What is considerably less self-evident is that while his novel speaks, on the lower frequencies and otherwise, for Americans Black and white, Ellison found himself in a position that was profoundly, and often uncomfortably, singular and isolated. Ellison's work responds to the limitations he saw contained in the legacy of the New Negro movement and to the restrictions he saw encoded in the forms of literary Naturalism and Black protest fiction to which Black writers were so often consigned. Far more often, Ellison cited the legacy of white writers and intellectuals like Herman Melville, Ralph Waldo Emerson, Mark Twain, and Stephen Crane. These are the writers who meant the most to him as a writer consciously pursuing art rather than as a writer pursuing Black art.

In "Justice for Ralph Ellison," which appeared in the *New Yorker* to celebrate the sixtieth anniversary of the publication of *Invisible Man,* David Denby points to Ellison's passionate reading habits as helping him internalize his chosen literary past and break new ground as a writer and intellectual willing and able to inject a tragicomic perspective that effortlessly moved between realism, surrealism, absurdism, formal strategies, and vernacular improvisations. Denby is correct in saying that Ellison's attraction to literary modernism certainly placed him in the lineage of James Joyce, T. S. Eliot, and William Faulkner.[2] But Ellison's vision was far more expansive than that lineage suggests. He also saw himself in conversation with Fyodor Dostoevsky and André Malraux.

Though it is not commonly framed in this way, Ellison's uneasiness with the way Black culture was understood throughout American culture reflects his deeper interest in the ways the cultural production of every race filters into and becomes absorbed by mainstream American culture. He is an anomaly in part because of his insistence in citing these influences. But he is also isolated and anomalous in his unwillingness to depart from his own closely held thoughts about the cultural meaning of the relationship of Black vernacular culture to American culture.

Ellison was clearly drawn to the Left at a formative moment of his development. But he came to see in radical ideology the danger of Black culture becoming coopted in support of an ideology primary intent on advancing its own political agenda. To Ellison's way of thinking, his friend Richard Wright had been used by the Left before becoming disenchanted with the ideology and the narrow role to which he became consigned. Ellison resisted that kind of manipulation. The same sense of isolation as a widely recognized American thinker became true after the publication of *Invisible Man* and the nation's movement to and through desegregation. Ellison saw the danger of Black people becoming reduced simultaneously by Black people and white liberals alike to a stereotype that emphasized qualities of racial victimization and that deemphasized the basic, fundamental value of Black humanity. The same could be said of Ellison's dismissal of 1960s Black nationalism, which aligned itself closely with a Pan-African reading of Marxist ideology that reduced Black experiences solely to their political usefulness at the expense of a diversity of Black cultural wholeness and cultural contribution. Too often, for Ellison, Black people were relegated by both white people and Black people to the periphery of their own experience by ideologies intent on speaking for a Black culture that was so diverse that it could only be coopted by way of reductively harmful stereotyping.

But that is not the end of the matter. All of this speaks to the reasons for recognizing Ellison as an important American intellectual and as an important Black intellectual. But part of the difficulty in recognizing Ellison in these terms is also recognizing that Ellison does not fit comfortably in either of these categories. He occupies a particularly unconventional position when these categories are situated within a broader ideology. Leftist ideology, racial ideology, and sociological ideology were all, in Ellison's assessment, overly engaged with speaking for stereotyped representations of Black Americans to support their ideology rather than fully acknowledging the depth and diversity of the very culture for which they claimed to speak.

Timothy Parrish captures Ellison's significance in *Ralph Ellison and the Genius of America* when he observes that "Ellison, within his lifetime, became the first 'canonical' black *American* author."[3] This is something that eluded other American writers who are now closely associated with the American canon like Edgar Allan Poe, Henry David Thoreau, Herman Melville, Emily Dickinson, Kate Chopin, and F. Scott Fitzgerald. This was particularly true for Black writers like Ellison's friend Richard Wright, who was certainly recognized while alive but whose work became canonical after his death, and Zora Neale Hurston, whose work was out of print in the last decades of her life. A significant part of that process of canonization had to do with Ellison's expansive consideration of how the nation's culture was formed to begin with, how the nation responded after Reconstruction, and how the nation would respond to its second Reconstruction, particularly after the Supreme Court handed down its landmark decision on *Brown v. the Board of Education of Topeka, Kansas,* and the passing of the Civil Rights Act of 1964 and the Voting Rights Act of 1965. It is also worth noting, as John Wright does in *Shadowing Ralph Ellison,* that "when Modern Library's 1998 panel of scholars and critics created dual lists of the twentieth century's greatest one hundred English-language novels and greatest one hundred works of nonfiction, Ralph Ellison stood in equipoised singularity, four years after his death, as the only writer to appear on both lists."[4]

In every person's life, there is an inflection point that casts a shadow on all that comes before and all that follows. At that point, the trajectory of all things that follow is changed and all things that have come before are understood differently. For Ralph Ellison, that point of inflection came when he published *Invisible Man* in March 1952 at the age of thirty-nine. The novel and the critical and popular response it received altered the ways we read Ellison's life leading up to and following its publication. The vast body of work that Ellison produced over the course of his lifetime is often considered in the broad shadow the novel cast on Ellison's subsequent public, intellectual, and creative activities. *Invisible Man* was not Ralph Ellison's first publication, nor was it his last. It is, however, the one through which most readers orient their understanding of a body of writing that includes leftist essays, short stories, an extensive collection of interviews and essays produced throughout his life and published as *Shadow and Act* (1964) and *Going to the Territory* (1986), and the publication of eight excerpts released over a period of more than fifteen years that were drawn from the second novel that Ellison worked on throughout the second half of his life. Speculation about the second novel began almost immediately after the publication of his first and continued even after his death on April 16, 1994. This is certainly understandable given the influence his first novel exerted on generations of readers and writers. Posthumously, the Ellison literary estate has published *Juneteenth* (1999), a selected collection of correspondence between Ralph Ellison and his good friend and fellow writer Albert Murray entitled *Trading Twelves* (2000), a scholar's version of the unpublished second novel entitled *Three Days before the Shooting…* (2010), and a selected gathering of his voluminous correspondence.

Invisible Man is undeniably his signature literary achievement. But it is certainly not his sole literary achievement. Although his reputation is often illuminated singularly by the intense light of scrutiny shone by the novel, his other work merits attention to understand the ways Ellison saw the world and how his view of the world so often contributes to the ways contemporary readers and writers understand and engage with the world. After its publication, *Invisible Man* became a kind of engulfing literary shadow. Its immense literary and cultural authority surrounded Ralph Ellison and influenced all conversations about him and his work. The impressions it created continued long after conversations about those impressions were complete. This remained the case throughout his life. The novel gave Ellison entrée to a world of ideas about race, identity, democracy, writing. Its success and insight on inter- and intra-cultural interactions became a primary credential for elevating Ellison from journeyman writer to Black public intellectual. The novel also elevated to visibility the kind of Black public intellectual that Ellison came to embody. Ellison became a primary interpreter and conservator of how the novel—and, by extension, the nation's attitudes about race relations—should be read and understood.

Nothing escapes history. The present cannot escape its past. In so many areas of his writing, Ralph Ellison often returned to several related ideas: America's complexity, personal and national identity (and the chaotic consequences of evading one's identity), cultural responsibility, skepticism, and the American intellectual tradition. The focus of this book is to look at the evolution of Ellison's thought as part of a process that was connected to memory, the past, and their deeply tangled relationship to American society. In 1965,

Ellison granted an interview to three emerging Black American writers: James Thompson, Lennox Raphael, and Steve Cannon. Ellison subsequently revised that interview from the original recordings and published the conversation in the March 1967 edition of *Harper's Magazine*. He later published the piece in *Going to the Territory* (1986). In the final question of the interview, they asked him to provide advice to an eighteen-year-old who aspires to become a serious writer. Ellison concludes his advice by emphasizing the importance of society's influence:

> I suppose what I'm saying is that this young writer should have a working model of society and of our national characteristics present within his mind. The problem of enriching that model and keeping it up-to-date is one of the greatest challenges of the Negro writer, who is, by definition, cut off from firsthand contact with large areas of that society—especially from those centers where power is translated into ideas, manners, and values. Nevertheless, this can be an advantage, because in this country no writer should take anything for granted, but must use his imagination to question and penetrate the façade of things.[5]

The emphasis Ellison places upon keeping the view of society current is, in some ways, the very thing that makes his protracted composition of the second novel so understandable. It is Ellison's evolving thoughts about literature and society that the present book tries to explore. Ellison was certainly no essentialist when it came to his conceptions of all that contributed to American identity, which for Ellison functioned around change. Readers should keep that realization in mind when considering the temporal and thematic scope of his fiction and essays. His work wrestles with large ideas and reflects the ways Ellison's own thoughts changed over the course of his writing life.

In the introduction to *Ralph Ellison and the Raft of Hope,* Lucas Morel focuses on *Invisible Man* to make the case that the novel speaks to the possibility of "political hope" by depicting "what the narrator is able to learn and teach through his own journey *up* the river to freedom and enlightenment" and by "what the novel as a novel conveys about Ellison's demonstration of the freedom and possibilities available to black Americans, white Americans, and human beings, simply, when faced with barriers to their development as individuals."[6] This is certainly an accurate assessment of Ellison's recognition of the complicated space that existed between individuals and democracy.

Morel's analysis suggests a framework for considering Ellison's significance beyond the confines of *Invisible Man*. More importantly, Morel implicitly raises the question of the implications of how Ellison might be considered in relation to the formation of national culture.

Several of the most influential treatments of Ellison focus intently on politics rather than on Ellison's reading of the formation of the nation's culture. In *Ralph Ellison and the Politics of the Novel,* for example, H. William Rice recognizes Ellison as a novelist but ultimately chastises Ellison for not achieving his own aspirations, which Rice sees as failing to provide the kind of national identity that Ellison demanded of the nation's other great writers. Although Rice's emphasis on evaluating Ellison's success as a political thinker is undermined by his relative inattention to close readings of Ellison's writing, he implicitly suggests the need to reassess the conclusion that consigns Ellison to the role of political "failure."

In *Heroism and the Black Intellectual,* Jerry Gafio Watts makes the provocative argument that he wants "to bring politics back into the discussion of Ellison and to do so without subjecting him to dogmatic ideological formulations."[7] In doing so, Watts asserts that "The Ellisonian concept of American culture, though easy to trace historically and to document empirically, was undoubtedly at times difficult to defend politically in a nation in which racial politics has seldom been as complex or fluid as its cultural identity."[8] Watts uses Ellison as a straw man for his critique that Ellison's deepest failure was his inability to acknowledge the limitations placed on Black Americans. Watts's critique ultimately combines art and politics when he paints Ellison as being an artistic failure that Watts describes as being the "elitism of heroic individualism." Unlike Arnold Rampersad's biography of Ellison, which saw a level of failure in Ellison's inability to complete his second novel, Watts draws that line of failure much earlier when he writes, "Whether or not Ellison ever publishes a stellar second or third novel, his forty-year effort to do so seems to indicate a creative failure of sorts" that may be tied to Ellison's desire "to prove himself in the eyes of white writers or the Western literati at large. The task of completing a writing project becomes increasingly difficult to the degree that Ellison inflates the greatness of those master white writers with whom he competes."[9]

In short, in claiming to know Ellison's motives, Watts accuses Ellison of being a Black intellectual who cannot adequately confront what Watts sees as an intrinsic sense of inferiority. He faults Ellison for not taking a more active role in the movement for civil rights, for not speaking out forcefully against the war in Vietnam, for not being Marxist, for not being a true public intellectual, and for being ungenerous with his time, particularly in comparison to Langston Hughes.[10] All of this "allows Ellison to write extensively about the most commonplace occurrences in his life and endow them with extreme significance and mythic proportions."[11] But all of this looks at Ellison through a lens so narrow that it fails accurately to take into account Ellison's place in and contributions to American intellectual thought. Watts is not a biographer, does not reveal much about Ellison's art, and does not trace Ellison's intellectual development in any systematic way. Watts reserves his deepest dislike for Ellison—or what he sees Ellison as signifying—for the final footnote of the volume, when he writes: "In some respects, Ellison's disrespect and trivialization of those who have actually struggled against tyranny as opposed to those, like himself, who merely write about the human desire for freedom, is myopic, selfish, and thoroughly disgusting."[12]

In *Wrestling with the Left,* Barbara Foley scrupulously reconstructs Ellison's composition of *Invisible Man* in the context of Ellison's involvement with, and subsequent disassociation from, radicalism. Specifically, Foley recognizes the influence of radical ideology on the novel's composition and warns scholars to avoid reading the novel through the anti-communist rhetoric that emerged during the Cold War and that was embraced by Ellison as he erased his radical origins. By untangling the relationship between Ellison's opinion of the Communist Party USA and his opinion of radical ideology, Foley argues that Ellison's movement right was a reflection of the inability of the Left to stay on course."[13] All of this seems to distill Ellison, particularly in the years during the composition of *Invisible Man,* to an essentialized, politicized version that reads Ellison from radicalism to the publication of *Invisible Man* in ways that privilege political influences over the cultural influences that also had their roots in the years before the publication of the novel.

For a great deal of his writing career, Ellison was consumed with thoughts about the form of the novel and the role of the novelist. This is particularly true after the publication of *Invisible Man*. He seemed to love the aesthetic and social possibilities of the novel as much as he distrusted the suitability of its form. Ellison's conception of the novel simultaneously looks backward to literary modernism and forward to more experimental novelistic explorations that followed. As early as 1941 in his essay "Richard Wright and Negro Fiction," Ellison edited from the essay an opinion that links the roles of the novelist to morality and the novel itself to democracy as securely as any other area of his subsequent commentary: "The future of democracy is seen wraped [sic] up in the development of the Negro."[14] It is not clear why Ellison chose here to remove this sentence from the draft, but the idea is one to which he returned in essays, lectures, *Invisible Man,* and *Three Days before the Shooting*.... The development of Black subjectivity is central to the ways Ellison situates the democratic impulse in the larger fabric of American culture. It is worth examining the moral component embedded in the most intricate aspects of how democracy functioned in America's past and how it continued to function in mid-twentieth-century America. His focus illuminates the ways democracy is fragile and requires constant attention to be sustained in even the most robust republic. His work emphasizes the disparity between the country Americans have always been told the United States is and the country in which they actually live.

But the knife of subjectivity and identity cuts both ways. While Black Americans sought to identify and locate themselves in a mainstream culture largely blind to Black presence and contribution, by 1970 Ellison had also recognized larger national insecurities about cultural identity: "On this level [popular culture], the melting pot did indeed melt, creating such deceptive metamorphosis and blending of identities, values, and lifestyles that most American whites are culturally part Negro American without ever realizing it."[15] By extension, Ellison saw most Black Americans as culturally being part white. Simply put, there is no way to define and isolate American experience that does not acknowledge the cultural appropriation that pluralizes and de-essentializes American experience in the first place. Ellison's biographers and numerous commentaries on his fiction and essays have made the point that the circumstances of Ellison's own lived experience create for him a unique lens through which to examine the ideas that animate so much of his writing. He was, after all, born and lived the first half of his life in a nation in which racial segregation defined all racial and institutional interactions.

In his introduction to *The Cambridge Companion to Ralph Ellison,* Ross Posnock points to Ellison's recognition of the cultural "appropriation game" in which groups and individuals in the nation commonly take from one another in ways that turn them into Americans. As Posnock argues, there is neither purity nor "Adamic innocence" in the nation's process of cultural appropriation and integration.[16] What he says decisively points to Lucas Morel's thoughts about the challenges of American inclusion that he proposes in his essay "In a Strange Country." Morel's argument emphatically speaks to the challenges of the color line on the ways "the 'land of the free' reposed a duty upon each member of that land to be 'brave' in their understanding and effort to be at home in America."[17] In a segregated nation, the distortion of Black individuality was a strategy used to deflect outside scrutiny. The distortion of the individuality of Black people was a response to a social and political system that equated being white with being American. The social and political system imposed social immobility. Its very presence imposes rigidly oppositional, mutually exclusive categories like white and Black, innocent and guilty, or reality and illusion that can be recognized as ways of differentiating one group from another and repressing the ambitions of Black Americans who wished to attain their highest aspirations.

In *Talking to Strangers,* Danielle Allen poses a question about collective autobiography to consider national habits and aspirations. In ways that echo Ellison, Allen acknowledges that "It's not as if all those currently in the United States have exactly the same experiences, or the same heritage or cultural horizons." Allen's work, which is firmly grounded in Ralph Ellison's central belief that sacrifice is a fundamental component of democracy, makes the point that citizens may have conflicting self-interests within the broader "contours of our collective political imagination."[18] This is certainly one of the struggles that Ellison's narrator faces most directly throughout *Invisible Man.* But Ellison also recognized the ways the social immobility imposed by segregation also functioned on the page: "Perhaps the most insidious and least understood form of segregation is that of the word.... For if the word has the potency to revive and make us free, it has also the power to blind, imprison and destroy."[19]

The article "Awakening to Race" by Jack Turner makes the argument that democratic individuality (particularly its Emersonian ideal) "plays an increasingly large role in contemporary political theory" and that "Ellison's contribution is significant—for it revises that conception to make it more fully adequate to the challenge of racial justice."[20] While his project is specifically an attempt to enlarge the idea of democratic individuality beyond the boundaries of whiteness, his focus on Ellison's presence by way of *Invisible Man* in that project is noteworthy. As chapter 4 discusses, Ellison's critique of democratic individuality was more than simply arguing against race consciousness. Instead, Ellison firmly turns *Invisible Man* into a race-conscious novel that recognizes the Black presence in the constitution of normative whiteness in the United States as a fundamental component of individual and collective national identities. Self-creation is illusory and virtually impossible to anyone whose self-reliant aspirations ignore the realities of American society and racialized experience. But Ellison's invisible narrator is not entirely a victim of the society that his experiences incriminate. He is thoroughly complicit in the very events and experiences that ultimately invoke his awareness of his invisibility and drive him to the underground apartment where he works so diligently to write his experiences. This is an illustration of Ellison's primary strategy of invoking and reworking the individual responsibilities contained in the tradition of American intellectualism in which much of his thought is firmly grounded.

Ellison's namesake, Ralph Waldo Emerson, made a similar remark in the Phi Beta Kappa address that he delivered at Harvard University in 1837, which he entitled "The American Scholar." As he notes, "The office of the scholar is to cheer, to raise, and to guide men by showing them facts amidst appearances. He plies the slow, unhonored, and unpaid task of observation." Ralph Ellison's invisible narrator has become the embodiment of a kind of Emersonian scholar who has somehow reconciled his own individual awareness of self with the democratic social context in which that self exists. College, where he was first introduced to Emersonian thought, is a place where he is most emphatically discouraged from using his education to craft his own reality in favor of accepting the illusory aspirations of the founder of the college. Society, at college and after his departure from college, fails to see and acknowledge him. But the narrator himself also fails to recognize and make visible those qualities that lift him toward wholeness and subjectivity. The narrator—invisible and obscured through much of the novel—reveals moral imperatives that have also been obscured and forgotten.

A TALL TALE TOLD BY INATTENTIVE IDEALISTS

That which we do is what we are. That which we remember is, more often than not, that which we would like to have been, or that which we hope to be. Thus our memory and our identity are ever at odds, our history ever a tall tale told by inattentive idealists.

RALPH ELLISON, "The Golden Age, Time Past"

Rather than seeking either to romanticize Ellison's artistic and intellectual contributions or to malign the nature and extent of his work, the purpose here is to provide an intellectual portrait that places his work in conversation with a broader intellectual framework of American social movement and cultural history. The broad outlines of Ellison's life are well-known. He was born in Oklahoma in 1913, six years after the former "Indian Territory" became the nation's forty-sixth state. He grew up in Oklahoma, which itself was navigating and trying to come to terms with its own assimilationist self-invention narrative. It arose from the diverse geographical and cultural areas acquired during the Louisiana Purchase in 1803 and after the Mexican-American War and merged into the nation's forty-sixth state in 1907 during Theodore Roosevelt's presidency. After the death of his father during an accident when he was delivering ice, Ellison's family descended into poverty that included jobs for Ellison in which he earned money by shining shoes, busing tables, and working in an Oklahoma City hotel. Ellison attended the Tuskegee Institute, which was founded on Booker T. Washington's accommodationist philosophy. Washington's thinking advocated a strategy of Black advancement that emphasized the development of practical skills (focusing on the trades) and self-reliance.

Ellison studied music in the years before jazz moved from being a collective art form often performed by large swing ensembles that merged blues-based art and popular culture. The swing music and the musicians that Ellison admired in his youth ultimately gave way to bebop, which replaced swing music's danceability with harmonic complexity, altered chords, and individual virtuosity and improvisation. Ellison first pursued music at the Tuskegee Institute in Alabama before departing for New York in the summer of 1936 without having either received his degree or embarking on the career in music to which he aspired. His trajectory south to Alabama from the former territories and eventually north to Harlem reflects the movement from South to North undertaken by countless Black Americans before the Civil War and by millions more who later migrated out of the South during the end of the nineteenth century and the first half of the twentieth century.

In Harlem, Ellison saw what he believed to be the inadequate responses of Black leadership to poverty, unemployment, and overcrowding. He also saw the influence of the radical Left, with whom he was associated for a period, and the effects of Black nationalist ideology. His Depression-era work initially included the kind of subsistence jobs that he had held in Oklahoma City. While he had relatively few publications during the early portion of this apprentice period, his talents were certainly recognized and encouraged by Alain Locke, Langston Hughes, and Richard Wright. Although there has been considerable discussion by Ellison and others about the extent of Wright's contribution to his political outlook and literary aspirations, it is abundantly clear that Ellison benefited from his interactions with Wright and from reading the manuscript for *Native Son* as Wright composed it.

Barbara Foley's refusal in *Wrestling with the Left* to accept at face value Ellison's insistence of radical marginality in the narrative he constructed after the publication of *Invisible Man* reflects a level of disappointment that, in some ways, echoes the ways Ellison was chastised by H. William Rice in *Ralph Ellison and the Politics of the Novel*. In place of Rice's blanket dismissal of Ellison's work—Rice writes, for example, early in his volume, that "It is hard not to attach these seemingly incomplete political gestures to Ellison himself, in particular his incomplete novel"—Foley provides a deeply researched appraisal of Ellison that calls into question the accepted narrative of his engagement with the Left, often put forth by Ellison himself in his responses to questions about how to read the novel and how to apply that reading to American culture. While it is difficult to accept Rice's complete rejection of Ellison's writing and politics, Foley's revision of the accepted narrative is illuminating. And yet, Ellison is much more than the sum of his political parts.

Though Ellison's association with radical politics was undeniable in his work for *Daily Worker, New Challenge, Negro Quarterly,* and *New Masses,* the depth of his commitment to radicalism is a bit more ambiguous. Ellison most certainly agreed with the ways the Left saw Black Americans as a leading edge of revolutionary social and political change. Ellison seems to have remained sympathetic to the radical agenda even after August 23, 1939, when Germany and the Soviet Union signed the Molotov-Ribbentrop Nonaggression Pact that effectively changed the political landscape of Eastern Europe. He remained sympathetic, to some extent, as the Communist Party USA abruptly changed its stance and began to advocate what many saw as nothing less than an abandonment of its antiracist, working-class objectives. In 1942, when *New Masses* published an issue dedicated to examining the relationship between race and the war effort, entitled "The Negro and Victory," Ellison seems to align himself squarely with the assertion made by the Communist Party USA that race should be sublimated to defeating fascism.

In "The Way It Is," originally published in *New Masses,* October 20, 1942, and subsequently included in *Shadow and Act,* Ellison writes of Black Americans that "Our desire to rid the world of fascism the most burning, and the obstacles placed in our way the most frustrating. Our need to see the war as a struggle between democracy and fascism the most intense, and our temptation to interpret it as a 'color' war the most compelling."[21] The paradox that he recognizes is that Black Americans daily negotiated the oppressive presence of Jim Crow segregation even as they were urgently asked to support the war effort against Axis fascism. Ellison soon afterward stopped contributing to Communist Party USA publications under his own name, though in his role as managing editor at *Negro Quarterly,* he encouraged Black Americans in a "Statement of Policy" editorial that appeared in the first edition of *Negro Quarterly,* published in spring 1942, fully to participate in the adversities of war now with the possibility of racial equality that would subsequently come from victory later: "Because our country is now engaged in an all-out war with the Axis forces, the full capacity of its man power must be thrown into the battle in order to insure full victory. This can be done more effectively when the barriers of Jim Crow in the Army, Navy, Air Force, and other national defense bodies are removed. Negroes must share equally in the hardship of war, as well as in the victory that is to come."[22] Abner W. Berry, who had begun organizing for the Communist Party USA in 1934 before joining the Harlem edition of the *Daily Worker* in 1942, published a piece announcing the publication of *Negro Quarterly* and emphasizing its editorial independence. Berry's welcome notice was published in the *Daily Worker* on September 15, 1942, under the title "The Negro Quarterly: A Vigorous Journal." The "Statement of Policy" contained in *Negro Quarterly* also emphasizes its editorial independence, but the comments it contains largely echo the position on the war held by the Communist Party USA. The *Negro Quarterly* ultimately published just four issues. After Germany invaded the Soviet Union, the Communist Party USA quickly pivoted in support of the war effort. Ellison is clearly torn between support for the revised agenda of the Communist Party USA and his belief that the Left had turned its back on the issues of racial justice that had been so much a part of how the Left thought of the wage earners who lacked capital, property, and whose only tool for survival was their labor.

In his biography *Ralph Ellison,* Lawrence Jackson paints a picture of Ellison's early life that looks at his pre–*Invisible Man* experiences—the death of his father when Ellison was a child, his poverty, his interests in music, his education at Tuskegee Institute, Harlem radicalism and his friendships with Langston Hughes and Richard Wright, and his critical development while working as an assistant editor for *Negro Quarterly* among them—as meaningful components of a cohesive whole. In this first act of his intellectual and artistic life, Ellison's association with and eventual withdrawal from radical politics should be weighed against its lasting contributions to his thinking about race, history, and the nation. In *Invisible Man,* the narrator recognizes that the Brotherhood, Ellison's imaginative re-creation of the radical Left, has given him an education as relevant as the education he left behind at college and the education he received from his dying grandfather. It provided employment when the invisible narrator first arrived in Harlem and was unable to find work. The Left gave him a system for thinking that allowed him to understand his own invisibility and, by extension, the invisible presence of Black Americans referenced in the nation's founding documents and responsible for building and sustaining the nation. Ellison recognized that the nation had in all respects been built by Black Americans from materials that were subsequently appropriated. Those contributions were vitally undeniable for those willing and able to see them, even in the face of longstanding institutional repression.

In *Invisible Man,* Ellison's awareness of the inseparability of black and white was clear in his description of the Liberty Paint factory that produces "the purest white [paint] that can be found." The paint is so white that the narrator's supervisor in the factory brags, in an overt reference to the founders of the nation, that it is "as white as George Washington's Sunday-go-to-meetin' wig," as "sound as the all-mighty dollar!" and so complete in its formulation that it can "cover just about anything."[23] But the paint can only achieve the level of whiteness it does with the addition of ten drops of a substance that makes the white whiter even as the black disappears. Deep in the factory's basement is a Black engineer named Lucius Brockway, invisible to others, who is the only person who truly knows how the factory works. In essays, public speeches, and college lectures for the remainder of his professional life, Ellison drew on this as a primary reading of race in America. He saw it reflected in the work of writers like Mark Twain who, in novels like *The Adventures of Huckleberry Finn* and *Pudd'nhead Wilson* recognized the indelible stamp placed on American culture by an invisible presence of Black people.

Though it was eventually removed from the final version of the manuscript, a section of *Invisible Man* dedicated to a character named LeRoy seems to echo the legacy of Ellison's relationship with the Left. In *Wrestling with the Left,* Barbara Foley identifies it as an important absent presence in the published novel that links Ellison more securely to the Left than subsequent narratives of his associations to radicalism imply. As she points out, citing Ellison's own notes, LeRoy "becomes, Ellison jotted, a 'benchmark' by which the protagonist's progress might be measured."[24] LeRoy had been born in the South, had moved to New York, studied for a bit at college, and had then begun to work on behalf of a multiracial maritime union. He was murdered while at sea and his body thrown overboard. When the invisible narrator moved into LeRoy's room at Mary Rambo's boardinghouse, he discovers books and a journal revealing LeRoy's radical ideas. In some ways, LeRoy may have been intended to anticipate the invisible narrator's own trajectory toward radicalism. LeRoy's journal paints a picture of revolutionary engagement in the present that was reflected in the past. LeRoy writes about race and the status of Black people living in America. But LeRoy is not entirely representative of the radical Left. The ideas reflected in the diary the narrator reads seem to be written from the dissatisfaction that Ellison himself had begun to feel toward the Left beginning in 1943. Ellison's publishers encouraged him to remove the LeRoy section entirely, which he did during the final stages of the novel's revisions. But the echo of LeRoy's diary in the novel suggests the ongoing relevance of his association with radical ideology. LeRoy is not a character in the novel. He is a memory, much like the memory of Ellison's earlier involvement with and influence by radicalism.

The passages containing the story of LeRoy reflect a kind of transition from Ellison's first act as an apprentice writer and Communist Party USA loyalist who abandoned the intellectual currency of interracial radical ideology that characterized his years as an apprentice writer. Ellison's second act can be characterized by the publication of *Invisible Man* and its expansive impact as a defining postwar American novel. Its influence was aided by Ellison's voluminous essays and numerous interviews that parsed its allegory, contextualized its relevance and objectives, and helped secure its position in the postwar American literary canon. This is perhaps the area of Ellison's life that most people know best. Ellison was certainly no early bloomer. He signed a contract with Random House on July 17, 1947. *Invisible Man* was eventually published after years of composition and revision when Ellison was thirty-nine years old. It became a bit of a touchstone—for Ellison and his reading audience—for all that followed. It was a celebrated novel that distinguished Ellison as one of the leading literary and intellectual focal points of the era. His lectures, public appearances, professorial appointments, essays, articles, and broad service to public and cultural endeavors speak to a novelist eager to make a place for himself in the kind of nation building that his work so often comments upon. This is also a period in which Ellison worked on and published sections from the novel in progress that remained expansively unfinished at the time of his death. Because Ellison wrote and revised large portions of the novel over so many years, it is, in its multi-thousand-page incompleteness, difficult accurately to place in the trajectory of Ellison's thought. The collection of essays, also written over a period of years and eventually published as in 1964 as *Shadow and Act,* comes much closer to achieving that goal.

Adam Bradley, writing in *Ralph Ellison in Progress,* comes closest to providing a vision of Ellison that argues for the benefits of recognizing the ways Ellison's work is very much reflective of a larger process of thought and composition that reveals a great deal about Ellison himself. By focusing on "the classic novel published in the first half of his life, and the unfinished novel never published in the second," Bradley contemplates Ellison's "novelistic judgment" in an effort better to understand his two works of fiction. The present book maintains the attention that Bradley gives to Ellison's compositional process and, by extension, argues that Ellison's essays most directly reveal important clues for considering Ellison himself and the central question: How does Ellison's work consider the production of national culture?[25] If, as Cheryl Alison observes in "Writing Underground," Ellison had difficulty "inhabiting the novel's roomier allowance," his essays provide a particularly useful way to distill some of the ideas that his longer fiction had difficulty bringing to closure.

Ellison never published an autobiography. Many readers have tried to see *Invisible Man,* which draws upon so many of the details of Ellison's life, as a kind of autobiographical document. But *Shadow and Act* reveals a writer searching the past—his own and the past of the nation—for an explanation of the components that contributed to the composition and success he encountered in the publication of *Invisible Man*. In examining the inherent tension between race and the nation, Ellison burnished his already widely acknowledged reputation as an essayist and social and cultural critic. In his "Introduction" to the collection, Ellison writes that his was an "attempt to transform some of the themes, the problems, the enigmas, the contradictions of character and culture native to my predicament, into what André Malraux has described as 'conscious thought.'"[26] Ellison describes a transformation away from the radicalism he had adopted when he first arrived in Harlem into the broadly inclusive universalism hinted at by the epilogue of *Invisible Man*. Ellison focused on democracy even as the movement for civil rights clearly illuminated the disparities and institutional and cultural obstructions that Black people living in America faced as they tried to access their democratic rights.

In some ways, it is unfortunate that Ellison was not in closer conversation with Frantz Fanon's thoughts. Fanon published *Black Skin, White Masks* around the same time that Ellison published *Invisible Man* in 1952. Both identified race as a central component of the modern world. But unlike Ellison, Fanon was deeply involved in the anti-colonial struggle, and his work was subsequently considered across academic disciplines like literary studies, anthropology, and cultural studies. Perhaps most importantly, Fanon's ideas provided a framework for reading race and oppression in Africa, Asia, and the United States. Conversely, while Black American writers like James Baldwin and Amiri Baraka, who was known early in his public life by his birthname LeRoi Jones, focused their attacks on political ideology and the institutionalized components of racism and disparity, Ellison insisted on explicating the problem of race in the context of technical craft and artistic responsibility that firmly sequestered the artist away from politics. Artistic and cultural integration was Ellison's solution to a problem dating back to the nation's origins in contrast to Fanon's widely influential body of work on behalf of the liberation of colonized people around the world or the kinds of separatist strategies eventually advocated in the United States by the Black Arts movement, which was the cultural division of the more encompassing Black Power movement.

The Black Power movement was a self-advocacy effort that developed out of the movement for civil rights. The master's tools might not bring about truly genuine and lasting change and dismantle the master's house but, for the Black Power movement, the master's house was not the only source of shelter and support.[27] The Black Power movement advocated the creation of a collective, Pan-African, political, economic, educational, and cultural community formed *by* Black people *for* Black people. Ellison saw this as little more than narrowly anti-intellectual.

In his study *The Black Arts Movement,* James Smethurst identifies the importance of the interactions that occurred between the new generation of militants and its ideological forebears. As he notes, "Another powerful and lasting interaction between the Old Left and the new cultural militants was the mentoring relationship that many older black writers and intellectuals with close ties to the remnants of the institutions and organizations of the Communist Left had with emerging black writers immediately before or during the early days of the Black Arts movement."[28] Ellison, who during his early years in New York had used the Left as a way of forming similar connections and advancing and sharing his work, was conspicuously absent in these mentoring relationships and remained so. Part of this may have been Ellison's antipathy to the work produced by the new generation of activist writers, which Ellison criticized for lacking craft and artistic merit, and part of this may have been his antipathy to the ideologies their work was founded upon.

His thoughts on the matter arguably had their basis in the radicalism that he had abandoned a generation earlier. Black Americans were present long before the birth of the nation. More importantly, the Black presence in America was responsible for all that the nation had become and everything to which the nation aspired. While Ellison did not disagree about the necessity of demanding the justice inscribed in the nation's founding documents, he firmly disagreed with a nationalistic strategy for achieving that justice. Separatism was, for Ellison, a loser's game because it demanded that Black Americans simply walk away from all that was rightfully theirs to begin with.

Although *Invisible Man* had implied the possibility of widespread cultural unrest, Ellison's second act seemed to produce a writer intent on distancing himself from the very consequences his most influential piece of writing seems to foreshadow. At the same time, Ellison also became increasingly inclined to devote more of his energy and attention to explicating and burnishing the legacy of *Invisible Man* during the 1960s and 1970s. Ellison's stances during this period put him in opposition to white liberals and Black radicals alike. He supported President Lyndon B. Johnson and the conflict in southeast Asia, even as opposition to the war intensified across the country. He regularly declined invitations to publish in Black-oriented journals that primarily focused on race and politics like the Pittsburgh-based magazine *Black Lines: A Journal of Black Studies, Black World* (formerly *Negro Digest*), which published a December 1970 edition entirely devoted to "Ralph Ellison His Literary Works and Status," a special edition of *College Language Association Journal* devoted to his work in the fall of 1970, and *Black Scholar*. He was seen by a younger generation of emerging Black writers like Ishmael Reed, John Henrik Clarke, John Oliver Killens, Amiri Baraka (particularly during the years when he was known as LeRoi Jones), John A. Williams, and Larry Neal as being uninterested in, and largely unimpressed with, their work.[29]

This is a central part of the narrative that Arnold Rampersad constructs in his biography *Ralph Ellison* to explain what he sees as Ellison's cultural and literary irrelevance and, perhaps more importantly for him, Ellison's inability to complete the novel on which he had been working for so long: "Ralph was bedeviled by too rigid ideas about culture and art, myth and symbol, allusion and leitmotif. His inability to create an art that held a clean mirror up to 'negro' life as blacks actually led it, especially at or near his own social level, was disabling him as a writer. As a novelist, he had lost his way. And he had done so in proportion to his distancing of himself from his fellow blacks."[30] What this ignores, however, is that Ellison, however imperfectly, decisively pointed in his published writing to an explanation of race and nation that the fullness of time has shown to be meaningful and relevant.

Culturally, this part of Ellison's life was characterized by Freedom Summer, urban unrest across the nation, the assassinations of John F. Kennedy, Medgar Evers, Malcolm X, the Reverend Dr. Martin Luther King Jr., and Robert Kennedy, among others, as well as cultural events like the Tet Offensive, the rise of the Black Panthers, the trial of Huey Newton, and the presidential election of Richard Nixon. This is also the part of his life in which a fire at his summer home in the Berkshire village of Plainfield, Massachusetts, consumed a portion of the second novel on which he had been working for over a decade. While the extent of the destruction is unclear, Ellison's biographer Arnold Rampersad suggests that Ellison may, over time, have embellished the extent of the loss to explain his delay in producing his widely anticipated second novel. Seen by many as speaking from a position of privilege,

Ellison clung to his assertions about aesthetics, the role of the artist, and the importance and consequences of technical mastery. In "Brave Words for a Startling Occasion," Ellison explicitly links moral consciousness with race consciousness and the work, ostensibly apolitical, of the writer. Central to Ellison's conception of novelists is the willingness and desire of writers to discern and make apparent for their readers the complex, and often chaotic, relationship between reality and illusion: "Here [in the realm of social and literary criticism] he [the novelist] is circumscribed by rules which are alien to his obsessive need to play with the fires of chaos and to rearrange reality to the patterns of his imagination."[31]

Ellison's third and final act is characterized by his position as Albert Schweitzer Professor of the Humanities at New York University from 1970 to 1979 and subsequent retirement. Curiosity continued about the status of his second novel, particularly since he had completed revisions of books I and II during the summer of 1972. He had teased the public with an excerpt entitled "Cadillac Flambé" that he published in *American Review* in 1973. "Backwacking, a Plea to the Senator," was the final excerpt from the novel that he published during his lifetime. It appeared in *Massachusetts Review* in 1977. Writing in a reminiscence after Ellison's death, James Tuttleton, who served as chair of the Department of English at New York University during Ellison's tenure there and who was a supporter of Ellison's at the university (and whom Ellison, in turn, had nominated for membership in the Century Club), memorialized Ellison by going so far as saying that,

> Although he wrote only one novel, I think it fair to say that Ellison also towered over his near contemporaries James Baldwin, LeRoi Jones (Imamu Amiri Baraka), William Melvin Kelley, and John A. Williams. Indeed, compared to Ellison's great achievement, the more recent contemporary adulation of Jamaica Kincaid, Alice Walker, and Toni Morrison seems grotesque. If these comparisons segregate Ellison from white fiction and seem to diminish him as merely "a credit to his race," let me go further and say that, in my view, *Invisible Man* towered over anything produced by Mailer, Bellow, Malamud, Roth, Updike, Cheever, Barth, Vonnegut, Pynchon, Hawkes, and Barthelme.[32]

Tuttleton's broad dismissal of Ellison's contemporaries in his elevation of Ellison notwithstanding, Ellison's time at New York University during the

1970s certainly reflects an increasing shift in expectation away from the second novel and toward a historicizing process contextualizing the significance of the body of work that Ellison had produced.

Chapter 1 of this book considers Ellison's ideas during the literary apprentice years between the late 1930s and his service in the United States Merchant Marine. This chapter reveals his thoughts about the difficulties of establishing a meaningful cultural self-definition in the context of a democratic process that pathologized racial self-definition. The hyper-visibility of Black racial difference transforms cultural awareness of individualized Black subjectivity into blindness and invisibility. In particular, the chapter addresses Ellison's movement away from activist radical ideology in favor of language that emphasized the artist and the contributions of Black vernacular culture on the broad outlines of a democratic vision of life in the United States. Ellison moved away from a vision that neatly aligned race with class.

When he arrived in New York, Ellison had documented Black vernacular culture in Harlem in the broader contours of the nation's segregated racial environment while working on a Works Progress Administration folklore project. His work certainly encouraged him to recognize the vernacular culture that contributed so much to what made Harlem distinct. Simply put, Ellison recognized a vibrantly expressive culture that he saw as being synonymous with American culture. This chapter argues for an understanding of Ellison's thought characterized by its sustained movement away from leftist ideology and literary naturalism. Ellison moved toward an apolitical modernism that aligned Black vernacular practices in America with aesthetic considerations and the responsibilities of the novelist. While Ellison recognized the shared experiences that existed between Black Americans, he also sought to differentiate his thoughts from the sociologists whose work so often pathologized those experiences by reductively essentializing race.

Ellison's deepest critique of social science was that it took from Black people any sense of agency. In doing so, Black culture became simply reactive. Ellison saw Black Americans living in the United States as being particularly generative because of their ability to produce a usable cultural intervention despite the limitations of profound social and political limitation. Both social science and the radical Left became inadequate tools for illuminating the complex alchemy of race and cultural production. By the end of the interwar period, Ellison wanted to express a Black vernacular culture that included but emphatically extended beyond the limitations of economic exploitation. This was certainly a time of transition for Ralph Ellison as much as it was his belief that this was an important time of transition for Black America.

Black vernacular culture became for Ellison a way of identifying the fragmentation and apparent lack of cohesion in modern culture. It became an ongoing point of contention for Ellison that Black vernacular conveys history even as it embodies its own kind of historical presence. Ellison's ideas about Marxism, the Communist Party USA, and leftist ideology had all changed since his arrival in New York and his attempts to situate himself as a writer within the Popular Front. But his thoughts about vernacular culture remained remarkably consistent, particularly his strategy for establishing a collective presence and linking that presence to symbolic representation. Ellison firmly embraced culture as a series of integrative gestures. From his earliest arrival in New York, Ellison was inclined to value craft far more than he valued ideology, even if he continued to employ Marxist language as a way of shaping and arranging his thoughts.

Chapter 2 examines the ways Ellison used music as a metaphor for his vision of literature and culture. While the jazz tradition became increasingly representative of the nation's cultural expression—and, to some around the world, completely synonymous with America's cultural tradition—Ellison recognized the ways in which it was simultaneously relegated to the nation's cultural margins. But as a metaphor, jazz particularly served Ellison's purpose of illustrating the relationship between literature and vernacular expression. Jazz's seemingly effortless expression reflected his sense of the fluid expression of democracy itself. Perhaps more importantly, as someone who was musically trained in both European classical music and jazz, Ellison recognized the role of technical mastery in achieving the highest levels of proficiency in literature and music. The same process that Ellison saw to be at work delegitimizing the contributions of Black American writers relegated jazz to the margin even as the art form increasingly came to occupy and define mainstream culture.

More precisely, Ellison's attraction to literary modernism easily extended to his thoughts about music. Ellison saw in jazz the attempt to trace and articulate the boundary even as the music sought to transcend that border. Jazz takes available, found cultural materials and transforms them into something that is both new and immediate. There was certainly fragmentation and apparent chaos in the process of making something new and compelling from found materials. But Ellison also recognized in the tradition a kind of unity reflecting the democratic ideal. Jazz registers Ellison's focus on craft and discipline and opens the possibility for Black American writers to move beyond the limitations of race literature or protest literature. But invoking the language of jazz is a two-way process. Jazz certainly invokes democratic possibility. But it also invokes cultural exclusion, particularly as that exclusion was reinforced by mainstream appropriation. Ellison recognized jazz as an appropriately authentic artistic form of cultural production that was generated from its own artistic and historical influences in traditions similar to the ways Black American literature was generated and located in American culture.

As Frederick Douglass and W. E. B. Du Bois had done before him, Ralph Ellison recognized the ways sonic production provided an important strategy for him to use in enlarging the possibilities of rhetorical production. The main point of this chapter is to demonstrate that, when Ellison makes the elaborate argument he does to illustrate the music that he sees as being relevant to his theory of culture, what he is really doing is attempting to articulate the role of an "authentic" art. He saw this "authentic" artistic production as being capable of summoning the importance of the histories and social movements of the people who made the music and the people who, like Ellison himself, consumed that art and whose lives were sustained and made meaningful by that cultural production. The final portion of the chapter examines the distinctions Ellison makes between the swing-era jazz that he grew up with and the emergence of bebop during the wartime years.

Ellison's view of the jazz produced after World War II is uniformly uncomplimentary and speaks to the distinction he makes between the performative mask and a musician's artistic production. This is especially true in the context of the ways Ellison saw bebop rewriting the performative practices of the style that preceded it. Bebop replaced a reliance on lyricism and danceability with a music favoring intricate individual improvisations that were consciously intended to be artistic, stage personas, and the elimination of direct audience interaction by some musicians. Ellison saw classical forms like jazz and the blues as simultaneously functioning as entertainment and a form of vernacular expression. For Ellison, the music produced in the postwar era isolated Black culture in America rather than acknowledging the depth of its relationship in the collective production of American culture from which it arose.

Chapter 3 considers the relationship of Ellison's art to his politics in the decades following the publication of *Invisible Man*. Specifically, the chapter examines his insistence on Americanism over ethnic particularism. The Black intellectual tradition was synonymous with the American intellectual tradition. For Ellison, the American intellectual tradition was under siege by Black intellectuals driven to the point of separation by fundamental frustrations with the nation's attitudes toward race. At the heart of Ellison's negative attitudes to the separatist rhetoric that had become so much a part of Black radical thinking by the middle of the 1960s was Ellison's argument that ideology—"sloganeering," as he dismissively referred to it—was taking the place of the real work in which writers and intellectuals should be engaged. Abstracting Black culture away from American culture simply did not refine it into something greater, regardless of the ideological basis from which that nationalist desire for separation arose. Ellison simply refused to merge aesthetic concerns with any kind of public response to social inequality, particularly as that conflation privileged ideology over art.

Ellison's focus on the form of the novel presupposes a direct and meaningful engagement with democracy over racial solidarity. Ellison increasingly came to occupy a position that saw the true role of Black artists and intellectuals as being to make clear to the American mainstream that the Black experience was synonymous with the nation's experience. There simply was, for Ellison, no intellectual basis for separatism. The nation was a cultural joint-stock company in which its component parts were inseparable from its whole. Ellison's democratic ideal functioned around an assimilated multiracial economy rather than around an ideology of separatism based on race. Ellison's view conflated race and nation in a mixture of shared history. But for Ellison, shared history most emphatically did not suggest an identical history. As Black nationalist writers moved toward ideological ways of considering Black identity, Ralph Ellison's pluralist vision of Black identity became seen by some as representative of a form of pathologizing race hatred.

The chapter examines the influence of New Criticism on Ellison's literary outlook, particularly in the context of Black nationalist criticism that relegated Ellison to being an establishment writer who pandered to white audiences by writing allegorical fiction and emphasizing aesthetics over politics in his essays. It concludes by examining Ellison's well-known, and particularly biting, review of LeRoi Jones's *Blues People*. This review is an important means through which to understand Ellison's complicated relation to Black nationalist writing and ideology.

At a time when the conversation about race and its effects on Black Americans was advancing very quickly, Ellison instead seems focused on reinterpreting his own frontier-born version of Black vernacular into a self-referential statement of his own intellectual and artistic maturation. This reflects the distinction Ellison's thinking makes between being a Black writer and being an American writer. In doing so, Ellison had created a nationalist vision that predates by almost thirty years the nationalist ideology that later consigned his thinking to being more reflective of the problem than representative of the solution. The shadow of the ideas Ellison presented in *Invisible Man* and *Shadow and Act,* particularly as those ideas related to cultural plurality, now served as the very point of departure from which a new generation of writers located their own origin narratives.

Chapter 4 focuses on one fundamental question: How are we to understand the implications of Ellison's primary belief that American democracy is inexorably connected to a meaningful engagement with race? Ellison often equated the nineteenth century with democracy. He saw in the nineteenth century an important reflection of twentieth-century attempts to reconcile democracy with individual identity and national character. Ellison's extended critique of his namesake Ralph Waldo Emerson is central to the ways Ellison situates democracy, particularly in *Invisible Man,* in the nation's experiences of the earliest democratic possibilities contained in its founding documents, the Civil War, the failures contained in Reconstruction, and legal segregation.

The true tension, as Ellison saw it, was between democracy, the nation, the novelist, and the legacies of nineteenth-century American literature. Ellison was not simply interested in race. He was interested in articulating race in ways that identified its presence in the origin of the nation's psyche. For Ellison, democratic individuality is impossible without eliminating normative whiteness and replacing it with historically contextualized, race-conscious interventions.

Chapter 4 includes an extended reading of Emerson's presence in *Invisible Man,* particularly as that presence relates to self-reliant identity and democratic individualism. Ellison's relationship to Ralph Waldo Emerson's ideas remained an important component of the way Ellison thought of himself as a writer and public figure. Emerson's ideas concerning race were as fragmented as the nation upon which Emerson tried to attach his idealized conception of a distinctly American ethos. Ellison's appropriation and ultimate repudiation of Emerson's thinking gave Ellison the useable past that he needed as the foundation for conceptualizing and articulating his vision of the world. Emerson explained America to itself, much in the way that Ellison subsequently sought to do. But while Ellison recognized the ways race was intrinsic to the American experiment, he also recognized that language used to describe the nation could also be used to critique the presence of Black people at the nation's heart.

America is more than simply a collection of individuals. In Ellison's conception, the individual is America itself. By revisioning Emerson, Ralph Ellison rewrites racial metaphor in ways that allow him to propose the possibility of the cultural pluralism that he saw resting at the heart of the democratic ideal. Pluralism was the nation's fact rather than its aspiration. The chapter concludes by arguing that what Ellison takes from Emerson is the conceit that the idea of America is simultaneously characterized by possibility and ambiguity, chaos and uncertainty. American democracy is an ever-changing concept that is inseparable from race itself and hindered by its own historical denial. One of the things associated with privilege is avoiding uncomfortable historical realities, even as the nation's founding documents and foundational thinkers like Ralph Waldo Emerson ostensibly envisioned a nation built on natural equality. This is the fundamental, tragic drama that *Invisible Man* and all his work after *Invisible Man* addresses: how to reconcile the moral hypocrisy encoded in the nation's acts and institutions.

Chapter 5 offers a sustained examination of the novel on which Ellison worked throughout the second half of his life and left unfinished when he died. The project's composition spanned the final years of Jim Crow, *Brown v. the Board of Education of Topeka, Kansas,* the movement for Black civil rights, America's involvement in Southeast Asia, the Black Power movement, and the identity anxieties that consumed 1980s America. Like *Invisible Man,* the second novel took the visibility of race as its main subject. The unfinished second novel is a fragmented maze of episodes. Some of those episodes were revised over a span of forty years. It is composed of thousands of manuscript pages from which it is impossible to know Ellison's true intentions regarding a definitive narrative arc.

It is not Ellison's best-known work, but it is the work to which he devoted himself for the last forty years of his life. It reflects Ellison's ideas about the unfinished—and unfinishable—process of American democracy. Part of Ellison's struggle was how best to integrate Black American identity with American identity during a period when Black identity in America was being rapidly redefined. From the second novel's inception, Ellison was clearly working on an epic project that he saw as being broadly assimilating. Specifically, Ellison wanted to distill the chaos of human experience into artistic form.

By closely considering episodes central to the unpublished novel, chapter 5 suggests that, because the nation's narrative of democracy is itself so contradictory, it should come as no surprise that the novel's form itself reflects and calls into question that narrative's unsettled, artificial form. Understanding the second novel, even in its incomplete, fragmentary form, requires a recognition that the novel repeatedly returns to a consideration of the ongoing influence of Black American culture on a nation so seemingly intent on remaking itself. The novel is a symbolic corrective to the kinds of cultural friction that Ellison saw being repeated in all aspects of American public life. In *Invisible Man,* Ellison had been able to create a cohesive novel whose meaning was firmly grounded in the tension presented by segregated life in the United States.

The novel in progress did not have a similar foundation. It was repeatedly transformed, reflected in Ellison's numerous revisions to the manuscript, by the changes in culture and identity that Ellison came to see as giving the novel its texture and meaning. Although his stated objective in composing the second novel was to provide a prism through which American history could be concentrated and surveyed, the nation's rapid cultural changes after the end of segregation took from him a primary lens through which to consider race and the human condition. Ellison saw America, particularly Black America, as needing its past in order to provide cultural unity and avoid disillusionment. Culture, without the authority of democracy, was reduced for Ellison to a homogeneity lacking individual subjectivity and historical awareness.

1

INVISIBLE TO WHOM?
The Uncreated Consciousness of the Race

"The title of Ralph Ellison's book was *Invisible Man*," Morrison said. "And the question for me was 'Invisible to whom?' Not to me."

TONI MORRISON, "Ghosts in the House"

BEFORE INVISIBILITY WAS IN VOGUE

You have got to pull the democratic and idealistic clothes off American utterance, and see what you can of the dusky body of IT underneath.

D. H. LAWRENCE, "The Spirit of Place," *Studies in Classic American Literature*

Given the question of how to understand the implications of the importance Ellison places on the ways national culture gets formed, what does Ellison's relationship to the Left, his obvious disdain for sociology, and the admiration he developed during his formative writing years for Kenneth Burke, ritual, and the Black vernacular tell us about how he conceptualized the issue in the first place? Even during his apprentice years, there was, somewhere in Ellison's mind, a commitment to an examination of race as a constituent part of national culture. The early fiction that Ellison produced during the time of his most active association with the Left reflects his attempts to go beyond describing the corrosive effects of racial oppression. He also wanted to recognize the ways Black national survival in the face of racism was sustained by cultural intervention.

What matters here is that, even as Ellison was actively trying to accommodate the transracial ambitions of the Left, he was also very consciously creating for himself a language that could contain radicalism and vernacular tradition, protest literature and cultural mythology, the epic and the particular in ways that meaningfully reflected the experiences of Black people in America. Paradoxically, that process contributed to his disengagement and isolation from the Left. As radicalism worked to construct a multiracial working-class movement to defeat fascism, Ellison was working to disengage race from class, even as he worked to formulate a perspective linking race more securely to nation.

This period in Ellison's life and the arc of twentieth-century Black American intellectualism's relationship to the Left in general has received critical attention from several differing perspectives. In *Wrestling with the Left,* for example, Barbara Foley sees Ellison as a leftist intellectual who distorted the depth of his relationship to Popular Front ideas without ever fully leaving either Marxism or the party behind. While Ellison very self-consciously crafted a narrative in which he highlighted the influences of modernism, Kenneth Burke, and mythology as well as his literary kinship to writers like Herman Melville, Mark Twain, Ernest Hemingway, and William Shakespeare, he was equally conscious of crafting a narrative that downplayed any meaningful association with the Left. This has largely been the accepted narrative that has persisted in discussions of Ellison and his work since he began to formulate it soon after the publication of *Invisible Man.* Some of this is understandable in the context of Ellison's desire to write as an American writer who was Black, rather than as a Black American writer. While Ellison engaged with a particular construction of the Left, especially in *Invisible Man,* Ellison's subsequent narrative clearly attempted to create and maintain a clear line of demarcation between critiquing the lived experiences of race in the United States without any obvious engagement with post–World War II political ideology or, subsequently, with 1960s Black nationalist political ideology.

More than a generation before Barbara Foley's critique of Ellison's relationship with the Left, Harold Cruse, writing in *The Crisis of the Negro Intellectual,* had accused white communists of making themselves spokespeople for Black affairs in ways that ultimately buried "the Negro radical potential deeper and deeper in the slough of white intellectual paternalism."[1] Cruse's polemic, written at the intersection of the movement for civil rights, integration, and Black nationalism, was a product of its time. Like Ralph Ellison, Cruse had come of age during the Great Depression and had been involved with the Left beginning in the mid-1940s before becoming disillusioned with radical ideology in the 1950s. Like Ellison, he was also unwilling to accept Black nationalism. *The Crisis of the Negro Intellectual* is a title clearly ironic in the face of a Black consciousness movement, characterized by Malcolm X and the Nation of Islam and subsequently embraced by the Black Power movement intent on displacing use of the term "Negro." It was a polemic that censured some of Harlem's leading cultural and political figures and named names, among them Paul Robeson, John Henrik Clarke, John Oliver Killens, Lorraine Hansberry, LeRoi Jones, and Ralph Ellison.

The book critiques Black intellectualism, often in ad hominem terms, but it takes the work of Black intellectuals and cultural workers seriously. Of Ellison's relation with the Left, Cruse notes that "The truth is that the radical leftwing will never forgive Ellison for writing *Invisible Man,* no matter what Ellison does or does not do about the 'struggle.'"[2] Cruse's assessment of Black American intellectualism between the Great Depression and the rise of Black Power, distanced as it was from its earlier radicalism, provides an important parallel narrative to the anomalous positions so often associated with Ralph Ellison (along with his lifelong friend Albert Murray and, eventually, Stanley Crouch). Cruse's final paragraph echoes Ralph Ellison's ideas about race and American history: "The farther the Negro gets from his historical antecedents in time, the more tenuous become his conceptual ties, the emptier his social conceptions, the more superficial his visions. His one great and present hope is to know and understand his Afro-American history in the United States more profoundly."[3]

Ralph Ellison's ideas are most often considered through the lens of *Invisible Man.* But the novel's influence overshadows the fact that some of the ideas that he pursued and worked to reconcile in his later fiction were hiding in plain sight long before he began work on *Invisible Man.* His ideas include considerations of race, nation, and the relationship between individual identity and cultural identity. At the center of his thoughts is his belief in the irreconcilable fact that "our cultural diversity is as indigestible as the concept of democracy in which it is grounded."[4] Ellison's earliest published fiction is the product of a writer who actively participated in the Popular Front and whose work reflects that association. Between 1935 and roughly 1939 (the years leading up to World War II), the Communist Party USA had worked to encourage and engage the broad assortment of cultural workers in the arts and intellectual circles who were brought together by circumstance, economic conditions, and politics.

American culture increasingly became seen through the lens of labor. This

Communist Party demonstration in Union Square, May Day 193?. Library of Congress, Prints and Photographs Division, LC-USZ62-35826.

is particularly true beginning in 1935 when the Communist Party USA actively collaborated with left-leaning political groups to build coalitions. This was a broadly influential social movement, especially as that influence was reflected in the work of its Black participants. Black artists recognized the opportunity to move beyond the limitations of the color curtain and open doors to the system of cultural production from which they had largely been excluded because of Jim Crow segregation. For the Left, popular cultural forms provided meaningful access to the working-class audiences they wanted to reach. The entry of the United States in World War II certainly changed that strategy and its related ideology, particularly as those elements related to Black Americans.

Black Americans certainly remained committed to fighting domestic and international fascism in the "Double Victory" initiative. But when the Communist Party USA abruptly adopted a pro-war policy, many Black Americans increasingly began to believe that the ability of the Communist Party USA meaningfully to address domestic racism had become irreparably diluted. Ellison's work here was produced long before he became a writer embraced by the literary mainstream and firmly placed within the American literary canon. Though disenchanted with the ideological direction of the Left, Ellison and other Black writers like Richard Wright, Chester Himes, and Langston Hughes, who subsequently became disillusioned to varying extents with leftist ideology, were certainly influenced by their association with the Left in meaningful and lasting ways. Ellison's work during this period reflects a preoccupation with class that is entirely appropriate for a writer who came of age in the 1930s and 1940s. But his position in these pre–World War II years relative to class is ambiguous because his attempts to foreground class (often in the context of the Black vernacular tradition) are often tempered by a broadly evolving conception of American democracy.[5]

It is not surprising that critical readings of Ellison's work so often background class-based elements of his writing. These readings often emphasize a more expansive view of his work that engages the language that Ellison himself developed after the publication of *Invisible Man* to situate his ideas. Barbara Foley's comprehensive examination of Ellison's engagement with the Left persuasively argues that "Ellison's detachment from the left was neither sudden nor painless" and that "the contradictions within Ellison, as both a man and a writer, cannot be understood apart from the contradictions informing his historical moment, which means, given his particular convictions, the contradictions informing the American left between the late 1930s and the late 1940s."[6] The short stories he published from the 1930s into the war years speak directly toward the way Ellison developed ideas that he had initially formulated during the time of his association with the Popular Front. The trajectory of Ellison's thoughts is far more nuanced than readings that plot his thinking along a rigid trajectory away from radical association and toward disengagement followed by an eventual repudiation of radicalism that ultimately concluded with the development of a counternarrative of universalist aesthetics and democratic liberalism. It is equally reductive to see his earliest explorations with fiction in the 1930s as representations in miniature that lead in an unbroken line to *Invisible Man* and to his most mature work.

The short stories he published during this time are illustrative of the ideas he was considering. "Flying Home" and "King of the Bingo Game" perhaps best reflect the complexity of symbol and thematic ambition of *Invisible Man*. But the other stories that Ellison published during the 1930s and 1940s reflect a genuine grappling on his part with how best to rework the constraints of Black protest fiction, sociology, and ideological limitation. These stories looked for ways that identified and counterbalanced racial oppression with descriptions of Black survival sustained by cultural intervention. It was not so much that Ellison was outside of the traditions of protest literature, radical ideology, vernacular traditions, and cultural mythology in his early work. Rather, he was consciously formulating a language during this period that could mediate these traditions in ways that spoke beyond their limitations and gave meaning to the immediacy of the experiences of Black people.

Ellison's essays during the war years reflect varying levels of commitment to radicalism. His work during the time also reflects a genuine commitment to artistic production and experimentation. In an essay he wrote for *New Masses* in 1941 entitled "Recent Negro Fiction," Ellison argues for "the mastery of life through the mastery of intense ways of thinking and feeling that are artistic techniques."[7] The connection between Ellison's earliest published fiction and his mature work is as much about the relationship between lived experience and artistic technique as it is about the point of disruption between the two. Ellison devoted the subsequent decades to developing a theoretical framework to address the integrative vision with which his early stories grappled. The decades he spent composing and revising his second novel, which he envisioned as an epic summation of America, speak to his inability to formulate a vocabulary to address the broad sweep of a complex and chaotic nation that was fundamentally challenged by the existence of racial division: "'In the beginning was the word.' The founders of this country understood very well that one of the problems was how to make a unity of diversity. How do you make a society in which for the first time you have to face the fact of race?"[8]

"Slick Gonna Learn," his first experimentation with writing fiction, was published in a Popular Front magazine entitled *Direction* in 1939. In it, Ellison describes a Black protagonist who is helped by a white truck driver after he has narrowly escaped death in an altercation with a white police officer. The story foreshadows the altercation that led to Tod Clifton's death and the narrator's rousing eulogy in *Invisible Man*. Slick Williams unintentionally punched a white police officer. Slick is subsequently abducted and harassed by the police for his infraction. They abruptly leave him by himself on a deserted road when they are called to rush to a nearby factory to stop a group of organizers from carrying out a labor action. For the authoritarian police who only enforce their version of the law, Slick, as a Black man, is as expendable as the labor they rush to repress. The truck driver who picks Slick up is an Irish laborer who forces Slick Williams and the reader to reconsider transracial relationships. Even though the truck driver indicates that he has risked his job by helping Slick—"I don't usually pick up riders, lose my job if I did. But hell! A man is still a man and it's nasty as hell tonight"—Slick is as suspicious of the help he receives from the white truck driver as he is of the white police officers who have harassed him in the first place. Though Slick's attitude remains ambiguous, the driver has indeed helped him by responding to Slick as a man rather than as a race. Slick is also indirectly saved as much by the striking workers whose job action caused the police to end their harassment of him so they can rush to the factory to suppress it as he is by the white laborer who recognizes their shared humanity and stops to assist him. The alliance of race and labor is fundamentally (though not seamlessly) connected and their broader objectives mutually supportive.

"The Birthmark," which Ellison published in *New Masses* on July 2, 1940, reflects a version of literary realism that focuses on a depiction of the confrontation of race, racialized violence, and authority that occurs too frequently. The story's central element is the death of a Black man whose lynching is so gruesomely vicious that he can only be identified by the birthmark that he has below his navel. The authorities try to disguise the cause of death as an automobile accident. But the dead man's brother recognizes the emasculation from the lynching and reveals the truth. The dead man's body lay covered by the comic section of a discarded newspaper under encircling buzzards. The story is an experimentation with the mode of social realism that Ellison soon abandoned.

Ellison published three Riley and Buster stories: "Afternoon" in a book collection entitled *American Writing* published in 1940, "Mister Toussan" in *New Masses* in 1941, and "That I Had Wings" in *Common Ground* in 1943. The stories focus on two young Black boys who interact in ways that emphasize their connections to Black history and Black vernacular. Their world is unapologetically Black and absent of the kind of racial inferiority to which the narrator of *Invisible Man* eventually succumbs. "Mister Toussan" is a story that affirms Black agency in the face of systemic, historical erasure. While their schoolbooks have eliminated the existence of any non-stereotyped Black presence, the boys embrace a counternarrative that celebrates Toussaint L'Ouverture's leadership during the Haitian Revolution. "That I Had Wings" is a story about the effects of Jim Crow aspiration. Riley's Aunt Kate represents the insidiously ingrained limitations of living in Jim Crow. Riley and Buster concoct a plan to help chicks fly by attaching them to parachutes. Though the chicks ultimately die because their wings were simply not yet strong enough to support their flight, Riley is able to see a vision of himself in the chicks. Taken collectively, the Riley and Buster stories assert a nationalist impulse based on valuing vernacular culture rather than emphasizing political ideology.

"King of the Bingo Game," published in *Tomorrow* in 1944, depicts the migration of a protagonist from South to North, from stasis to chaos, and from the external to the inner world of experience. He is invisible to potential employers and unable to find work because he does not have a birth certificate. The protagonist wants to win the bingo jackpot to be able to pay his wife's medical expenses. His gamble quickly goes from being real to being surreal when he wins and qualifies to compete for the $36.90 jackpot. In order to do so, he must spin a wheel that illustrates the precarious relationship between fate and self-determination. The spinning wheel brings him to an epiphany about self-identification so powerful that it leads those around him to assume him to be insane. They respond to that assumption by leading him from the stage before he can enjoy his success.

"In a Strange Country," which Ellison published in *Tomorrow* in July 1944, addresses issues of nationalism. The protagonist is a Black American sailor who has been beaten by his shipmates and rescued by a group of men from Wales. Regardless of the inferior treatment he receives from his own country, the sailor realizes that, although these Welshmen see him as more than his race, they can never see him as anything but an American. When he hears America's national anthem, he realizes something very similar: "only now the melody seemed charged with some vast new meaning.... For the first time in your whole life, he thought with dreamlike wonder, the words were not ironic."[9] Ellison subsequently published the first chapter of "Invisible Man" in *Horizon* in 1947. Though he published an excerpt from the prologue of *Invisible Man* in 1952 in *Partisan Review* in advance of the novel's publication, this was the final short story he published before the publication of *Invisible Man* five years later.

In 1944, while still serving in the United States Merchant Marine, Ralph Ellison wrote and published the short story "Flying Home" in a book collection entitled *Cross Section*. In a foreshadowing of Ellison's subsequent compositional experiences with *Invisible Man* and his unfinished second novel, Ellison completed the story, which he had been unable to accomplish, in 1943 with the encouragement of his friends Stanley Hyman and Shirley Jackson just hours before his first deployment to the North Atlantic. The story appeared in an anthology published as *Cross Section, 1945: A Collection of New American Writing* that included Richard Wright's novella *The Man Who Lived Underground*, Norman Mailer's novella *A Calculus at Heaven* (Mailer was only twenty-one at the time), Arthur Miller's play *The Man Who Had All the Luck*, and contributions by Shirley Jackson and Langston Hughes, among others.

The story is the culmination of the leftist critical and theoretical work with which Ellison had been engaged through the early 1940s. It was written eight years before Ellison published *Invisible Man* and a full year before he even wrote the novel's opening line, in which the unnamed narrator speaks intimately and knowingly about invisibility. "Flying Home" tells the story of a Tuskegee airman named Todd who crashes during a flight into a Black sharecropper's cotton field in Alabama. Lawrence Jackson's biography of Ellison notes that the story also incorporates Ellison's signature interest in the relationship between the absurd and the realistic when "[h]e brings his Tuskegee flier to earth with a lowly buzzard, a bird reduced to a spray of blackness and blood as it covers the plane's windshield"[10] The story describes the idea of invisibility to which Ellison returned in *Invisible Man*. "Flying Home" also examines the broader issues of cultural collectivity, the Black presence in America, and the disparities between the lived experiences of Black people in the more expansive context of the nation's founding principles. Ellison returned to these issues frequently throughout his long career as a writer and public intellectual. These ideas also resonate in the second novel, which remained incomplete at the time of his death.

As a merchant marine, Ellison was well acquainted with the stories of other Black soldiers who complained of serving the United States only to return home to humiliating daily experiences of Jim Crow racism. Ellison's own father had fought in the Philippines in 1899 during the Spanish-American War. Though there is no evidence to support the claim, the story told by the family was that he had also served on San Juan Hill with Theodore Roosevelt's Rough Riders, in the Philippines, and in China to suppress the Boxer Rebellion. Regardless of the embellishments attached to his service, he nevertheless returned from serving in the US Army to face the paradox of equality in foreign conflict but not at home, where he was demoted to private from the rank of lance corporal and eventually dishonorably discharged. Ellison was certainly aware of Black American airmen "who after being trained in segregated units and undergoing the abuse of white officers and civilians alike were prevented from flying combat missions."[11] The restrictions became abundantly clear when, after hesitating over training Black American pilots, the US Army Air Corps decided instead to confine Black pilots to the dangerous and difficult role of pursuit pilot. They further hampered the effectiveness of these Black American pilots by refusing to train them in fighter aircraft.

Though happy about the decision to train Black pilots at a newly formed flying school at Tuskegee Institute, many, including Ellison, saw the whole affair as an example of racist bias that was never intended to give these Tuskegee Airmen, as they were known, a fair opportunity for the success they deserved.[12] The Tuskegee Air School was, after all, segregated, and the first class of pilots it graduated in 1942 were delayed for almost an entire year before being deployed in active duty in April 1943. Ellison references these tensions in "Flying Home" when Todd remembers the last letter he received from his girlfriend, where she says "I don't need the papers to tell me you had the intelligence to fly. And I have always known you to be as brave as anyone

G. S. Roberts, B. O. Davis, C. H. DeBow, R. M. Long, Mac Ross, and L. R. Curtis, members of the first graduating class of African American pilots in the US Army Air Corps at Advanced Flying School, Tuskegee, Alabama. Visual Materials from the National Association for the Advancement of Colored People Records, Library of Congress, Prints and Photographs Division, LC-USZ62-94039.

else. The papers annoy me. Don't you be contented to prove over and over again that you're brave or skillful just because you're black, Todd. I think they keep beating that dead horse because they don't want to say why you boys are not yet fighting. . . . I sometimes think they're playing a trick on us."[13] But the fact that these pilots were being trained for such technically challenging work was a cause of pride for many Black Americans and was seen by many as the realization of an important stage of Black aspiration and social progress.

In the composition of the story, Ellison recognized that his view of the conflict had been simplistic and incomplete. The pilots whose experiences he was attempting to transform in fiction had indeed suffered the animosity of white officers who refused to see beyond race to recognize highly trained pilots who wanted to serve their country and improve their economic status. Ellison realized that there was something to be rendered in fiction that was far more ambiguous. In his hyper-visibility to white people, the narrator of "Flying Home" was paradoxically invisible. Equally importantly, class and cultural difference made him invisible even to himself: "A man of two-worlds, my pilot felt himself to be misperceived in both, and thus at ease in neither."[14] More than simply creating a story about the debilitating frustrations of racial disparity, Ellison found himself writing about the cultural difficulties of self-definition in the broader circumstances of race, culture, history, and the pathologies contained in the democratic process.

As well trained and conscientious as he was, Ellison's pilot Todd was eager to please a military that could not fully see him and that was reluctant fully to allow him to prove himself. Todd was also uneasy with his relationship to the Black tenant farmer named Jefferson who helped him but whose primary cultural connection to him—given their differences in class, education, and social aspiration—is the legacy of slavery that they share. Todd is an Icarus who has flown too close to the sun. Now he worries whether his superiors will ever let him fly again. Ellison's implication is that the freedom that Todd experiences in flight is mitigated by the freedom of those with cultural power to curtail that freedom in favor of the color line. Todd recognizes that he is being tested and that his crash somehow suggests that he is not fit fully to contribute to the nation in the ways to which he aspires.

Ellison understood what Black people in the United States were able to contribute to American culture and society. His understanding of the precariousness of that contribution was reflected in Todd's anxieties about his crash. But as much as Todd aspires to soar beyond the limitations of the color line, and beyond the social limitations of people like the sharecropper Jefferson, the influences of race and the nation's past make that impossible. Ellison recognized these tensions even in his earliest explorations with fiction and struggled with how best to represent and cultivate those ideas. In some ways, the difficulties that Ellison faced as he worked to reconcile those same ideas in his unfinished second novel were already present in the short fiction he produced eight years before the publication of *Invisible Man*.

Todd spends most of the story lying injured after crashing his airplane on the land that Jefferson works but does not own. He spends most of his time considering the ways his crash has curtailed his attempts to occupy a racial and cultural modernity that he can see but cannot necessarily occupy. Todd is humiliated by crashing in the South as a Black American reaching for individuality but knowing that he is being judged collectively: "*Now* the humiliation would come. When you must have them judge you, knowing that they never accept your mistakes as your own but hold it against your whole race—that was humiliation. Yes, and humiliation was when you could never be simply yourself; when you were always a part of this old black ignorant man. Sure, he's all right. Nice and kind and helpful. But he's not you."[15]

Todd cannot move without Jefferson's help and feels himself transported backward in time: Todd's crash has knocked him "back a hundred years"; Jefferson's oxen make "queer, prehistoric shadows against the dry brown earth"; Jefferson's fingers are "like gnarled wood."[16] Todd resents Jefferson because of what Jefferson represents to him and because of what he represents to Black Americans like Jefferson. Initially, Todd was proud of the attention he received from Black men like Jefferson. But their fawning acknowledgment of his accomplishments eventually made him feel a sense of shame and distaste. In some ways, their ignorance about his technological understanding became condescending to him. Todd's aspiration is to receive the appreciation of his white officers, not the acknowledgment of the uneducated Black people from whom he was trying to fly away. Todd wants white cultural inclusion rather than Black cultural acknowledgment.

While the democratic ideal asserts unity in diversity, Todd's actions symbolize the disassociation he feels with sharecroppers like Jefferson whom he thought he had left behind in a temporal and cultural past. Because of the hubris of flying too high and too fast when he goes into a spin, he hits a buzzard—a "jimcrow," as Jefferson calls it—and crashes. Todd's return "home"—to the South, to the "negro sound" of Jefferson's vernacular speech, to an ever-receding, quasi-mystical past that points toward a chaotic, unknown future—is made complete when Jefferson tells him his own story about flight. Todd quickly recognizes this as a story as old as the Black presence in America. It can be read as a story of resistance, escape, and freedom. It can also be read as a story of Black commonality that connects Black people in America to shared cultural experiences that ultimately reconstruct the past. It is an archetypal story that is woven throughout the diaspora. Todd remembers it as "an old tale" told to him years ago and long forgotten.

Ellison's emphasis on home and flight raises some important questions: Did belief in flight fuel Black American cultural resistance? Or conversely, was Black American resistance an act that could be rendered most efficiently in the metaphor of flight? Todd's story of flight is a story of both hubris and control: "[H]e had been flying too high and too fast. He had climbed steeply away in exultation. Too steeply, he thought. And one of the first rules you learn is that if the angle of thrust is too steep the plane goes into a spin."[17] It is also a story that is told in a way that looks forward to the conversational call-and-response style that Ellison favored between the Reverend Alonzo Hickman and Senator Sunraider in the second section of *Three Days before the Shooting....* Like the invisible narrator and Senator Sunraider, Todd desperately wants to leave his southern roots behind. But Jefferson returns him to the common ground they share.

In Jefferson's story, a long-forgotten old story that Todd immediately recognizes, Jefferson has died, gone to heaven, and been awarded the gift of flight. But flight for Black angels was restricted by a harness intended to diminish their power. Jefferson ignores the constraint "and got to flyin' fast enough to shame the devil."[18] Upon his expulsion from heaven, he was given a parachute and a map of Alabama. Jefferson's story is an obvious retelling of the Tuskegee Airmen who, like Todd, were trained to fly but constrained because of the limitations imposed by their race. Although Todd has grudgingly interacted with Jefferson through his feelings of anger and humiliation, Jefferson returns him home by integrating their experiences of race and class. As he is being carried by Jefferson and his son Teddy out of the field in which he has crashed, Todd thinks to himself that "it was as though he had been lifted out of his isolation, back into the world of men. A new current of communication flowed between the man and boy and himself."[19]

Todd's story echoes the myth of Daedalus and Icarus. Theirs is a myth that describes their use of wings to escape from the island of Crete. Icarus is most often associated with the flying skill that he develops and with his descent into the sea when he flies too close to the sun and the wax that secures his wings begins to melt. This mythical story of ambition, accomplishment, escape, hubris, and arrogance is coupled with Jefferson's exuberant vernacular tall tale of narcissistic flight and subsequent repression. The cultural space that Todd and Jefferson bridge is the space separating culturally aspirational Black people from the rural vernacular of their uneducated Black American counterparts. Ellison's friend and literary supporter Richard Wright had certainly experimented with similar literary subjects and techniques. Ellison's contribution was that he was able successfully to create a literary style that managed to incorporate classical literary form and allegorical concerns with vernacular expressions like jazz, the blues, and the rich variety and signification of Black American folk culture.

While the ideas Ellison presents about identity, racial justice, and cultural recognition certainly reverberate throughout his later work, "Flying Home" represents for Ellison a transition away from the leftist ideology reflected in the short fiction and reviews that he had previously published. By 1944, Ellison's vision of social reform had begun to focus on the artist and the role of art in that reform. Ellison's disillusionment with leftist ideology certainly had a great deal to do with leftist wartime strategies that downplayed racial activism. In a broader context, Ellison saw the war effort and the nation's eventual entry into the war as consequences that resounded across Black America. As Black people migrated in historic numbers from the rural South to urban centers in the North and the West to participate in wartime industrial production, the nation's contradictions became increasingly apparent. Black Americans served in segregated units in the military, were educated in segregated schools, and lived and worshipped in deeply segregated communities.

Black grievances were reflected in a series of protests that occurred across the nation in 1943. These protests suggest that Ellison was not alone in his assessment that Black Americans were at a crossroads of thought and identity that he identified as the first of its kind since Reconstruction. Conflict in Detroit, Michigan, took place June 20–23, 1943, and was the direct result of social tensions caused by the conversion of the city's automotive industry to wartime production. White workers on the Packard Motor Car Company assembly line, who had long worked with Black workers in the plant, refused to work side-by-side on the line with the Black workers who, in accordance with the anti-segregation policy of the Department of Defense, had been assigned to assembly jobs. Circumstances were worsened by housing and employment shortages due to the migration of southern Black and white people to the city in search of the higher wages offered by jobs involved with military production. Shipyard workers had attacked Black Americans in Beaumont, Texas, June 15–17, 1943, on the rumor that a white woman had been raped. The conflict, much like similar conflicts that occurred in Mobile, Alabama, was concentrated by wartime tensions that had become exacerbated as people, white and Black, from across the South arrived in search of work.

Harlem descended into civil conflict on August 1–2, 1943, when members of the Black community retaliated against white-owned property when a white policeman shot a Black solder and the rumor spread among Harlem's Black residents that the soldier had been killed. Racial conflicts had broken out earlier that summer in a series of conflicts June 3–8 in Los Angeles, California (and echoed elsewhere across the country), in a conflict between white American servicemen and Mexicans and Mexican Americans. In the review he published in the December 2, 1941, edition of *New Masses* for William Attaway's novel *Blood on the Forge,* Ellison's Marxist-influenced outlook saw northern factories as places of racialized power.[20] All of these circumstances pointed directly to anger at domestic racism rather than resentment about foreign fascism. For Ellison, creating and sustaining cultural forms were the keys to rejecting white culture's process of pathologizing Black culture. In a truly democratic act, Black Americans shape themselves in an American context rather than a separate history. As he asserts in "Harlem Is Nowhere," folklore and the vernacular served most potently as the "guide to action."[21]

While Ellison's thoughts evolved rather quickly during the period between the late 1930s and the completion of his service in the United States Merchant Marine, Ellison's conception of the vernacular and the people who comprised it was certainly influenced by Communist Party USA political ideology. In 1942, just a few years before he wrote "Flying Home," Ellison, in an unsigned editorial that appeared in *Negro Quarterly,* described World War II as a "people's war" and argued that, among other colonized peoples, Black Americans should be recognized as having produced "a culture and the basic outlines of a truly democratic vision of life."[22] For Ellison during this period, Black American culture radiated from the political and cultural components of its working class but nevertheless remained largely invisible and, in practical terms, unarticulated.

The place Ellison seems to be moving toward is the belief that race was not necessarily synonymous with class. Particularly in the late 1930s, leftist thought certainly encouraged an ideological strategy that organized relationships between workers, liberals, the Democratic Party, middle-class leaders engaged in the movement for Black civil rights, and others to construct a multiracial working-class movement robust enough to defeat fascism. It was certainly a radical act to encourage the importance of a multiracial nation that would reject the casual association of Black culture with the most negative elements of American culture. But the reality was that the alchemy of race and class can make for a profoundly unstable relationship. This is reflected in Ellison's early stories like "Flying Home," "Slick Gonna Learn," and "King of the Bingo Game."

Ellison subsequently illustrates the point in his descriptions of the narrator's experiences in *Invisible Man,* of Welborn McIntyre in book I of *Three Days before the Shooting...,* and of the Reverend Alonzo Hickman in subsequent sections of the unfinished novel. These main characters are simultaneously outside of the boundaries of the communities they describe while being inextricably tied to the limitations and possibilities that characterize those communities. In "Flying Home," for example, Todd believes that his aeronautical training somehow provides him with the possibility of transcending the historical past to enter a modernity for which other Black Americans remain unprepared. He is brought home to the land worked by sharecroppers like Jefferson, with the obvious ties to slavery, the failures and disappointments of Reconstruction, and the recognition that, although their futures may indeed diverge, their past and present circumstances share a great deal of similarity.

Ellison's relationship to vernacular culture was anything but casual. Beginning in 1938 and continuing until he accepted the appointment of managing editor of *Negro Quarterly* midway through 1942, Ellison worked for the Federal Writers' Project in New York City under the direction of folklorist Benjamin Botkin. Ellison's job in his assignment to the Living Lore Unit was to interview Harlem residents who had recently migrated to New York. His work documented a vernacular world in Harlem within the racial dilemma of American culture. The Black vernacular culture of everyday Harlem residents—musicians, ministers, and Pullman porters among them—revealed a world to Ellison in which culture was actively created rather than simply passively reflected. While some of the interviews arguably inspired some of his subsequent depictions of Harlem in *Invisible Man,* the work Ellison involved himself with during this period of employment with the Federal Writers' Project most certainly caused him to recognize a Black vernacular culture in Harlem largely invisible to those outside of it. It became for him representative of an expressive culture that existed on its own terms and according to its own rules and conventions.

Unlike the sociologists who reduced Black American vernacular culture to a pathologizing of American culture, Ellison's work revealed Black culture to be synonymous with American culture and disputed the assertion that it was little more than a pathologized version of the highest aspirations of American culture. During these years of literary apprenticeship, a period during which he is widely regarded to have been a friend and protégé of Richard Wright and Wright's sociological approach to literature, Ellison actively supported the work Wright produced in *Native Son* (1940) and subsequently in *Black Boy* (1945). But his reaction to Gunnar Myrdal's work serves as an important point of modulation that looks backward to the ideas that he had developed during the 1930s and forward to the ideas that he promoted throughout the 1950s and 1960s. Specifically, Ellison began to turn away from an emphasis on the vernacular itself and toward a sustained critique of the foundational role the Black vernacular tradition plays on aesthetic considerations. His assertion became one in which the Black American writer's role is to harness Black vernacular experiences in the service of communicating an otherwise unarticulated racial consciousness: "In Negro culture there is much of value for America as a whole. What is needed are Negroes to take it and create of it 'the uncreated consciousness of their race.' In doing so they will do far more; they will help create a more human American."[23]

This calls into question the very idea of how literature is historically contextualized. John Wright, writing in *Shadowing Ralph Ellison* about Ellison's trajectory toward *Invisible Man* suggests that "What also drew Ellison's conception away from the privatist preoccupations of most 1940s war novelists, and toward the unifying political focus of *Invisible Man,* were exactly those democratic moral visions of social reconstruction with which so many of the 1940s Anglo-American novelists had become disillusioned. In that conceptual void, race provided the heuristic and the metaphor that pulled Ellison's postwar fictional musings on the problem of collective and individual freedom toward the perplexing social figure of the hero and the democratic quandaries of public leadership."[24] Ellison was certainly in a moment of intellectual and ideological transition in the mid-1940s. This transition is commonly read as coalescing in the publication of *Invisible Man*. But as "Flying Home" suggests, Ellison, before he had begun composing *Invisible Man,* seemed to be moving away from cultural authoritarianism and toward a worldview that embraces a vision of democratic pluralism firmly influenced by Black vernacular culture. When seen in this context, it becomes much easier to read Ellison as also making a transition from a journeyman writer working predominantly in the language of leftist ideology. The unifying focus of *Invisible Man* was not ideologically political at all. His is a movement toward a mature writer who has left behind the limitations he saw contained in Marxism in favor of a non-politicized view of the world. This perspective emphasizes aesthetics, the role of art, and a view that sees the novelist as responsible for being a conduit for cultural insight to readers naive to the realities of American culture.

Ellison moved from serving as Works Progress Administration collector of Black vernacular traditions to becoming a journalist contributing class-conscious, working-class commentary to *New Masses* and the leftist *Negro Quarterly*. Both emphasized the need for cross-racial alliances. In *Ralph Ellison,* Arnold Rampersad is particularly critical of Ellison at this point of his life by castigating him as "writing mainly as a hack" for *New Masses* and characterizing his work as being little more than an endorsement of party ideology.[25] But Ellison was moving through an increasing skepticism about leftist naturalism toward a modernism that was decidedly apolitical. Regardless of the depth and extent of his association with the Left, Ellison certainly had grievances with leftist ideology as that ideology related to race. That sense of frustration, particularly during this period, is reflected in the writing he produced that reveals a certain level of conflict as he worked through his thoughts about Black self-determination in an American context.

Ellison was certainly working toward a revised view of Black self-determination, particularly as it related to the relationship between race, radicalism, and the working class. Black American radicals like Paul Robeson, Claude McKay, Langston Hughes, Richard Wright, and C.L.R. James had already begun to raise many of the same questions. Ellison was undoubtedly not alone in questioning the ideologies that were so pervasive during the era of the Popular Front. In many ways, he chose a path like the ones taken by Richard Wright and Chester Himes. His ultimate decision, enacted in the years during and after the publication of *Invisible Man* and far more anomalous and isolating than the responses of other Black radicals at the time, reflects a movement away from leftist ideology in favor of a socially acceptable universalist, homogeneous liberal democracy based in aesthetics that was acceptable in the nation's social and political Cold War atmosphere.

For Ellison, there are no separate histories *among* Black Americans, regardless of present circumstances or future possibilities. The point of separation comes *between* Black people who are distinctly American and the nation in which they live that is unable to recognize the depth of that American presence. America's entry into World War II at the end of 1941 signaled for Ellison a fundamental transformation in the ways Black Americans thought and acted that was unrivaled by any social change in the country since the conclusion of the Civil War and Reconstruction.

Filtered through his own evolving thoughts about Marxism, Ellison saw the United States as being in a state of radical change that forced Black Americans, many of whom had migrated out of the South in search of opportunity, in direct confrontation with the lack of humanity associated with urban industrialism: "Historically, American Negroes are caught in a vast process of change that has swept them from slavery to the condition of industrial man in a space of time so telescoped (a bare eighty-five years) that it is literally possible for them to step from feudalism into the vortex of industrialism simply by moving across the Mason-Dixon line."[26]

Ellison's review, originally written in 1944 for *Antioch Review* but not published until 1965, of Gunnar Myrdal's *An American Dilemma: The Negro Problem and American Democracy,* is perhaps the clearest indication of how far his thinking had traveled from his earliest stories and Marxist analyses of the nation's problematic relationship to race. By the mid-1940s, Ellison was actively opposed to the kinds of naturalistic representations of race so often contained in the work of his friend and literary supporter Richard Wright. Instead, Ellison's outlook began to focus on the influences of psychology and culture on the formation of a distinctly Black folk culture in the United States. These influences are largely distinct from the kinds of naturalistic claims that Wright preferred. This is what an early story like "Flying Home" suggests and what Ellison ultimately succeeded in capturing in *Invisible Man.*

This is not to suggest that Ellison's relationship to the sociological theorists he so often disparaged was not without some intricacies. The line upon which Ellison's thought treaded was his desire to acknowledge that Black Americans had encountered some very real and ongoing racial injustice and repression without characterizing the entire Black American experience as a function of repression. Black people were victims of systemic discrimination, but the experiences of Black people living in America were not solely defined by passive victimhood. In other words, Ellison had to reproduce the most compelling features of sociological approaches to race even as he sought to transcend what he saw as the reductive limitations of those ideological aspects. In doing so, Ellison fashioned a line of thinking that transformed itself into what became the basis of his aesthetic ideology.

While Ellison was expanding class-based ideology to lead him to his vision of the importance of folklore and culture, some of sociology's most prominent scholars, Gunnar Myrdal and Talcott Parsons among them, had moved toward an outlook that moved beyond the limitations of social determinism in order to concentrate more deeply on the influence of culture and its collective psychology on the nation's experiences of race. Like Ellison, for example, Myrdal recognized a fundamental tension between the nation's professed beliefs in equality and the realities of its biases and prejudices. Myrdal saw the role of the intellectual as bridging the gap between a range of incompatible and conflicting value systems. The idea around which Ellison framed his own thoughts was that Black culture needed to be understood in ways that allowed alienated working-class Black Americans to assert their social and political relevance: "Not quite citizens and yet Americans, full of the tensions of modern man but regarded as primitives, Negro Americans are in desperate search for an identity. Rejecting the second-class status assigned to them, they feel alienated and their whole lives have become a search for answers to the questions: Who am I, What am I, Why am I, and Where?"[27]

ON THE HORNS OF THE WHITE MAN'S DILEMMA

Thus despite the bland assertions of sociologists, "high visibility" actually rendered one un-visible—whether at high noon in Macy's window or illuminated by flaming torches and flashbulbs while undergoing the ritual sacrifice that was dedicated to the ideal of white supremacy.

RALPH ELLISON, "Introduction to the Thirtieth-Anniversary Edition of *Invisible Man*"

Sociology played absolutely no role in the formation of national culture, at least as far as Ellison was concerned. For him, sociology was a discipline, in the most generous use of the word—he considered social science to be fundamentally pseudoscientific—that was preoccupied with diminishing the contributions of Black culture and replacing those contributions with a perspective that pathologized all aspects of Black life in America. It was a tool that relied on stereotype. Vernacular expression certainly ran the risk of romanticizing experience but certainly not with the same kind of stereotyping, ideological threat that sociology posed. Reading Ellison in relation to sociology is a paradigm that has gone largely unremarked upon by critics of postwar literature, who often fail to consider the negative historical implications of social science on public policy and individual attitudes.

To Ellison, sociology was the nation's clumsy response to addressing the failures of Reconstruction. As Stephen Schryer argues in *Fantasies of the New Class,* the basis of the revised version of democratic liberalism in the reformist possibilities was suggested by the Progressive and New Deal eras. Ellison's response replicates a shift present in the discourse of other intellectuals writing in the post–World War II era like Lionel Trilling. There was certainly a national shift as the middle class expanded economically and educationally. The New Critics saw a fundamental conflict between their outlook and sociology's fundamental assertions about the causal relationship of socially determining elements like family structure, education, and economic insecurity on human behavior and individual action.

While Schryer connects this revision of discourse to a reformist agenda, Ellison's response to sociology's ideological simplifications and its influence on public policy emphatically moves away from political reform and instead toward his evolving belief that the focus of intellectuals should be aesthetic sensibility (in his case, firmly grounded in vernacular tradition and its cultural contributions) rather than public policy and ideological rigidity. Donald Pease outlined this in *Visionary Compacts* when he argued that postwar critics like Leslie Fiedler, F. O. Matthiessen, and Richard Chase established an Americanist canon that failed to acknowledge the inherent tension between collectivism and individualism. According to Pease, postwar intellectuals failed to recognize an important element of the American Renaissance when they increasingly discredited the importance of the public sphere. They were unable to see the kinds of collectivist politics that characterized the 1930s in relation to the experiences of individuals who were anxious about their role in homogenously collective ideologies.[28]

Though he does not make the case in specific relation to Ralph Ellison, Wolf Lepenies in *Between Literature and Science* draws the battle lines between literature and sociology as being characterized by the diametric opposition of sociology, which wants to quantify modern society but only succeeds in alienating individuals from the world in which they live, and literature, which recognizes intuitive experiences of humanity.[29] Ellison did not frame it precisely in this way, but sociology threatened to intrude on humanism at a time when Ellison increasingly wanted to abandon mimesis and ideology as organizing principles. But sociology and literature were not always mutually opposed. Frankly, naturalist writers like Richard Wright were very accepting of sociology, seeing it as an organic way of describing the correlation of experience, class origin, and economic determinism.

The basis of Ellison's antagonism to the politicized expression of social science in general and particularly to sociology has been identified as stemming from his time as a student at Tuskegee Institute. While there, he encountered the ideas Robert Park presented in *Introduction to the Science of Sociology,* which had been published in 1921.[30] Ellison had studied the work with Professor Ralph Davis and was understandably angered by the broadly influential theorizing about group identity that Park's work engaged in.

Park, along with W. I. Thomas, was an influential figure in what emerged in the early decades of the twentieth century as the Chicago School of sociology. Park's ideas centered on group identity and cultural engagement as the most important markers of Black social mobility in the United States. Since migration and the movements of immigrant populations to and within the United States were a primary focus of Park's work, he drew correspondences between immigrant culture and Black American culture. Cultural comparison was the foundation of his approach. For immigrants, he observed the collective mechanism that replicated Old World social and cultural structures as a way of warding off feelings of disconnection and detachment.

For Park, immigrants aspired to cultural status by way of their assertion of a separate identity. Park's ideas about Black American migrant populations within the United States were an extension of his theories about migrant populations to the United States. But since Black Americans carried the additional burdens of racism and American cultural history, the movement from rural to urban America would necessarily require a very conscious process of reimagining the role and cultural destiny of urban Black America. Basically, Black Americans, like their immigrant counterparts, would need to find ways to leave behind rural folk culture and instead infuse urban America with elements and contributions that were specifically Black American.

Park had worked with Booker T. Washington on race issues at Tuskegee Institute between 1905 and 1914. His initial ideas were about the ways Black

Booker T. Washington. Library of Congress, Prints and Photographs Division, LC-USZ62-119897.

people had created a cohesive Black community in the American South. He shifted his focus during his tenure at the University of Chicago between 1914 and his retirement in 1933. In his work at the University of Chicago, Park began to emphasize the ways migration from the South to northern industrial centers had a profound influence on the development of what he saw as a cohesive Black American cultural presence.

Specifically, his argument was that Black Americans, largely relegated to segregated urban communities in the North, collectively benefited from proximity that led to educational opportunities, economic development, and the advancement of Black leadership. Park remained in complete agreement with Booker T. Washington that the development of a robust middle class was a necessary condition for Black social mobility. But for Park, cultural production also served a crucial role: "Literature and art when they are employed to give expression to racial sentiment and form to racial ideals, serve, along with other agencies, to mobilize the group and put the masses *en rapport* with their leaders and with each other. In such case literature and art are like silent drummers which summon to action the latent instincts and energies of the race."[31] Park's theories of race and sociology influenced Alain Locke and Charles S. Johnson and, by extension, their conception of the New Negro movement. Alain Locke, for example, similarly places Black Americans in a global perspective in *The New Negro* when he writes that "Harlem has the same role to play for the New Negro as Dublin has had for the New Ireland or Prague for the New Czechoslovakia." Building on Park's thoughts in *The New Negro*, Alain Locke saw Harlem as a place that would consolidate the varied experiences of Black people living in the United States into "a common consciousness" rather than simply serve as the geographic location for "a common condition."[32]

Park was also a proponent of using history to deflect racial stereotypes. During the early years of his collaboration with Booker T. Washington at Tuskegee Institute, Park proposed a project in which he would write a self-help reader that amounted to a history of Black Americans. He envisioned the reader being distributed to Black students throughout the South. Park's hope was that the history would be used as a tool to instill a sense of race consciousness among Black Americans. In line with his relentlessly comparatist approach, Park saw the experiences of Black Americans as being aligned with experiences of European populations: "[N]othing short of the history of Italy in the period of the Renaissance or France during the Revolution seems to me equal to the story of this people—if you consider it as the story of a *people,* a race and not a history of political controversy, as it is usually considered [*emphasis in original*]."[33] Park's interest was reinterpretation rather than adaptation. Black American cultural advancement would be achieved through reconfiguring the cultural relationships that already existed between mainstream American culture and the elements unique to the history of Black Americans living in the United States. Black culture would itself be the mechanism for collective mobility.

While Ellison was willing, perhaps grudgingly, to acknowledge the usefulness of some of Park's work, Ellison was clearly most agitated by Park's assertion, which Ellison quotes in his review of *An American Dilemma,* that Black Americans have collectively "always been interested rather in expression than in action; interested in life rather than in its reconstruction or reformation. The Negro is, by natural disposition, neither an intellectual nor an idealist, like the Jew; nor a brooding introspective, like the East Indian; nor a pioneer and frontiersman, like the Anglo-Saxon. He is primarily an artist, loving life for its own sake. His *métier* is expression rather than action. He is, so to speak, the lady among the races." There are any number of value judgments contained in this passage that Ellison included in his essay that have absolutely nothing to do with scientific methods involving data collection. But what seems to linger with Ellison is his intense disapproval of Park's casually reductive assertion that Black Americans are the "lady among the races."[34]

Park's ideas anticipated the ways in which interracial conflict would influence Black social status. In anticipation of Gunnar Myrdal's work a generation later, Park speculated that democratic principle would outweigh the effects of racial discrimination. He also speculated that urban spaces rather than rural environments would be the places where Black Americans could take advantage of the economic, social, and educational opportunities available to develop leadership sufficient in influence to redefine the possibilities of social mobility. One of the elements that Park's ideas failed to consider, as his students like E. Franklin Frazier pointed out, was the extent to which the experiences of Black communities in the United States were influenced by white people who lived outside of those Black communities. Park is also indifferent to the kinds of social stratification that E. Franklin Frazier identified

Gunnar and Alva Myrdal. Library of
Congress, Prints and Photographs
Division, LC-DIG-ppmsca-12446.

that occurs when people in the middle class begin to make decisions based
on class rather than group identity.[35]

Frankly, much of this echoes Ellison's own thoughts about race in the
United States. After all, Park is actively trying to address racial inequality,
albeit from a sociological framework. But Ellison's antagonism toward so-
ciology and more broadly toward the reductively essentializing tendencies
of the ways social sciences address race is the basis of his dispute. While Park
overlooked the collective pressures of white influence on Black communities,
Gunnar Myrdal's examination of race in the United States seems, at least for
Ellison, to overvalue that very element. Beginning around 1935, the Carnegie
Corporation indicated an interest in supporting an extensive examination of
Black Americans. That interest culminated in Gunnar Myrdal's exhaustive
fifteen-hundred-page study that was published in 1944 as *An American Dilemma: The Negro Problem and Modern Democracy*. The root of the dilemma
he outlined was that Americans face a fundamental tension between a patina
of egalitarianism and the reality of the nation's actual treatment of Black
American citizens.

The study was completed in the shadow of World War II amid the urban unrest that consumed Detroit and Harlem in 1943. Myrdal was a Swedish sociologist who had been brought to the United States in 1937. His study was intended to be a fresh look at an old American problem and was widely regarded as a rigorously researched influential tool in the fight against segregation. Myrdal actively collaborated with and engaged the ideas of prominent Black thinkers on the subject like Ralph Bunche and Sterling Brown. But for Ellison, Myrdal's report missed the boat by focusing on Black American reaction rather than on the rituals and cultural elements actively developed by Black people in response to their lived experiences that were at the core of those reactions. If the nation's race problem was really a white problem, as Myrdal argued, then the Black Americans most affected by the cause of the problem were reduced to a series of characteristics, at best, or at worst made invisible and eliminated completely from active engagement with this dilemma.

Ellison conveys this challenge to his readers on numerous occasions as he reaches beyond reductionist constructions of race. The review of the study that Ralph Ellison was asked to write by the editors of *Antioch Review* was completed in 1944. While it was arguably an important conceptual movement for Ellison away from sociological approaches for making sense of his experiences and toward understanding the experiences of other Black Americans, the review remained unpublished for twenty years until the publication of *Shadow and Act* in 1964. It is unclear if the article remained unpublished for so long because the views Ellison expressed were overly acerbic, because the comments contained in the review largely ignore Myrdal's copious text in favor of Ellison's own overly broad assessment of sociology itself, or even because Ellison's thoughts were unfocused as he considered the reality that he would, at some point, be required to respond to the notification he had received from the draft board informing him that he was required to report for active armed-forces service. He ended up shipping out with the United States Merchant Marine during the winter of 1945, near the time of the German counterattack in the Battle of the Bulge in January of 1945. In a letter to Paul Bixler at *Antioch Review* dated November 30, 1944, Ellison himself deprecatingly referred to the review as "a mess of loose ends." Lawrence Jackson suggests in his biography that the cause of rejection for the review had to do with the pointedness of Ellison's views. Conversely, Arnold Rampersad points in his biography to the broad, unfocused relation of Ellison's ideas to the book itself as the cause of the essay's rejection. Whatever the reasons, Paul Bixler ended up rejecting the review for publication in the journal.[36]

Early in the review, Ellison notes that, "Since its inception, American social science has been closely bound with American Negro destiny." The comment looks backward to the white philanthropists who arrived at Tuskegee Institute intent on shaping the future of Black Americans and forward to Ellison's own caricature of the white philanthropist who arrives at the narrator's college spouting empty assertions about his relation to Black destiny in *Invisible Man*. By arguing that sociologists do little more than attempt to use "their graphs, charts, and other paraphernalia to prove the Negro's biological, psychological, intellectual, and moral inferiority," Ellison's primary objective seems to be to use the review as a way of attacking sociology as a dangerous pseudoscience that does little more than justify southern exploitation of Black Americans and northern indifference to that exploitation. In short, Ellison dismissed Myrdal's pseudoscience—and, by extension, the pseudoscience that he saw at the foundation of all sociology—as doing little more than propagating a condescending theory that pathologized Black American culture in the United States.

This pathologizing process had its roots in Reconstruction, when the North functioned as little more than an observer of what was occurring in the South. The North endorsed sociology's flawed methods and assumptions by sanctioning a flawed response to the country's own flawed response to the failures of Reconstruction. Specifically, Ellison argued that "the North simply lost interest in the Negro" following the Civil War. But the North also recognized that it needed to normalize economic relations with the South and, to do so, had to address the experiences of Black American citizens. It did this, however clumsily, by establishing and promoting Black education in the South, inserting itself into the economic and political circumstances of Black Americans, installing Booker T. Washington as a de facto representative of Black America (and Tuskegee Institute as the segregated site of his authority), and by employing sociology as a preferred method for justifying the methods of its response. At the center of that response was the process that pathologized Black Americans as themselves being the root of the problem, just as Ellison believed Myrdal had done. For Ellison, Myrdal may indeed have been an outsider to the problems he described in the United States, but that did not guarantee his impartiality. Nor does it mean that Myrdal was without his own bias and agenda. If leftist ideology had moved Black Americans further left, it had also done something similar for New Deal politics. At this moment in Ellison's thinking, class struggle and the economic components of anti-Black racism were inseparable from power and the manipulation of that power. While Myrdal employs America's professed belief in democracy, equality, and individualism, the reality for Ellison is that he also employs those very same elements as tools for denying the very existence of class struggle in the United States. Perhaps more specifically, Ellison's reading accuses Myrdal of ignoring the fact that social science stands at the point of connection between several distinctly American principles, each of which are kept in balance by social science itself.

What particularly seems to infuriate Ellison is that Myrdal's study takes from Black Americans any sense of agency in their own existence. White Americans are privileged with agency over Black Americans, and Black Americans are reduced to the role of passive reaction: "[T]he Negro's entire life and, consequently, also his opinions on the Negro problem are, in the main, to be considered as secondary reactions to more primary pressures from the side of the dominant white majority."[37] For Ellison, the value for Myrdal is for Black people to be American and, more pointedly, for Black people to be assimilated into America. The cultural exchange goes in one direction. Black Americans had to give up the African parts of their Americanness in order truly to become American: "But can a people . . . live and develop for over three hundred years simply by *reacting* [emphasis in original]? Are American Negroes simply the creation of white men, or have they at least helped to create themselves out of what they found around them? Men have made a way of life in caves and upon cliffs; why cannot Negroes have made a life upon the horns of the white man's dilemma?"[38] Ellison's review highlights his belief that Black Americans have survived specifically because of their active production of folklore and culture.

This is a marker of the ways Ellison's thought had shifted from the late 1930s to the occasion of this long-unpublished review from the mid-1940s. While Black cultural practice and production remained at the center of Ellison's thought, the Black Americans at the center of the process of producing a useable culture out of the realities of the social limitations in which they were produced became a primary concern for him. Myrdal's pseudoscientific assumptions—and, by extension, the pseudoscientific assumptions that Ellison eventually began to associate with the radical Left—are simply inadequate for the task of illuminating the interactions of race and cultural production. Ellison had reached an important point of transition, perhaps influenced by his own dissatisfaction with the Left, the weight of World War II, and his own impending involvement in the war. Cultural production had become for Ellison, and steadfastly remained, an individual and collective act that was itself inherently political, perhaps because the act of cultural production was such an emphatic indication of the democratic process.

While Myrdal clearly recognizes the existence of Black cultural production, his sociological approach renders that production a pathological issue that liberal goodwill would eventually assimilate—that is, marginalize, dilute, and make inconsequential. The history of Black vernacular production would be converted and absorbed into a Eurocentric model of cohesion and conformity. Myrdal's assessment simply had no space for a vernacular culture based in the blues. The study itself represented the expression of a pathology best avoided by Black Americans. For Ellison, the expression of Black culture that Myrdal's study reductively proposed assimilating into American culture was the highest indication of a cultural and political process that was generative, rather than simply reactive, in the face of the nation's cultural oppression.

The year 1944 was certainly a time of transition for Ralph Ellison. As his remarks in "Introduction to the Thirtieth Anniversary Edition of *Invisible Man*" indicate, Ellison's thoughts had turned very acutely to the relationship between the South and the North and, more specifically, toward the process of migration that became so much a part of *Invisible Man,* numerous essays, and the unfinished second novel. Perhaps World War II, his increasing disillusionment with the Left, the coalescence of the thoughts contained in pieces like "Flying Home" and the review of *An American Dilemma,* and the development of his thoughts about his work leading to *Invisible Man* represent the most significant ways in which his thoughts were evolving. Ellison himself migrated to New York from the South as the energy generated by the New Negro movement was dissipating. The element of migration is apparent in "Flying Home" when Todd migrates back to his southern roots, in *Invisible Man* when the unnamed narrator migrates from the South to Harlem and then to the recesses of Harlem's underground, and in *Three Days before the Shooting…* when Bliss geographically migrates spatially from south to north and internally from Bliss to Senator Adam Sunraider.

The recurrence of geography and the movement of people through and across geographies is clearly both a necessary component of explaining the vernacular and in explaining race. In that sense, Ellison and Richard Wright, his literary, political, and intellectual mentor, clearly reflect their desire to revise a primary impulse of the New Negro movement to address the relationship between aesthetic considerations and the Black populations about whom they wrote. Often, the space between aesthetics and the folk was invoked by fiction writers, poets, sociologists, and historians and mediated by their use of vernacular cultural traditions like spirituals, the blues, the sermon, and jazz improvisation.

The vernacular was also a way to bridge the space between Black America and its influence on and by modernity. But the *designation* of folk is as relentlessly amorphous in its definition as it is in the strategies used to *invoke* folk. "The folk" and their vernacular traditions are most often used to invoke a collective identity that may not actually exist and is certainly broadly contested. But this attempt of the New Negro movement to assert an essentialized racial collectivity, subsequently opposed by Wright and Ellison alike, was in some ways a natural progression toward a race consciousness that stands in the place of the origins erased by slavery.

The New Negro movement, by its own definition, self-consciously corrected conceptions about the alchemy of race, art, and cultural identity. Its critique and reformation of these elements is a powerful reminder that not only is the very conception of race a social invention largely produced by politics and ideology but that the conception of racial identity and consciousness is itself an intrinsically modern conceit. It is also a reminder of the ways the vernacular is so often mediated.[39]

This sense of modernity, particularly as it relates to the work of Wright and Ellison during the interwar period, is reflected in their attempts to represent a Black vernacular presence that extended beyond the limitations of the middle class. Their vision during this period of vernacular influence is inseparable from class and modernity. In his article "Notes on Deconstructing 'The Folk,'" Robin D. G. Kelley makes this point more broadly in his observation that folk culture, by its very definition, is intrinsically tied to race, gender, and the modern: "'[F]olk' either signifies what people imagine to be preindustrial survivals or, when one is not talking about Europe, the cultural practices of the Other (in this case, African-American, Asian, Latino, Appalachian, or whoever the Other might be) that have not been mass marketed."[40] "Flying Home," for example, describes a young Black man on the cusp of modernity who crashes into a sharecropper's field that itself stands in as a representation of the economic and sociopolitical position of many Black Americans. In this respect, particularly given Ellison's relationship to the Left during this period, vernacular culture functioned in direct relationship to the effects of racial oppression and economic exploitation.

While invoking vernacular culture certainly has political implications, Ellison's ideas about vernacular culture, particularly as those ideas were deployed during his closest association with Richard Wright during the 1930s and early 1940s, evolved from a politicized use into something more comprehensive. Vernacular culture became increasingly representative of a broader cultural imagination in the face of oppression and racial violence. Ellison's thoughts steadily began to move him to the margins of Black vernacular experience even as his work increasingly described the cultural workings of a heterogeneous Black consciousness to an audience that was not Black. Richard Wright was doing similar work during the period in, for example, his essay "How 'Bigger' Was Born" and in the very creation of Bigger Thomas in *Native Son*. Race, as Ellison viewed it during the years he moved away from leftist thought, was not class.

Early during the nation's involvement in the war, in an unsigned editorial comment that Ellison wrote for the summer 1942 *Negro Quarterly*, Ellison referred to the conflict as the "peoples' war."[41] His conflation of politics and the folk was published in the shadow of Richard Wright's *12 Million Black Voices: A Folk History of the Negro in the United States,* published in 1941. It is a history that functions around enslaved Black migration from Africa and the eventual exodus of Black people from the American South. It is about cultural birth, death, and rebirth from Africa through slavery and Reconstruction to Black American. At the conclusion of the text, the narrator emphasizes each of these elements by saying "hundreds of thousands of us are moving into the sphere of conscious history. We are with the new tide. We stand at the crossroads. We watch each new procession. . . . Voices are speaking. Men are moving! And we shall be with them."[42] Here, Wright, as Ellison echoes, recognizes Black culture as a distinct national culture that had both survived and thrived during multiple migratory experiences. Wright sees that culture in terms that were linked to the Black working class that was emerging in the North. Richard Wright's thoughts about folk culture, which he developed during the Depression and expanded during the war, saw Black folk culture as a vestige of the history of Black people in the United States that could not be assimilated into modernity. Though Ellison's thoughts were certainly influenced by Wright, particularly during the closest years of their association, Ellison's thoughts by 1944 had begun to focus on the cultural importance of the ways Black vernacular culture expressed itself.[43]

Ellison's early writing quickly diverged from Wright. That process was largely complete by the wartime years when Ellison was consciously moving away from Marxist ideology. While Wright hypothesized in *12 Million Black Voices* that modernity would bring with it the culmination of a viable Black folk culture, Ellison began to organize his thoughts around the possibility that one of the strengths of Black folk culture lay in the possibilities of Black migration from the rural South to the urban North. Ellison accepted Wright's vision that Black America was in transition from vernacular culture to a consciousness that was increasingly democratic and urban. Wright's modernity brought with it the death of the rural vernacular in favor of a modernity that functioned around workers, Black and white. Specifically, southern vernacular traditions were largely useless in urban modernity. In both his influential 1937 essay "Blueprint for Negro Writing" and in *12 Million Black Voices,* Wright locates Black vernacular culture firmly and inextricably in the American South.

"Blueprint for Negro Writing," published in the first issue of *New Challenge,* focused on Wright's conception that the new culture emerging from the shadow of the New Negro movement was produced by a sense of nationalism that was reflected throughout Black American culture and particularly its vernacular culture. This outlook certainly has echoes of Robert Park and the Chicago School of sociology inasmuch as Park saw Black migration as forming the basis of Black nationalism. Wright recognized in the progressive Black writer a nationalist impulse stemming from the consequences of Black interdependence. For Wright, the Black author mediates collective experience and the social processes contained in a Black nation that exists within the geographic borders of the nation.

This Black Belt thesis had become part of Communist Party USA policy at the Sixth Comintern in 1928. It asserted the Marxist position that Black Americans were an oppressed nation within the nation and deserved the

Richard Wright in his study. US Farm Security Administration/Office of War Information Collection, Library of Congress, Prints and Photographs Division, LC-USW3-030278-D.

right to self-determination in the area of the country—the Black Belt—in which Black Americans constituted most of the population. In articulating a Black consciousness, the true push was toward worker solidarity. Though Wright's "Blueprint for Negro Writing" retained a strong attachment to racial self-determination, the Communist Party USA had begun to move beyond that objective in favor of a broader focus on disenfranchisement and civil rights. Wright had very publicly become disenchanted with the Communist Party USA as its position moved away from Black self-determination in favor of supporting the German-Soviet Nonaggression Pact in 1939, opposing the war into 1941 when Germany invaded the Soviet Union, and then supporting the war. Before Germany's invasion of the Soviet Union, for example, the party had endorsed Black civil rights to slow the pace of the nation's buildup to entering the war.[44]

In *12 Million Black Voices*, Wright describes a romanticized southern Black peasant vernacular experience where "In summer the magnolia trees fill the countryside with sweet scent for long miles. Days are slumberous, and the skies are high and thronged with clouds that ride fast. At midday the sun blazes and bleaches the soil. Butterflies flit through the heat; wasps sing their sharp, straight lines; birds fluff and flounce, piping in querulous joy." Its urban counterpart, which he centers in the kitchenette, is palpably bleak in its difference: "The kitchenette is our prison, our death sentence without a trial, the new form of mob violence that assaults not only the lone individual, but all of us in ceaseless attacks. The kitchenettes with its filth and foul air, with its one toilet for thirty or more tenants, kills our black babies so fast that in many cities twice as many of them die as white babies." Perhaps unlike Ellison, Wright was looking for ways to describe his migratory experiences in terms that could encompass the broad spectrum of experiences that Black Americans encountered. Black writers could embrace the modernity that Wright envisioned by synthesizing vernacular experience with the science produced by sociology and the ideology provided by Marxism.

The critique that Ellison produced in his early writing largely corroborated Wright's deployment of Marxist ideology. Ellison was certainly committed at this time to Black self-determination and the Black Belt position. Moreover, Ellison began to envision writers, like the one he was becoming, as the embodiment of a kind of consciousness that united his vision of nationalism with a movement—cultural, social, and political—that embraced yet transcended race. His first publication was a book review that was published in the same initial issue of *New Challenge* magazine that contained Wright's "Blueprint for Negro Writing." It makes a Marxist argument in favor of employing Black folk material as a strategy for moving beyond the middle-class limitations imposed by the New Negro movement.

But as his thinking migrated away from leftist ideology, Ellison saw Black vernacular as a living, ongoing process that continued to link Black Americans to the most central elements of American culture and its democratic aspirations. Most pointedly, Ellison saw urban Black vernacular as central to modern working-class consciousness and saw it as a fundamental element for understanding Black American experience. As Ellison's narrative shifted from organizing itself around leftist ideology in favor of an aesthetic orientation, Ellison clearly wanted to see himself and his work as being part of a larger cultural conversation.

Ellison's shift away from focusing on the class-based elements of vernacular culture in favor of an aesthetic focus indicates his desire to observe the complexities of race without reproducing the limitations inscribed in race. Vernacular culture, for Ellison, should certainly not be equated with artistic production. While Ellison made a compelling argument beginning in the years following the publication of *Invisible Man* for the contributions of Black Americans in the American literary production of writers like Herman Melville, Mark Twain, Ernest Hemingway, T. S. Eliot, and William Faulkner, the reality is that artists do not necessarily participate in the culture that they self-consciously interpret for consumers of their art. From the mid-1940s onward, Ellison's work increasingly focused on exceptional individuals—often profoundly flawed individuals but exceptional individuals nonetheless—who were somehow representative of vernacular expressive influence.

Vernacular expression gives meaning and resonance to culture even as the vernacular is so often homogenized into a romanticized collective. This was the heart of Ellison's angry review of Myrdal's *An American Dilemma* and reflected the distance that Ellison's thoughts had traveled from his earlier endorsement of Richard Wright's proletarian vision of Black vernacular influence. Wright saw himself as an outsider to American politics. Ellison worked to fashion a trajectory that presented himself as an artistic insider mediating the Black American vernacular culture that formed the core of the nation's culture.

In the fullness of his divergence from Wright's conception of the vernacular, Ellison replaced the ethos of labor and the working class with the ethos of culture itself. If Wright's formulation established the working class as the agent for social and political change, Ellison came to see vernacular expression, that is, culture itself, as the most effective instrument for social change. In an essay published in the winter–spring 1943 *Negro Quarterly,* Ellison observes that "Much in Negro life remains a mystery; perhaps the zoot suit conceals profound political meaning; perhaps the symmetrical frenzy of the Lindy-hop conceals clues to great potential power—if only Negro leaders would solve this riddle."[45]

While the trajectory of Ellison's thoughts on the broader effects of Black folk culture continued to evolve, this moment in 1944, culminating with his review of Myrdal's book, is a point of transition for Ellison relative to both the Right and the Left. His comments indicate a profound dissatisfaction with the Right, embodied in Myrdal's book, which he sees as little more than a capitalist-inspired tool that was a *"blueprint for a more effective exploitation of the South's natural, industrial, and human resources [emphasis in original]."*[46] The Left, which he had come to see as refusing to recognize and acknowledge the true complexities of race as it is lived and experienced in America beyond the encircling boundaries of ideology, fared little better.

ELLISON'S FIELD OF BATTLE:
SYMBOLISM, MODERNITY, AND THE VERNACULAR

[A]ll symbolism can be treated as the ritualistic naming and changing of identity.
   KENNETH BURKE, *Attitudes toward History*

Ellison's transition through radical ideology and his denunciation of sociology were both contained in his search for a vocabulary that could transcend the limitations of race even as it embraced the realities of race as a lived experience and as a cultural construct in America. For all the distaste Ellison had for sociology, *An American Dilemma* was a liberal response that substituted the redistribution of cultural capital to white people as a strategy against racism instead of the redistribution of wealth to the Black community. Both Ellison and Myrdal suggested the viability of a Black presence capable of revising the nation's relationship to culture and race relations. For Ellison, this is central to his consideration of how national culture gets formed in the first place. As Stephen Schryer observes in *Fantasies of the New Class*, "Myrdal and Ellison ... could not help but reflect the ways in which racial prejudices are shaped by a complex interplay between cultural attitudes and economic interests."[47] Even with Ellison's fierce opposition to sociology, each did indeed emphasize in the work of the other how cultural attitudes informed national interests.

Kenneth Warren observes in *So Black and Blue* the ways this stage of Ellison's thought embodies the sociological approach that he subsequently rejected in his critique of Richard Wright and literary naturalism when he writes: "even as Ellison elaborated his understanding of the blues in his 1945 review of Richard Wright's *Black Boy,* he also embraced certain characterizations of black life that were not all that distant from some of the claims later made" by sociologists.[48] This is certainly true, though the direction of his thought at this point was to formulate a more complex theory of race, culture, and American race relations. Ellison's was a response against the liberal paternalism that acknowledged the existence of Black culture but focused instead on the damage inflicted by slavery on that culture rather than on the contributions that culture had made to the nation's formation. Ellison fought the battle of white paternalism a generation before the Black Power movement fought a similar battle. Ellison's dissent was against the sociological attitude that placed the conversation in the hands of white people who simply referred to Black people as the primary exhibit of what the damage of racism had caused.

Ellison's critique of Myrdal was, according to Barbara Foley in "Ralph Ellison as Proletarian Journalist," little more than a reprise of the ideas that Ellison had encountered during his more active engagement with the Left. In arguing that Ellison "clearly remains wedded to a Marxist paradigm" and that "Ellison here remains within the rubric of Marxist political and cultural critique,"[49] Foley's project is to tie Ellison more securely to a Marxist ideology between 1937 and 1944, from which Ellison worked to distance himself in subsequent decades. Ellison's thought displays ideas that he ultimately rejected precisely because this review stands as a point of delineation—however awkwardly that delineation was made—between his leftist writing and the cultural argument that he had begun to formulate and subsequently embrace. But in making that transition, Ellison needed a framework upon which to overlay his ideas about culture and aesthetics, which is what his intellectual relationship with Kenneth Burke provided.

Kenneth Burke's influence on Ralph Ellison has long been firmly established, perhaps most persuasively by Bryan Crable in *Kenneth Burke and Ralph Ellison*. Crable argues not only for a reading of their relationship that acknowledges Burke's influence on Ellison, going so far as to say that "Ellison's novel also includes implicit critiques on Burke" and that the novel presented what he calls a "clear indictment of Norton's—Burke's—lack of vision" in the college section of the novel.[50] In speculating, as he does in the chapter "Was Kenneth Burke a Racist?" about Burke's willingness and ability to address race in America, Crable suggests that, while Kenneth Burke may have stopped short of embracing a language capable of engaging race in America, Ellison formulated from their intellectual relationship a language of race and nation. Ellison clearly wanted to think about—and beyond—race in America. But he also found it impossible to consider one without the other. *Invisible Man,* portions of which grew out of the conversation between these two men, ultimately envisions and responds to the particularly binary view of race that characterized Jim Crow America. Ellison's conversation with Burke also influenced the composition of *Three Days before the Shooting…,* and the unfinished novel can be seen in the context of Ellison's attempt to wrestle with and expand the binary view of race in America that characterizes *Invisible Man.*

Ellison's thoughts about culture, vernacular and otherwise, constitute for him a central strategy for understanding and explaining experience. While his definition of culture was refined and specialized, particularly during the period of broad social changes that occurred throughout the nation from the 1930s into the 1970s, the genealogy of Ellison's evolving conception of culture theory predates his engagement with leftist ideology and the ideas contained in his earliest published work. Ellison had encountered a variety of cultural theories before he became radicalized, and these encounters finally had a significant effect on his formative thoughts about culture in ways that ultimately superseded political ideology.

Invisible Man, with its assertions about cultural relativism and the ability of individuals to make their own meaning of an unrelentingly complex world, was a late contribution to literary modernism. Ellison's ideas about modernism as a strategy for describing a world that was fragmented and chaotic had begun to take shape much earlier and certainly spoke to his early endorsement of proletarian prose. Some of the criticism of *Invisible Man* echoes a broader critique of modernism's aesthetic self-consciousness and aesthetic questioning of the very nature of being and identity. With modernism's insistence that meaning comes from an individual experience of culture, Ellison could tell stories from multiple perspectives, as he did in *Invisible Man* and as he attempted to do in the structure he set out in the unfinished second novel. Perspective was everything. Certainty was distorted, elusive, and ever-changing. Meaning and sense could be dislocated from its contexts. Cultural values could be questioned. History could be rethought through the lens of myth. Modernity could become synonymous with complexity and the unconscious mind synonymous with chaos. Language could become experimental, improvisatory, dismissive of sentimentality, and thick with allusion.

Ellison regularly identified T. S. Eliot as a major influence on the ways he came to see the role folklore and vernacular production influenced how culture was produced and understood. By way of Eliot, Ellison was able to see that an important value of myth and folklore was the way they provided both structural and thematic possibilities. In what became an often-repeated explanation, Ellison claims to have found his way to "The Waste Land" during the year he worked in the library at Tuskegee Institute. Ellison gave a speech to the plebe class at West Point on March 26, 1969, which he subsequently published as "On Initiation Rites and Power." His comments focused on *Invisible Man,* which the students had been assigned to read. Early in the speech, he references Eliot:

At Tuskegee I found myself reading *The Waste Land,* and for the first time, I was caught up in a piece of poetry which moved me but which I couldn't reduce to a logical system.... I had a sense that all of these references of Eliot's, all of this snatching of phrases from the German, French, Sanskrit, and so on, were attuned to that type of American cultural expressiveness which one got in jazz and which one still gets in good jazz. But between feeling intuitively that this was what was going on and being able to confirm it, there was quite a gap. Fortunately, Mr. Eliot appended to the original edition of *The Waste Land* a long body of footnotes, and I began to get the books out of the library and read them. That really was a beginning of my literary education, and actually it was the beginning of my transformation (or shall we say, metamorphosis) from a would-be composer into some sort of novelist.[51]

His understanding of what he had experienced followed more slowly: "Years later when I began to try to understand Eliot and Pound, and so on, to see how they worked putting these things together, I began to look back and understand, 'Oh yes, I was involved with folklore,' but this was the result of certain sorts of conscious experience based upon literature. I discovered the folklore because I had become a literary person."[52] The folklore that Ellison saw in T. S. Eliot—"Eliot is full of American folklore"[53]—was largely invisible to him in Deep Deuce, the vibrant Black community in which he had grown up in Oklahoma City, and in the work of the Black American writers he read: "I was reading all these people very intensely and I felt something missing in them that I ran into in Eliot, the folk tradition they had and didn't know what to do with."[54]

While it is unclear precisely what Ellison saw in Eliot's use of folklore that he found lacking in the Black American writers whose work he was reading, the worth that Ellison attaches to folklore and vernacular culture is the value of individual and collective self-definition. This impulse toward self-definition was especially important after the end of segregation, when Ellison increasingly saw racial and political affiliation as inadequate containers for identity. The legal conclusion of segregation made this especially important, as Black Americans identified new strategies for shaping and explaining their experiences. Just before the end of legalized segregation, Ellison observed in an interview that folklore mediates the past and present as groups look toward the future: "For us the question should be, what are the specific *forms* of that humanity, and what in our background is worth preserving or abandoning. The clue to this can be found in folklore which offers the first drawings of any group's character. . . . These drawings may be crude but they are nonetheless profound in that they represent the group's attempt to humanize the world [*emphasis in original*]."[55]

It is understandable why the alchemy of self-identification and self-preservation were so important to Ellison, particularly then. After all, Black American vernacular culture had grown and expanded into the American mainstream during a tortuous historical course in the Americas, and Ellison very self-consciously wanted to be sure that vernacular experience was recognized, particularly given the selective nature of the nation's historical memory. In a letter to his lifelong friend Albert Murray, whom Duke Ellington called the unsquarest man he knew, from June 2, 1957, Ellison notes "The trick is to get mose lore [*a blanket term that Ellison used to refer to ordinary Black people in folk terms that he often used to signify bluesmen, tricksters, and folk philosophers*] into the novel so that it becomes a part of the tradition."[56] The importance was the Black presence in American culture: "[W]e keep talking about 'black awareness' when we really should be talking about black American awareness, an awareness of where we fit into the total American scheme, where our influence is."[57] To some extent, Black vernacular experience served as a corrective tool intended to remedy the myopic lens through which the nation viewed its own history, particularly as that history related to race. For Ellison, American culture, consciously and unconsciously, had already insinuated Black vernacular elements into the deepest recesses of its national literature.

Vernacular expressive culture is often seen as a kind of preliterate expression that is invoked in the oral tradition (like sermons, storytelling, and song lyrics), gospel, the blues, and vernacular visual expression. Ellison's ongoing project was to use literature to invoke the preliterate as a way of explaining the fragmentation and chaos of modern culture. Migration had certainly modified vernacular expression, but it had not destroyed its ability to explain and give meaning to individual and collective experience.

Ellison is often read as primarily being interested in revealing the unseen Black presence in American literature. But the most meaningful part of Ellison's interventions into American literature was to recognize the ways Black Americans were marginalized in a body of literature that relegated Black American experiences to less-meaningful representations. Ellison saw this as having to do with literary intention. As an Oklahoman with parents from Georgia and South Carolina, Ellison was acutely aware of the ways in which the experiences with which he most closely related were written out of the American literary tradition. He saw tradition as being the best technique for moving Black American experience from the margin to the center: "I wanted to tell a story. I felt that there was a great deal about the nature of American experience which was not understood by most Americans. I felt also that the diversity of the total experience rendered much of it mysterious."[58] The vernacular translated the mysteriousness of that experience into something resembling symbolic myth and archetype.

When Ellison first arrived in New York during the Depression, he worked on a folklore project administered by the Works Progress Administration in which he was given the assignment of collecting children's rhymes. These rhymes undeniably had connections to the American South and to African retentions. He came to see migration as an important component of folklore: "Mark Twain understood the importance of the Mississippi River (as did T. S. Eliot and others) to the fluidity of American literature and folklore. Where you get people going back and forth you get literature, art. Kansas City and Chicago were great towns for jazz because they were great railroad towns. People would come up and tell their stories."[59] Culture, by its very definition, functions around exchange rather than isolation.

For Black American folklore, the terms of the cultural exchange were limited by its development and existence in a broader cultural environment. That environment undermined the acknowledgment of the experiences it described and diminished its contributions to the nation and to its role in the lives of the Black Americans who produced it: "One ironic witness to the beauty and the universality of this art is the fact that the descendants of the very men who enslaved us can now sing the spirituals and find in the singing an exultation of their own humanity."[60] Ellison focuses here on the universality of Black vernacular. The greater implication is that vernacular culture both conveyed history and, embodied in its own rituals, was its own kind of historical presence.

Ritual, like the vernacular itself, provides a glimpse of the Black presence that evolved into his broader thoughts about the democratic ideal. Ellison was far less interested in exploring folklore and ritual in ways that provided textual structure than he was in the ability of vernacular traditions to illuminate the changes created by migration and the expansion of urban centers. The role of the artist was also an important component of the vernacular inasmuch as art provides order and context to individual and collective experience in an otherwise fragmented, chaotic world.

Ellison regularly ascribes his awareness of the importance of folklore to his early reading of T. S. Eliot. It is worth noting, as Ellison does himself, that it was the work of Kenneth Burke that most strongly solidified the direction of his thinking about folklore that he had begun with his reading of Eliot.[61] Two years before Ralph Ellison became acquainted with Kenneth Burke's thinking, he and Richard Wright had attended a lecture given by Ernest Hemingway. Hemingway had been asked to give the keynote address to the Second American Writers' Congress, which took place June 4–6, 1937. The League of American Writers had been organized by the Communist Party USA as a response to fascism. Hemingway delivered his address on Saturday, June 5. Hemingway, who had recently returned from the Spanish Civil War, used his address to denounce fascism and to enlist writers for the cause.

Ellison, during his time at Tuskegee Institute, had begun to see Hemingway as a consummate illustration of modernist potential and as a contributor to the ways Ellison envisioned the confluence of art and politics. When Ellison heard Hemingway speak at the conference, Ellison was new to New York and new to meaningful engagement with the Popular Front. But as much as Ellison may have liked the work he read during his college years, Lawrence Jackson's biography of Ellison suggests that his response to Hemingway's keynote may have been fairly negative. At the very least, Wright and Ellison left disappointed by what they considered a lack of sophistication in Hemingway's view of politics in western Europe.[62]

Two years later, Kenneth Burke gave a reading entitled "The Rhetoric of Hitler's Battle" at a session that was part of the Third League of American Writers' Conference. Ellison immediately saw in Burke's presentation the sophistication of thought that he had found lacking in Ernest Hemingway's keynote presentation from the previous conference. (In a 1977 interview, Ellison misremembered the date of Burke's presentation of "The Rhetoric of Hitler's Battle" when he says, "I first became interested in Burke after hearing him read his essay, 'The Rhetoric of Hitler's Battle.' It was a critique of *Mein Kampf,* and the time was 1937." Burke made this presentation at the conference on June 4, 1939. Ernest Hemingway gave the keynote address two years earlier at the Second American Writers' Congress in 1937.)[63] Kenneth Burke was active with the League of American Writers and an enthusiastic supporter of Popular Front causes, particularly those objectives that focused on protecting the Soviet Union. Burke later repudiated his support of Stalin: "I believed that Stalin was alright. I didn't believe the goddam charges against Stalin at the time. I really didn't. I thought the guy was straight."[64] Ellison drew from Burke a lens through which to focus the intersecting threads of language and culture: "I was just starting out as a writer, and as I went on struggling to understand his criticism, I began to learn something of the nature of literature, society, social class, and psychology as they related to literary form. I began to grasp how language operates, both in literature and as an agency of oral communication. In college and on my own, I had studied a little psychology, a little sociology, you know, dribs and drabs, but Burke provided a Gestalt through which I could apply intellectual insights back into my own materials and into my own life."[65]

Burke's work did not address issues of race with the same intensity as Ellison's. What Ellison was able to distill from Burke's work, and from the correspondence they exchanged beginning in the mid-1940s, was a clarification of literary perspective and rhetorical sensibility. For Ellison, the history of the nation was race. Burke seemed to struggle with the issue but was willing to engage with Ellison's thinking. In a letter to Richard Wright from August 24, 1946, Ellison wrote, "We were out to Kenneth Burke's place in N.J. several weekends ago, where he gave me a letter he had written in answer to one of my own last year. He had tried to answer some of my opinions concerning the racial set-up and our culture, but was so dissatisfied with his answers that he could never mail the letter. In it he attempted to set down a formula for a Negro character who would incorporate all of the contradictions present in the Negro-white situation in this country and yet be appealing to whites."[66] The intellectual relationship began in the context of leftist ideology between Burke and Ellison and extended through the correspondence they maintained. It illustrates Ellison's development as a young writer eagerly seeking artistic inspiration and the analytic vocabulary necessary to bring his aspirations to fruition.

Burke's presentation was in response to the recent publication of *Mein Kampf* in English. Burke's assertion was that Hitler's political distortions represented a symbolic representation that brought together disparate German worldviews into something that was considerably more cohesive. In this presentation, Burke had found a way to fuse the ideological (Marxism) with the psychological (Freud). "I was very curious about how one could put Marx and Freud together. No real problem now, I suppose, but coming from where I did, it was puzzling. I was to discover that it was also a problem for Communist intellectuals and for any of their opponents. Either Marx was raised up and Freud put down, or Freud raised up and Marx put down."[67] Burke and Ellison were able to share an intellectual exchange that began in a radical environment and that extended beyond the relationship either of them had with radicalism. In his first letter to Burke, from November 23, 1945, Ellison writes that "I am, as you say, becoming quite at home in that amalgam of sociology, psychology, Marxism and literary criticism, and I'd go further and say that without it, coming from where I do in American society, I would not be at home in this rather cockeyed world. I suppose that is why I feel really indebted to you. Essentially the Negro situation is irrational to an extent which surpasses that of the rest of the world, though God knows that sounds impossible. Your method gave me the first instrument with which I could orient myself—something which neither Marx alone nor Freud alone could do"[68]

What Ellison absorbed as a beginning writer from his interactions with Burke and, presumably, others, in the years leading up to and during World War II was a relationship between literature and social formation. In "Revolutionary Symbolism in America," from the First League of American Writers' Conference in 1935, Burke had argued that the myths that writers reproduce in their work provides a tangible way to describe pattern and relationship. Ellison came to see Black vernacular culture as a viable framework for providing an intervention between vernacular expression and artistic expression. Although he was always careful to limit the extent of his commitment to leftist ideology after the publication of *Invisible Man,* Ellison came to see his role, which he eventually related to his thoughts about the novel, as being to create a form robust enough to harness the power of symbolic action. Literary details gather associations, those associations gather meanings, and those meanings speak to the reader's sense of significance: "These [imagery and the incidents of conflict] come from all kinds of sources. From literature, from the spirituals and the blues, from other novels and from poetry, as well as from my observations of socio-psychological conflicts and processes. It comes from mythology, fool's errands, children's games, sermons, the dozens, and the Bible."[69]

Ellison readily acknowledged that Kenneth Burke's way of thinking had contributed a great deal to the possibilities he eventually saw available to him when he began to organize his own thoughts about race, literature, and culture. The environment of radical ideology in which Ellison first encountered Burke's ideas also contributes a great deal to the ways he understood and drew upon what he saw to be a uniquely synthesizing intellectual approach. Clark Henderson makes a strong argument in "Transforming Action" for a fairly substantial alignment of their politics during the period: "Both Burke and Ellison attended the second and third Writers' Congresses, were associated with the Communist-influenced League of American Writers, and published in the left periodicals *New Masses* and *Direction*. They converged and participated within a Communist-inflected Popular Front scene and were part of what Michael Denning refers to as the 'cultural front.' Their shared political perspective might be called Marxist, communist, or simply leftist, words that each on occasion would embrace."[70] As part of the same conference and at a time when the League of American Writers was at the height of its influence in 1939, Hyde Partnow and B. A. Botkin, who were writers at the Folklore Department of the Federal Writers' Project, gave a presentation at a session entitled "Folklore and Folksay." Richard Wright gave a presentation at a session on the novel. Langston Hughes and Alain Locke spoke at a session entitled "The Negro in Fiction." Kenneth Burke's influences on Ellison's thinking and Ellison's consistent acknowledgment of those influences is not new information to those who have studied Ellison. Burke's contributions influence both the conception and composition of *Invisible Man,* as well as Ellison's broader ideas about history, the novel, and American culture. For Ellison, this outlook grew directly from the literary tools he took from T. S. Eliot and Kenneth Burke at the outset of his writing career. Ellison was able to use these elements to attach his writing to his larger vision of American democracy.

Ellison's ambition was large and unwieldy enough that it may have complicated his composition of the second novel, which, like *Invisible Man,* was meant to be transformative and epic. Eliot's ideas about folklore became coupled with Ellison's ideas about the ways Black vernacular could serve as a place of connection between Ellison and his reading audience. The association of these ideas suggested for him some of the possibilities of how artistic production could actively intervene in the ways the complexities of the nation were understood. Even during these journeyman years of his writing career, Ellison chafed under the assumption that political ideology should be the reason to produce writing rather than being one of many things about which writing might concern itself. Writing certainly mattered in politics, but it was not solely the expression of politics.

Ellison was only twenty-five years old when he heard Burke present "The Rhetoric of Hitler's Battle" during a session entitled "The Writer and Politics" at the 1939 League of American Writers' Congress. Ellison took away from the presentation Burke's attempts to put Marxist ideology and Freudian psychology in conversation with modern cultural analysis. What Burke had done was to provide commentary and a methodology for that commentary to examine the recent unabridged translation of *Mein Kampf* that had been published in English on February 28, 1939. The Book-of-the-Month Club had offered it to its members as a featured selection. While other reviewers had decisively dismissed the book, Burke had provided a close reading of the book intended to arm Americans against subsequent ideologies that might use similar rhetorical strategies. Burke's analysis provided historical context and critical social engagement. In the November 23, 1945, letter to Burke, Ellison writes: "My real debt lies to you in the many things I've learned (and continue to learn) from your work.... That is a debt I shall never stop paying back and it begins back in the thirties when you read the rhetoric of 'Hitler's Battle' before the League of American Writers. I believe you were the only speaker out of the whole group who was concerned with writing *and politics* rather than writing as an *excuse* for politics [*emphasis in original*]." Ellison concluded his letter by saying that he had begun work on the novel that became *Invisible Man* and felt that "if it is worthwhile it will be my most effective means of saying thanks. Anything else seems to me inadequate."[71]

Burke's intervention clearly imposed itself on the composition of *Invisible Man* and on the ways Ellison's thoughts about aesthetics, politics, history, and the writer subsequently evolved. Ellison perhaps saw in Burke a moral purpose that was unavailable to engage solely through the lens of sociology, psychology, or political ideology. For all that has been written about Ellison's relationship to the Left, particularly in his pattern beginning after the publication of *Invisible Man* of blurring the depth of his engagement with leftist ideology in favor of universalizing discussions about aesthetics, it is important to recognize that he clearly emerged as a writer within the framework of the Popular Front. Though the depth of his commitment to official Communist Party USA objectives may be difficult to ascertain with any certainty, his desire to create a presence as a writer who was able meaningfully to engage the influences of history, culture, nation, and aesthetic production was unambiguous.

Ellison came to recognize that this was a deeply chaotic, ambiguous role. Writers existed as much as mythologized and mythologizing figures as they did as the exemplars of the critic/intellectual capable of describing ambiguities of American experience and placing the complexities of that experience in a broader context of meaning and historical significance. Burke was more than simply a "stimulating source" who had contributed to Ellison's ideas for more than two decades, as Ellison described Burke near the end of his introduction to *Shadow and Act.*

By the time *Shadow and Act* was published in 1964, Ellison was a widely read writer. He had evolved a great deal from the twenty-five-year-old recent arrival to the New York literary scene who was radicalized and encouraged by Richard Wright and Langston Hughes and who then encountered Kenneth Burke's ideas about symbolic action. In his biography of Ellison, Arnold Rampersad comments that "The influence of [Langston] Hughes and [Louise] Thompson, in the context of the Depression and his raw ambition, virtually ensured Ralph's radicalization." But views of this moment of Ellison's radicalization are exceptionally difficult to align with any certainty. In *Communists in Harlem during the Depression,* for example, Mark Naison includes a comment from Louise Thompson: "We used to have discussions in our home with him [Richard Wright], Paul Robeson, Langston [Hughes] and Jacques Romain, a Haitian poet we greatly admired.... Ralph Ellison used to be part of that scene as well. He used to be at my house almost every day." But in *Ralph Ellison,* Lawrence Jackson places considerably more distance, as Ellison so often did himself, from Ellison's acceptance of leftist ideology by saying that, while Ellison was attracted to the ideology, Ellison became associated with the movement far to the right of Richard Wright and maintained a certain amount of distance during the period of his deepest involvement.[72]

What is clear is that Burke's ideas reflected the kind of radicalism in which Ellison had participated as he grew and developed as a writer. After all, the ideas that Burke proposed in the 1930s—identity and symbolic action—remained the ideas to which Ellison remained most faithful throughout his career. Ellison's thoughts about Marxism, the Communist Party USA, and leftist ideology all evolved a great deal after his earliest attempts to situate himself as a writer within the Popular Front. His thoughts about Black vernacular as an instrument for establishing and maintaining a collective presence linking action with the symbolic remained remarkably consistent.

All of this suggests a conscious theory for explaining the ways the process of producing art was a reenactment of the American democratic process itself. Vernacular culture was one of the few ways that Black Americans, particularly during the two centuries and a half when they were an enslaved people, could exert individual and collective agency. Neither race, class, nor politics presents the kind of identification and autonomy—that is, identity—that artistic production provides and sustains. One of the things that Ellison saw during his association with the Left, as well as with the assertions made a generation later by the Black Arts movement, was that individuals and the circulation of their ideas were made secondary to the relationship of individuals and their ideas to ideology. What Ellison saw in the work of T. S. Eliot and Kenneth Burke and subsequently embedded into his own evolving thoughts about art, culture, and the vernacular was the possibility of broader associations with the world than those that could be obtained through race or political ideology alone.

Ellison saw nineteenth-century writers like Mark Twain as addressing that precise issue in *The Adventures of Huckleberry Finn* when Huckleberry chooses, against the conventions of the society in which he lived, to side with his friend Jim in Jim's predicament as a person escaping slavery rather than siding with a society that could only see Jim as enslaved and nothing else. Huck's decision to help his friend is arguably predicated on the social privilege that Huckleberry Finn enjoys as a white boy in a society that offers him opportunities for autonomy and self-identification that Jim could never expect to share. But Huckleberry, however briefly, had found a reservoir of empathy that he was able to access and extend to Jim. As Ellison saw it, Huckleberry Finn had not irreparably extinguished his connections to a world that he found inherently immoral. Huckleberry had not even really made a choice about his relationship to the world at all. He had simply chosen Jim, however briefly, over the prescriptions of the world in which they lived.

Ellison resisted the limitations that he saw imposed upon him by racial, political, or even artistic prescription that took from him the integrative characteristics he associated with culture itself. Ellison's initial attraction to leftist ideology was eventually replaced with the broader conception of universalism that is associated with the epilogue of *Invisible Man* and reflected in his disputes with Irving Howe and the Black Arts movement. Irving Howe's critique of Ellison centered on his view of Ellison's break with Richard Wright and the kind of protest literature that Wright produced. Ellison's resistance was based, certainly in part, on what he saw as his extension of Wright's approach rather than a complete disruption of that approach. Ellison's resistance to the Black Arts movement represented a more fundamental resistance to racialized ideology and Black separatism.

Ellison's preferred metaphors tended toward culture, complexity, chaos, and democratic possibility. Specifically, for the work in which Ellison envisioned himself engaged, artistic commitment, grounded as he saw it in the vernacular, made individuals responsible for democratic possibility. Democratic possibility was part of a broad thread of continuity that for Black Americans linked slavery, Reconstruction, segregation, vernacular culture, and migration to the nation's founding documents. In *Invisible Man,* Ellison suggests that time itself is circular and bends like a boomerang rather than proceeding in ways that are linear and progressive. Separating Black Americans from democratic possibility meant that Black Americans were relegated to a position in which Black experience could only represent the particular and never the universal: "For then through the symbolic action of his [the novelist's] characters and plot he enables the reader to share forms of experience not immediately his own. And thus the reader is able to recognize the meaning and value of the presented experience and the essential unity of human experience as a whole. This may, or may not, lead to social change or bring the novelist recognition as a spokesman. But it is, nevertheless, a form of social action, and an important task. Yes, and in its own right a form of social power."[73]

While the focus here is to examine this prewar period as an intervention in the ways readers think of Ellison's development into an artist and intellectual, it is important to recognize that Ellison's pathway into a mature writer was not an uncomplicated arc from prewar Marxism to the universalist, liberal democratic, cultural hybridity that he embraced later in his writing career. It is also unreasonable to reduce Ellison's evolution solely to an increasing disillusionment with the Left that, fueled by the evolution of his thoughts about T. S. Eliot, Kenneth Burke, and New Criticism, led in an unbroken line to the universalism that characterizes the epilogue of *Invisible Man* and to the democratic liberalism that increasingly characterized his thinking after *Brown v. the Board of Education of Topeka, Kansas.*

The wartime years represent a significant progression of Ellison's thought, even as he often continued, particularly in the essays he contributed to *New Masses,* to use a Marxist lens and to employ Marxist language as the thematic and rhetorical mechanisms for organizing his thoughts. But Ellison had indicated from the earliest days of his arrival in New York that he valued craft as much as he valued social change and far more than he valued ideology. In

"Richard Wright and Recent Negro Fiction," an essay from 1941 that appeared in *Direction,* Ellison observed that serious writers "know that the safety of American culture depends as much upon the spread of their craft knowledge as upon the growth of trade unions and other organizations of social struggle."[74] (*Direction* published a shortened version of the essay entitled "Richard Wright and Recent Negro Fiction" that *New Masses* published in 1941 as "Recent Negro Fiction.") *Direction* was a recognized publication, though not an official one, of the League of American Writers. It was first conceived during the first American Writers' Congress in 1935.[75]

The idea of consciousness to which Ellison's work frequently referred during this period was an extension of the ideas he had supported in Wright's "Blueprint." His use of the word "identification" was drawn from Kenneth Burke's conception of the term as a referent to collective solidarity. In *Attitudes toward History* (1937), Burke observes that

> Bourgeois naturalism in its most naïve manifestation made a blunt distinction between "individual" and "environment," hence leading automatically to the notion that an individual's "identity" is something private, peculiar to himself. And when bourgeois psychologists began to discover the falsity of this notion, they still believed in it so thoroughly that they considered all collective aspects of identity under the head of pathology and illusion. That is: they discovered accurately enough that identity is *not* individual, that a man "identifies himself" with all sorts of manifestations beyond himself, and they set about trying to "cure" him of this tendency. It can't be "cured," for the simple reason that it is *normal* [emphasis in original].[76]

Many of Ellison's prewar writings focus on social transformation in ways that had not yet embraced a broader American narrative of coherence and meaning. In his introduction to *Flying Home and Other Stories,* John Callahan argues that the stories Ellison published before *Invisible Man* "point to Ellison's remarkably consistent vision of American identity over the fifty-five years of his writing life." The nine short stories that Ellison published between the early support he received from Richard Wright, his active engagement with radicalism, and the publication of *Invisible Man,* as well as the fiction that remained when he died in 1994, often focused on class conflict and unifying resolution that embraced but also transcended racial identification. The transracial agency that Ellison presents in "Slick Gonna Learn" in 1939, for example, contrasts with the intra-racial agency that he describes in "Mister Toussan" just two years later. The stories that Ellison produced during the war years reflect an expanding belief in the roles of history, vernacular culture, and the importance of inter- and intra-racial alliance as a starting point for social change. The stories also show Ellison grappling with the difficulty of presenting psychological and political response in the broader context of the social situations that cause that response.[77]

2

THE GOLDEN AGE, TIME PAST

Without the presence of Negro American style, our jokes, tall tales, even our sports would be lacking in the sudden turns, shocks and swift changes of pace (all jazz-shaped) that serve to remind us that the world is ever unexplored, and that while a complete mastery of life is mere illusion, the real secret to the game is to make life swing.

RALPH ELLISON, "What America Would Be Like without Blacks"

LOUIS ARMSTRONG, BEBOP, AND THE LIMITS OF JAZZ

I wouldn't be a jazz critic for love or money. . . .

RALPH ELLISON, Letter to Albert Murray, September 28, 1958

Which reminds me that here, way late, I've discovered Louis [Armstrong] singing Mack the Knife. Shakespeare invented Caliban, or changed himself into him—Who the hell dreamed up Louis? Some of the bop boys consider him Caliban but if he is he's a mask for a lyric poet who is much greater than most now writing.

RALPH ELLISON, Letter to Albert Murray, June 2, 1957

What does Ellison's use of jazz as a vernacular metaphor of democracy and the nation's cultural integration tell us about how he conceptualized the issue, particularly in his use of Louis Armstrong's cultural presence? Jazz and Black vernacular culture represent Ellison's ongoing commitment to an examination of race as a constituent part of national culture. Ellison's thoughts about Louis Armstrong are a starting place for the restoration of Armstrong as a consequential Black activist who, like Ellison, pursued his forms of activism—often in the face of harsh criticism—in the ways he found personally meaningful. Ellison's music writing should be attached more securely to his writing about literature, culture, and democracy. The reappraisal of Armstrong can help to revise the general critical consensus that dismissed Ellison as unable to hear the new forms of jazz—American music, as he called it—that developed during and after World War II.

David Yaffe suggests in *Fascinating Rhythm* that Armstrong was not, for Ellison, an ideal. Rather, Armstrong was "an alternative to the politicized factions of Harlem life."[1] This seems particularly true given the fact that Ellison, the musician who became a writer, most often talks about Armstrong in cultural terms rather than musical terms specific to technique or sound. Ellison's sources of literary inspiration often isolated him and made him seem a bit anomalous as a writer and thinker. The same is certainly true here, where Ellison turned to Louis Armstrong during his composition of *Invisible Man* to historicize the influence of Black culture in America at precisely the time when the earliest jazz forms were themselves being historicized. Yaffe goes so far as to argue that Ellison's thoughts about "Armstrong were so contrary to standard judgments that his revision to his novel was also a revision to jazz history."[2] There is certainly a great deal of accuracy to this claim, especially because Ellison was so willing to choose Armstrong as an alternative to politicized faction, particularly as the bebop generation of musicians criticized Armstrong for being musically and culturally dated.

Like Armstrong, Ellison is often accused of a kind of antiquated provincialism, particularly when it came to the jazz that was produced after World War II. Ellison certainly objected to the ways he saw bebop fracturing the community that previous generations of musicians had formed. And it is certainly true that the jazz produced in the second half of the twentieth century reflected the ways that psychic and cultural continuities were being revised. But Ellison's record collection, now housed at the National Jazz Museum in Harlem, reveals some of the range of Ellison's listening habits. In his essay "Sounds and Meaning," Todd Weeks reveals "a truly comprehensive collection of Western classical, jazz, blues, Cante Flamenco and many oddities" contained in a record collection containing about 540 pieces composed of about 360 LPs, some 45s, and some ten-inch and twelve-inch 78s. Duke Ellington is well represented in the 78s and the LPs, along with Xavier Cugat, Fred Waring, and Les Brown. There was a lot of dance music, but the collection also contained Western classical music composed by, among others, Johann Sebastian Bach, Johannes Brahms, Igor Stravinsky, Gustav Mahler, Ludwig van Beethoven, Giuseppe Verdi, Sergei Prokofiev, and Ernest Bloch. Twentieth-century composers like Benjamin Britten, Paul Hindemith, Aram Khachaturian, and Alban Berg are contained in the collection along with performances by Russian virtuosi like Mstislav Rostropovich and Sviatoslav Richter. Ellison wrote warmly about singers, and there are recordings by, among others, Joan Sutherland and Leontyne Price. The collection contained three recordings by Charlie Parker, three by Ornette Coleman, and, perhaps unsurprisingly, none by Miles Davis or John Coltrane. (Weeks noted the conspicuous absence of Armstrong's recording of "[What Did I Do to Be So] Black and Blue.") The breadth of the collection certainly calls into question the assertion that Ellison was somehow uncomfortable with musical innovation, particularly since Ellison wrote approvingly about musicians like Charlie Christian, the pioneering guitarist for the Benny Goodman Orchestra who expanded jazz's musical vocabulary in ways that were subsequently recognized and explored by the bebop generation.[3]

Ellison saw jazz as a medium through which the chaos and complexity of culture could be understood and endowed by the artist with meaning and significance. This is not meant to suggest that the influence goes only in one direction. Jazz and blues influence culture and are, in turn, influenced by cultural change. The artists to whom Ellison so often returns, particularly Louis Armstrong, represent people who have expended the effort necessary fully to master their chosen medium. What comes of that is freedom. An artist like Armstrong can claim an individual presence in American culture because of the labor required to transcend the limitations of his art. Armstrong does not produce art without a certain level of intention. By extension, that intention reflects American democracy itself. American democracy was an intentional act of revolution and creation. All of this reflects the ways in which the artist mediates experience. But Louis Armstrong is also a representative figure in the history of jazz and race in twentieth-century America. He is undeniably a point of origination of jazz as a cultural entity. Unlike Charlie Parker, Dizzy Gillespie, Miles Davis, Charles Mingus, Cecil Taylor, and John Coltrane, for whom Ellison had very little regard, Louis Armstrong had successfully moved jazz from a marginalized race music to a music with international influence. Jazz became a central aspect of America's cultural production in much the same way that Ellison saw the Black presence as being central to the nation itself.

While Ellison himself may have disliked modern jazz, his ideas have had a significant influence on how his critics think about the form and its relationship to the broad ideas that were of interest to Ellison. Kevin Bell's essay "The Embrace of Entropy" speaks to the questions of how "free" or "avant-garde" jazz moves beyond the explorations of bebop to articulate "a new and improvisatory agency within the voided margins outside the framing confines of 'identity,' 'history,' or 'genre.'" "For these movements, not unlike their historical idiomatic precursors, especially bebop, think and aspire toward a certain conceptual and performative freedom that is at philosophical variance with significant Enlightenment meditations on freedom. This critical swerve sounds itself perhaps most sharply in its performance of the abandonment of mandates of 'proper' musical classification and indeed of 'proper' performance itself."[4] This is an important intervention because, although it goes far beyond the boundaries that Ellison himself imposed, it investigates improvisation and freedom in ways that are intimately intertwined with the conceptual dimensions that Ellison opened in *Invisible Man*.

For as much as Ellison thought and wrote about jazz and culture, particularly in the ways he theorized about the mutually supportive functions of each, Ellison's view of the jazz he wrote about was largely relegated to the musicians to whom he listened around the time he entered college, like Louis Armstrong, Duke Ellington, Mahalia Jackson, Charlie Christian, and Jimmy Rushing. Many of these musicians had direct connections to the Territory Bands who performed throughout Oklahoma beginning in the 1920s. Bands like Walter Page's Blue Devils originated from Oklahoma City and counted Count Basie, who joined the band in 1926, among its members. These bands were very consciously representatives of popular culture. Succeeding generations of musicians held relatively little interest for Ellison as essay subjects, perhaps because their place in culture was so very different from the cultural place the musicians who were part of Ellison's youth occupied. Part of Ellison's detachment from subsequent generations of the music may have had a great deal to do with the movement of jazz away from its dance origins or because jazz had created an audience robust enough that its musicians could focus on the very sense of individualized self-creation that Ellison's writings most seemed to value in the music.

Ellison remained deeply attached to his geographic origins and to the music that geography nurtured and produced. As the host of a television broadcast called "Jazz: The Experimenters," which was recorded in 1965 at the Village Gate in New York, Ellison remained committed to jazz as an "outlaw art" that privileged freedom over "status and respectability." Even as modern jazz musicians like Cecil Taylor and Charles Mingus performed on the show, Ellison clung to the assertion that jazz—or, at least, the jazz that he valued—"was an attempt to humanize the world in terms of sound, an effort made with musical means to impose the Negro American sense of time upon the larger society and upon the world of nature."[5] Modern jazz was undanceable and overly serious for Ellison precisely because he saw modern jazz musicians as craving the very status and respectability that the music, in Ellison's opinion, had avoided in the form he grew up with. In a 1976 interview with Robert G. O'Meally, Ellison critiques those musicians by saying, "I would think we've [Black American culture] lost something important. And I think it came out of a kind of misunderstanding of the institution—some of this on the part of the musicians who began to take themselves too seriously, I guess, in a kind of political way, wanting people simply to sit still and listen to them when they aren't always that exciting, *at best.* And all of the politicizing of jazz, which came with bebop, sort of turned people off. They couldn't follow the beat, and it was no longer as pleasant [*emphasis in original*]."[6] Ellison had never felt entirely comfortable with the ways naturalism placed politics in the foreground, and that discomfort clearly influenced his dissatisfaction with what he saw as the politicization of jazz. What Ellison sought, beyond the limitations of naturalism and protest literature, was an artistic language that could describe the value of Black American experiences in the United States. Perhaps what Ellison saw in the directions that jazz had taken after the arrival of bebop was an expression that was technically proficient but not particularly aesthetically relevant to the ways he saw culture being reflected through literary modernism.

Fred Moten, in his book *In the Break,* attempts to place Black jazz from the 1950s and 1960s in conversation with a broad selection of Western thinkers like Sigmund Freud to consider Duke Ellington's music, Martin Heidegger in his consideration of Amiri Baraka's thoughts on Black music, and the conceptual artist and philosopher Adrian Piper, whom he places in conversation with Ellison's *Invisible Man.* In each conversation, there are points of convergence and tension. For Moten, Black performance is radical precisely because of his broader argument that Black performance is improvisation. The book is essentially a meditation on what is to be radically Black. The volume itself is an improvisation on language, linking a disparate group of thinkers around the investigation of the performance of Blackness. What Ellison saw in that performance of Blackness was a cultural working-out of the promise of America's pluralism. As Paul Anderson puts it, "For Ellison, the music of invisibility at its best gestured toward an American future of pluralistic integration along the lines of mutual and reciprocal recognition. His championing of the aesthetic and cultural promises of pluralistic integration moved in tandem with his focus on African-American popular music as a singularly prophetic American landmark." Pluralism, particularly in the context of democratic individualism, certainly seems to come closest to Ellison's vision.

Steve Pinkerton's article "Ralph Ellison's Righteous Riffs" focuses directly on the ways jazz serves as the model for Ellison's democratic vision. This is the narrative that Ellison himself put forth, particularly in his writing about music, and this essay provides a supportive function for those ideas. But what much of the writing about Ellison and jazz overlooks is that the argument that Ellison offers (often in collaboration with his longtime friend Albert Murray) is dependent on a very selective discourse around jazz before the arrival of bebop and its cultural resonance. In *The Craft of Ralph Ellison,* Robert O'Meally observes Ellison's relative antagonism to "virtually all jazz beyond Basie and Ellington."[7] Though his record collection suggests otherwise, this is largely true of the choices Ellison made in his letters and essays. It is particularly true of his antipathy to bebop in general and to Charlie Parker (and what Parker came to represent culturally) in general.[8]

For all the ways that postwar jazz expanded the sonorities and cultural presence of the swing-era jazz that Ellison preferred, his view of it was uniformly dim. In the prologue to *Invisible Man,* his narrator describes smoking marijuana and descending, like Dante, into the depths of the music playing on his phonograph. The tranquility he seeks is drowned out by a blaring trumpet and a hectic rhythm. The narrator finds the music as raw and disorienting as Ellison himself finds the music. In a letter to his good friend Albert Murray from September 28, 1958, he describes his experience participating in a critics' symposium at the 1958 Newport Jazz Festival and listening to the music that was performed, much of which he found "simply pathetic." Ellison disparages Miles Davis as "poor, evil, lost little Miles Davis, who ... sounded like he just couldn't get it together," and John Coltrane "with his badly executed velocity exercises." Of the saxophone players he heard, Ellison dismisses these musicians as being poor imitators of the late Charlie Parker, whom he considered to be "miserable, beat, and lost." Ellison's assessment to Albert Murray of what he heard at the festival was dim and completely representative of his critique of the ways modern jazz's countercultural impulse fell short of true artistic production. Rather than being true artists contributing to culture, he saw these performers as being a "screwedup" [sic] "bunch of little masturbators" interested only in playing for their own pleasure. Ellison sees no evidence of the pluralistic collectivism he recognizes in the previous generation of musicians who serve as the foundation of his thoughts about jazz and culture.[9]

The exception to what Ellison described as a disappointing festival was a reunion between Count Basie, a star of that generation who was performing at the festival with his current band, and the blues shouter Jimmy Rushing, who was from Oklahoma City and who had performed with Count Basie between 1935 and 1948. Their performance elicited from Ellison a deep sense of nostalgia for a musical era now supplanted by those he saw as musical imposters: "It was like the old Basie band playing the Juneteenth ramble at Forest Park in Okla. City."[10] Rather than the narcissism that Ellison disparaged in the postwar jazz scene, the music preceding jazz modernity offered something approximating his vision of democracy's individuality in collectivity:

> But these [Black American institutions], like his folk personality, are caught in a process of chaotic change.... [E]ven his art is transformed; the lyrical ritual elements of folk jazz—that artistic projection of the only real individuality possible for him in the South, that embodiment of a superior democracy in which each individual cultivated his uniqueness and yet did not clash with his neighbors—have given way to the near-themeless technical virtuosity of bebop, a further triumph of technology over humanism.... One "is" literally, but one is nowhere; one wanders dazed in a ghetto maze, a "displaced person" of American democracy.[11]

Charlie Parker was a primary architect of the new music that transformed dance-based swing-era music into the music that came to be known as bebop. He was quickly venerated as the patron saint of bebop and improvisation's possibilities for freedom and creativity. His larger-than-life presence was reflected in the "Bird Lives" graffiti that began to appear around New York City soon after his death in 1955 at age thirty-four. The veneration was

Charlie Parker on saxophone, Miles Davis on trumpet, Tommy Potter on bass, and Max Roach on drums at the Three Deuces, New York, around 1947. William P. Gottlieb Collection, Library of Congress, Monographic. Photograph. LC-GLB23-0694 DLC. www .loc.gov/item/gottlieb.06941/.

not without merit. Parker was, after all, a self-taught musician who, along with Dizzy Gillespie, Thelonious Monk, Max Roach, and Bud Powell, among others, revolutionized jazz into a music of complex, inventive phrasing and innovative, technical brilliance.

In "On Bird, Bird-Watching and Jazz," Ellison focuses on Parker as a figure legendary, beginning at the time of his death in 1955, for the excesses, musical and personal, that surrounded him. Ellison sees Parker as a hero to some but a hero who is ultimately unable to live up to his own legend. More specifically, Ellison saw Parker and those associated with bebop as having defined themselves by rejecting the conduct of the generation of musicians that preceded them (particularly Louis Armstrong) and, by extension, reduced their music "to a matter of race."[12] Armstrong became representative of a strand of entertainment that to some bore the imprint of minstrelsy.

Armstrong's attention in the 1930s had certainly turned to projects that were increasingly directed toward popular audiences. He appeared in several Hollywood feature films and short films, often as himself, like *A Rhapsody in Black and Blue* (1932 short), *I'll Be Glad When You're Dead You Rascal You* (1932 short), *Pennies from Heaven* (1936), *Artists and Models* (1937), *Every Day's a Holiday* (1937), *Doctor Rhythm* (1938), *Going Places* (1938), and *Birth of the Blues* (1941). He collaborated with Bing Crosby and Hoagy Carmichael and even recorded Hawaiian instrumentals.

While Armstrong may have crossed to increasing success beyond the limitations of a jazz audience, he nevertheless remained a Black artist belittled by the racism directed at him by club owners, promoters, police, and hotels in the United States and internationally. Although his stage persona launched Armstrong into multi-genre success, it also reinforced many of the racial stereotypes that appeared throughout the media. What Ellison saw in Armstrong's persona is an undeniable Black essence that seamlessly combined artistic success with vernacular culture: "By rejecting Armstrong they [bebop musicians] thought to rid themselves of the entertainer's role. And by way of getting rid of the role, they demanded, in the name of their racial identity, a purity of status which by definition is impossible for the performing artist."[13] For Ellison, the performing artist—*any* performing artist, including those who consciously saw themselves as artists like Jascha Heifetz, Glenn Gould, or the Modern Jazz Quartet—was by definition an entertainer. But

Louis Armstrong. New York World-Telegram and the Sun Newspaper Photograph Collection, Library of Congress, Prints and Photographs Division, LC-USZ62-127236.

Ellison saw a profound difference between the performative mask and the musician's artistic production.

Though disparaged by some of playing the role of "Uncle Tom," Armstrong was a consummate artist who, like Charlie Parker and Dizzy Gillespie in their cofounding of modern jazz, had been equally revolutionary: "Consider that at least as early as T. S. Eliot's creation of a new aesthetic for poetry through the artful juxtaposing of earlier styles, Louis Armstrong, way down the [Mississippi] river in New Orleans, was working out a similar technique for jazz."[14] Parker, marginalized by his race, his addiction, and his role in developing a new jazz vocabulary, struggled against the Dionysian urges that put him in conflict with social institutions. While Ellison believed Parker's personal shortcomings kept him from truly attaining the status of deification to which he was elevated after his death, Ellison recognized that Parker's playing had at times "captured something of the discordancies, [sic] the yearning, romance and cunning of the age and ordered it into a haunting art."[15]

Berndt Ostendorf observes in his essay "Ralph Waldo Ellison" that, "With Louis Armstrong in the twenties, jazz stopped being a collective folk music and became a Modernist art whose hallmarks were originality and innovation."[16] Seen through that lens, what makes Armstrong so compellingly distinctive were the musical qualities he displayed that were encompassing and integrative of all that had come before and inclusive of so much of what was occurring in popular musical culture. Parker, much like Rinehart in *Invisible Man,* was too many things to too many people and therefore without a center (or, as Ellison observed of Rinehart, the embodiment of chaos). He could not, except as a performing artist, escape the chaos and disorder that engulfed his life. Modern jazz may well reflect the chaos and fragmentation of modern life, but as modern jazz musicians increasingly defined their cultural place, Ellison clung to the music produced by the musicians who had defined for him the sound and ethos of jazz in the years preceding World War II. The prewar jazz that Ellison venerated certainly offered a lyricism that was stylistically very distinct from bebop's musical angularity. The lyricism to which Ellison was drawn can certainly be seen as a metaphor for Ellison's penchant for seeking coherence within the absurdities caused by fragmentation and chaos.

As far as Ellison was concerned, bebop consciously set aside performance practices common to the style that preceded it. The emphasis shifted from large ensembles producing music appropriate for dance to small groups that focused on producing virtuosic, complex, intricate improvisations that were intended to be art rather than danceable entertainment. The music pioneered by Charlie Parker and Dizzy Gillespie was a radical disruption of audience expectation. The ritual elements of its disruption, like stage personas and the elimination by some musicians of direct audience interactions, were as important to Ellison as its musical disruption because of the ways Ellison transferred the qualities of the musical medium to the literary. In a letter to his good friend Albert Murray dated June 2, 1957, Ellison made clear his belief that "Bessie Smith singing a good blues may deal with experience as profoundly as [T. S.] Eliot, with the eloquence of the Eliotic poetry being expressed in her voice and phrasing. . . . Human anguish is human anguish . . . only expressed in a different medium."[17] This is precisely what Ellison did in *Invisible Man* when he correlated the narrator's rhetorical expression of invisibility with Louis Armstrong's musical expression of invisibility.

For all that Ellison thought of Armstrong and his cultural presence, Armstrong was not Ellison's first choice to be the inspiration who inhabited the narrator's thoughts in the prologue to *Invisible Man*. In drafts of the novel, Ellison used the cornetist Charles Joseph "Buddy" Bolden in that role.[18] Bolden is particularly suited to occupy the position of an invisible jazz presence in the mind of an invisible man. Bolden's place in jazz has itself been largely invisible to historians of the music. He was an improviser who left behind no written music. He played in the decades before recorded sound. The only record of his presence has been the stories that circulated (and which were undoubtedly embellished) about his playing. Only one grainy photograph from sometime around 1905 exists of Bolden with his band. He died in a mental institution and was buried in an unmarked grave. By the time Ellison was writing *Invisible Man*, in the early years of bebop, Buddy's musical legacy had been largely forgotten.

It is unclear what Bolden's legacy meant to Ellison. What is clear in Ellison's revision in the manuscript from Bolden to Armstrong at the suggestion of his editor Albert Erskine was that Ellison was also revising Armstrong's presence, even as the bebop musicians Ellison wrote about at Minton's Playhouse were deconstructing it. Bebop was musically radical. Ellison was as averse to it as he had become to the Left and as he became to Black radicalism a generation later. It is not without irony that by the 1960s Ellison himself, as a Black writer whose work was also enthusiastically consumed by a white audience, became the target of many of the same kinds of criticism that had for so long been directed at Armstrong.

Ellison largely ignores the race records that Armstrong recorded between 1926 and 1928 in favor of Armstrong's presence as a Black artist in a broadly white cultural context. This is particularly true in Ellison's decision to have his invisible narrator take underground Armstrong's recording of "(What Did I Do To Be So) Black and Blue" by Thomas "Fats" Waller and Andy Razaf. Armstrong had performed the song as a member of the Broadway pit orchestra of "Hot Chocolates." It was a pop song, but in Armstrong's recording, it was transformed into a powerful protest song. It addressed race and colorism in ways that subvert its popular origins and transcend the limitations imposed upon it by cultural context or the circumstances of its performance.

The rituals associated with the bebop generation and those it influenced broke with ritual in ways that also modified form: "[R]ites are there to form and test character, and I believe speaking abstractly that this is the way I want my fiction to work."[19] By dispensing with the rituals Ellison associated with the music (or perhaps by creating their own collection of stereotyped characteristics), Ellison could no longer recognize any intrinsic link between the artist, the performance, the performative production, and the audience. The Charlie Parker whom Ellison disparages in his essays is as dissimilar from a more fully historicized version of the actual musician as the versions of Louis Armstrong and Duke Ellington whose work he admires.

Perhaps Ellison's ridicule of postwar jazz can be taken at face value as a reflection of his disappointment that, although technically brilliant, the newer generations of musicians interacted with the music and with their audiences in ways that Ellison saw as nothing less than egotistic and antidemocratic. Ellison nostalgically saw swing-era musicians as interacting with their music, their fellow musicians, and with their audiences in ways that spoke to the ideas of jazz and democracy that Ellison and Albert Murray developed. Ellison's opinions are often contradictory, though. In some ways, Ellison chronicles the breakdown of publicly performed cultural coherence into a fragmented, self-centered parody of what had come before. But his writings about jazz, particularly the influential essays he produced after the end of legal segregation in 1954, provide his view of a future best described by and understood in relation to a past that was quickly becoming transformed by the mid-1940s.

In the essay "Ralph Ellison's Righteous Riffs," Steve Pinkerton joins Ellison's jazz as directly as any to a creative process linking art and nation when he writes "Jazz for Ellison must model an idealized democratic liberty, not show forth democracy's limitations in their naked and inevitability rough state. To do the latter would be to give free rein to the chaotic, when the artist's task is to order it. The goal of jazz and literature both, as Ellison declares time and again, is to tame and control precisely the kind of chaos he intuits in bebop and other postwar jazz forms."[20] Pinkerton, who connects the performative aspects of jazz to the sacred and the profane that he argues to be an affirmation of an integrated, "total culture," is correct in what he observes about Ellison's forward-looking thoughts about the direction the music was taking. But Ellison's attempts to impose a patina of order on chaos also had a retrospective component to it that spoke as directly to the origins of national culture as it did to its implications. Ellison's thoughts about modern jazz, particularly what he has to say about Charlie Parker, bebop, and its movement away from swing-era lyricism, suggests a retrospective approach to a distinctly prospective musical form. He does, however, register jazz's ongoing relationship to contemporary culture: "Not that it isn't recognized that it [jazz] is an art with deep roots in the past, but that the nature of its deep connections with the social conditions here and now is slighted."[21] Ellison almost seems to warn against the arrival of the very national identity composed of cultural pluralism and democratic individualism that he saw defining the nation's exceptionalism. Like *Invisible Man* and his unfinished second novel, Ellison's work looked backward for ways to impose order on the chaos reflected in Black migration and urbanization. This was Ellison's view of culture, and it sharply distinguished itself from musicians like Charlie Parker and movements like Black Arts.

Ellison clearly had little regard for listening to bebop and the music that grew out of it. At a conceptual level, he also had little regard for its cultural implications. The most intimate areas of Charlie Parker's life had become inseparable from his public personae. There was no mask to mediate the interactions between the public and the private. Ellison clearly recognized that Louis Armstrong, for all his virtuosity, wore a mask that the bebop generation came to associate with a kind of performative minstrelsy. But that mask was a conscious stage presentation that did not ultimately undermine his art: "Certain older jazzmen possessed a clearer idea of the division between their identities as performers and as private individuals. Offstage and while playing in ensemble, they carried themselves like college professors or high church deacons; when soloing they donned the comic mask and went into frenzied pantomimes of hotness—even when playing 'cool'—and when done, dropped the mask and returned to their chairs with dignity." The performative mask of entertainment enabled artistic production rather than inhibiting the depth of its production.

Except for Dizzy Gillespie, who maintained a bit of the comic mask in his stage presence, Ellison saw Charlie Parker, Miles Davis, and others as having simply traded one mask for another, which served as a representation for authentic creation. These musicians represented for their audience, an increasingly white audience rather than the predominantly Black audiences that Ellison experienced during his youth in Oklahoma City and at the time of his arrival in New York, a commodification that Ellison found distasteful.

The audience was no longer participatory in the production of cultural experience reflective of democratic possibility and instead simply consumers of a product.[22]

In "Ralph Ellison's Music Lessons," Paul Allen Anderson sees Louis Armstrong, as he is deployed in *Invisible* Man, as being simultaneously representative of underground expression and the white mainstream when he suggests that, "For Ellison, the music of invisibility at its best gestured toward an American future of pluralistic integration along the lines of mutual and reciprocal recognition."[23] By explicitly repeating Ellison's attempt to link Armstrong to time in the novel, Anderson sees in Armstrong a conscious shift in registers "from blues individualism to idealistic nationalism." Ellison sees none of that either in the arrival of bebop itself or the cultural commentary its arrival produced. "Ellison's criticisms of bebop," Anderson writes, "as the post-war lingua franca of 'modern jazz' were so sweeping because they were primarily cultural rather than musical."[24] This is certainly true of Ellison's critique of bebop that extends into the review he published in the *New York Review* on February 6, 1964, of LeRoi Jones's *Blues People*. Along with Ellison's disapproval of the ways Black music is described in terms of ideology and his suspicions about the limits of sociological approaches for understanding the experiences of Black people, his view of *Blues People* is that it reinforces a mutually exclusive division between art and entertainment:

> Jones makes a distinction between classic and country blues, the one being entertainment and the other folklore. But the distinction is false. Classic blues were both entertainment *and* a form of folklore. There are levels of time and function involved here, and the blues which might be used in one place as entertainment (as gospel music is now being used in night clubs and on theater stages) might be put to a ritual use in another. Bessie Smith might have been a "blues queen" to society at large, but within the tighter Negro community where the blues were part of a total way of life, and a major expression of an attitude toward life, she was a priestess, a celebrant who affirmed the values of the group and man's ability to deal with chaos.[25]

While Ellison was willing to consider *Blues People* as a reflection of the ways LeRoi Jones historicized himself in the turbulence of the 1960s, he was unwilling to accept the book's assessments as a viable theory of Black American culture. Like his perception of bebop, he saw the book as unnecessarily isolating Black American culture rather than acknowledging Black American culture as being a function of American culture. For Ellison, this pluralism is as true of Black people who render their experiences through the culture they produce as it is for literary artists who render their experiences in words and for musicians who render their experiences in the world of sound: "For as I see it, from the days of their introduction into the colonies, Negroes have taken, with the ruthlessness of those without investments in cultural styles, whatever they could of European music, making it that which would, when blended with the cultural tendencies inherited from Africa, express their own sense of life, while rejecting the rest."[26] The ways bebop supplanted swing-era music, which had displaced traditional jazz, reflected the cultural changes at work in the ways the term "Black" replaced "African American," which had itself replaced "Negro" and "Colored."

Taken collectively, these changes revealed a fundamental reconception of the ways Black cultural production was created and consumed. For Ellison, Negroes existed in a space that, broadly speaking, actively produced culture. Black people, reflected in bebop, the Black Arts movement, and the publication of *Blues People,* passively consumed culture without actively participating in the collective production of that culture. As Robert O'Meally observes in his introduction to "Blues People" that appears in *Living with Music,* "Dissention brings out an unrelentingly aggressive side of Ellison"[27] (particularly the dissension contained in "The World and the Jug," "Change the Joke and Slip the Yoke," and his review of *Blues People*). But Ellison's musical dissension tends to look backward to a departed past made meaningful by the blues.

Ellison's distaste for bebop, Charlie Parker, and the ideas about music and culture put forth by the Black Arts movement are balanced by his unwavering admiration of Louis Armstrong. Armstrong is widely regarded as an influential figure in the development of jazz who expanded the role of the soloist relative to the ensemble. He was certainly not the first musician to play the style that became widely known as jazz, but he was the innovator who enlarged the music's vocabulary and changed the ways jazz was produced and consumed. The jazz that was created in New Orleans during the early decades of the twentieth century largely featured ensemble playing except for brief one- or two-bar breaks where individual musicians were given the opportunity to display their skills. When Armstrong left New Orleans in 1924 to become a member of the Fletcher Henderson Orchestra, he had the opportunity to participate in what was perhaps the best jazz orchestra of the era. Armstrong was able to display a level of virtuosity that stood out in a band filled with musicians who could sight-read musical scores but who had not yet made the transition to the sense of swing and the extended solo that soon became so much a part of jazz.

Until Armstrong's arrival, jazz was either presented in orchestrated arrangement that left little room for individuals to stand out or in more loosely arranged traditional "Dixieland" ensembles that emphasized collective improvisation over individual improvisation. Armstrong brought a musical style that helped define the sound of jazz as well as the sound of the trumpet itself. Armstrong's playing became influential among musicians and popular to the public for his tone and the expressivity of his solo playing. Trumpet players of his generation quickly moved to emulate his style to the point that it was not until the development of bebop twenty years after Armstrong's earliest recordings that musicians like Dizzy Gillespie and Miles Davis began to look for other musical and performative role models. Armstrong was also a singer with a distinctive, rough, throaty voice with phrasing and interpretive innovation as unique as his instrumental playing. His approach to music altered the way space was used between musical phrases.

Additionally, Armstrong performed both New Orleans standards as well as freely improvised popular songs taken from the American songbook that composers like Irving Berlin, George Gershwin, Cole Porter, and many others wrote for Broadway and Hollywood musicals. For many, Armstrong's versions of these songs were recognized over the ways they originally appeared on stage and on film. That is, Armstrong's improvised, rhythmically complex reinvention was favored over the "straight" version the listener expected. Armstrong's popularity signaled a unique confluence of art and popular culture. Technology allowed his recordings to be widely consumed, and films and newsreels made him widely recognized as a musician and entertainer. As a fellow trumpet player (Armstrong permanently switched from the cornet to the trumpet in 1926), Ellison recognized Armstrong's technical abilities. But Ellison also saw in Armstrong an entertainer whose performative qualities were as important and influential as his musical abilities. Armstrong was comedic, technically brilliant, and embracing. In short, Armstrong was as much a cultural presence as he was a musical presence.

During the Cold War years, Armstrong and jazz musicians like Dizzy Gillespie, Dave Brubeck, Ella Fitzgerald, and Duke Ellington traveled internationally as jazz ambassadors in international tours sponsored by the State Department. The State Department's objective was to counteract the Soviet Union's criticism of America's racism and racial tension. The United States used jazz in much the same way that the Soviet Union used ballet as a way of displaying the best the culture had produced. Jazz, as a uniquely American art form created by Black people, was seen, according to a headline that appeared in the *New York Times* in 1955, as the nation's "Secret Sonic Weapon." International audiences often responded enthusiastically. In his biography of Louis Armstrong's later years, Ricky Riccardi notes the adulation that Armstrong received abroad. In *Satchmo Blows Up the World,* Penny Von Eschen goes so far as to characterize his 1960–61 tour to Africa, particularly his visit to what soon became the independent nation Ghana, as being moving both for Armstrong and the audiences for whom he performed when she writes, "Armstrong the American embraced his African roots and caused Africans to embrace him." Von Eschen is careful to note that, "if Armstrong was moved and inspired by his experience of an African country on the eve of independence, this did not blind him to the struggles the Ghanaian people still faced as they grappled with the legacies of slave trading and colonial subjugation."[28] But Armstrong's presence nonetheless was electrifying and enthusiastically received. When Armstrong arrived in Congo during a tour through Africa in 1960, for example, he was greeted by drummers, dancers, and a parade through the city on a throne.[29] But even though Armstrong had staunchly supported civil rights, many criticized him for a performance presence that they saw as pandering to a white audience. Ironically enough, this is the critique that Ellison directed toward bebop. He disliked bebop musically and particularly objected to the ways he saw it as pandering to white audiences. But his greatest concern seems to be that it alienated jazz from the authentic audience from which it arose.

Armstrong became seen by some as an ingratiating representation of an era supplanted by activism and Black political consciousness. By the 1950s, bebop was undeniably jazz's preferred style among the younger generation. In his autobiography, Miles Davis complained of his dislike for the way Louis Armstrong would grin and "clown" for white audiences. Modern jazz became the music of that Black political consciousness. While bebop rejected the posture of entertainment, Armstrong specifically saw himself as an entertainer whose power was to project a positive image of Black and white musicians sharing the stage. Armstrong recognized that his audience was predominately white, and he recognized that some of their attitudes were undoubtedly racist. But his job was to entertain, and the fact that he did not embrace the changes that bebop brought was a function of his awareness that his audiences came to hear him play the style of music he had pioneered a generation earlier. For Ellison, Armstrong changed the ways the nation understood Black cultural influence. Whether the nation knew it or not, American culture was Black culture. And Armstrong's popularity and influence made the nation abundantly aware that Armstrong's vernacular presence confronted racial hierarchy in ways that bebop could not. Armstrong's performative presence did more than simply imply the Black presence in American culture. It represented the Black presence as the very fabric of that culture.

What Ellison wrote in his appreciation "Homage to Duke Ellington on His Birthday" is equally true of Armstrong in his observation about musicians following Ellington's example in "attempting to make something new and uniquely their own out of the traditional elements of the blues and jazz."[30] Mastering personal histories and cultural histories are qualities essential to individual and cultural progress. Ellison makes this point in his essays, in *Invisible Man,* where the narrator struggles through much of the novel precisely because he is unaware of his relationship to the boomerang of history, and in *Three Days before the Shooting…,* where much of the novel's narrative tension functions around personal and cultural histories that are obscure and indistinct. Armstrong represented for Ellison, in ways that Parker and the bebop revolution did not, a meaningful cultural response to modernity.

Louis Armstrong's trumpet specifically appears in the prologue and the epilogue of *Invisible Man.* Armstrong serves as a figure representing Ellison's democratic impulse in the sense that Armstrong's music and performative presence link art and culture as both an artist and as a culturally connected representative of identity and agency. Ellison's description of Black people is very similar to the terms he often uses to describe jazz musicians: "He [the Black American] is a product of the interaction between his racial predicament, his individual will, and the broader American cultural freedom in which he finds his ambiguous existence. Thus he, too, in a limited way, is his own creation."[31] Armstrong embodies the higher callings of art and culture by invoking the sense of communal engagement between the audience and the performer in ways that post–World War II jazz, with its emphasis on technique and intellectualism, does not. Jazz in the postwar era was part of the threat of chaos for which true art is meant to provide order. This is precisely what the Reverend Alonzo Hickman, the jazz musician who traded the jazz secular for the religious sacred in *Three Days before the Shooting…*, means when he says "our hard-driving style gave a little more order to what even *white* folks were feeling. Gave form to all that freewheeling optimism and told folks who they were and what they could be [*emphasis in original*]."[32] Ellison's work offers two diametrically opposed views of the world. One view is characterized by the fragmentation, chaos, and complexity that so often characterize his vision. The work of the novelist, for example, is intended to help create continuity and explication in a multiplicity of meanings. But the essays that Ellison devotes to music are particularly backward-looking discussions about a world that has now been supplanted by a modernity often consciously detached (in his view of postwar jazz, for example) from the collectivity of democracy, history, the past, and its cultural roots.[33]

JAZZ, BLUES, AND THE WORD

We invented the blues. The Europeans invented psychoanalysis. You invent what you need.

ALBERT MURRAY, quoted in Scherman, "The Omni-American"

Who better than Ralph Ellison has considered jazz in combination with the question of how race is at the foundation of the American experiment and how American democracy is inexorably connected to a meaningful engagement with race? As far as jazz is concerned, Steve Pinkerton argues in "Ralph Ellison's Righteous Riffs" that, "For Ellison, American democracy insists that we strive both artistically and politically to *resolve*, to seek an end that is both aesthetic and pragmatic, transcendent and embodied [*emphasis in original*]."[34] As he notes, the jam session is the quintessential example of the tension contained in reconciling individual presence with collective will. His comments resonate with Ellison's numerous aesthetic assertions about the literary task of bringing order to chaos and fragmentation. In "Ralph Ellison's Zoot Suit," Larry Neal even goes so far as to call *Invisible Man* "one long blues solo," though it is a blues solo that gives the illusion of improvisation even as its composition and subsequent revisions expanded to nearly a decade.[35] Ellison's writing was anything but free jazz.

As Steve Pinkerton points out, "Ellison was evidently not a great writer of first drafts; like a film actor doing multiple takes of a single scene to erode the sense that she is acting, he seems to have required multiple revisions to create the sense of an apparently 'natural,' improvisatory style."[36] While Ellison's work itself was thoughtful, disciplined, and considered, his reliance on jazz as a metaphor emphasizes his belief that freedom itself results from discipline and the careful application of form, thought, and cultural resonance. His dislike of postwar jazz amplified his distrust of artistic forms that were unable to manage the chaos that defined the world. Adam Bradley observes in his discussion of the unending revisions that Ellison made to the second novel, "It is possible for an artist to be too free."[37] Structure, like the blues form itself, provided the foundation and necessary limitation that improvisation embraced and ultimately transcended. Black Americans, much like the music their culture created, are the product of the place where individual and collective interests intersect in American culture. This insight represents the relevance of the formation of national culture, particularly as that culture is informed by race.

Ralph Ellison arrived at Tuskegee Institute in 1933 with the intention of using the scholarship he had received to pursue his interest in music. He was on scholarship to study trumpet and symphonic composition. He practiced studiously to improve his skills in both European classical music and American jazz. Duke Ellington and Louis Armstrong had been important to him before he matriculated at Tuskegee Institute and remained so during his time there and afterward. He used the diligence he brought to his musical studies when he began to study the techniques that made literature literary: "Having given so much attention to the techniques of music, the process of learning something of the craft and intention of modern poetry and fiction seemed quite familiar."[38] The same was true when he arrived in New York and became friends with Richard Wright.

Ellison recalls Wright encouraging him systematically to examine a body of literature to understand the craft of the writing process: "'You must read so-and-so,' he'd say. 'You have to go about learning to write consciously. People have talked about such and such a problem and have written about it.

Duke Ellington at the Aquarium, New York, about 1946–48. William P. Gottlieb Collection, Library of Congress, Monographic. Photograph. LC-GLB23-0251.

You must learn how Conrad, Joyce, Dostoevsky get their effects."[39] Richard Wright's instruction even went so far as to encourage Ellison to study the writing of Henry James and practice repunctuating the writing to master grammar and the art of precision, being conscious of the techniques and the effects they produced.[40] Ernest Hemingway had long been of interest to Ellison. Ellison had first been introduced to Hemingway's work long before his arrival in New York. Ellison read the popular, sophisticated, outdoorsman articles that Hemingway contributed to *Esquire* magazine in Oklahoma City in the summer before beginning his third year at Tuskegee Institute. Ellison was fascinated by the prose and remained so for much of his writing life. In the essay "Ellison's Hemingways," Brian Hochman examines Ellison's intellectual engagement with Hemingway's work and reaches the conclusion that "Perhaps no other novelist in the American tradition struggled with Hemingway—with his strengths, with his shortcomings, with his bequest to twentieth-century writers, white *and* black—more openly and insistently than Ralph Ellison. Perhaps no other novelist wrote more honestly, more courageously, and more artfully on Hemingway; at the same time, no other novelist wrote more unpredictably, and seemed to change his mind more often [*emphasis in original*]."[41] This is a provocative assertion, but it certainly speaks to the complicated relationship Ellison had with Hemingway's writing. In short, Hochman reveals a connection between the ways Hemingway contributed to Ellison's thought in relation to modernism and jazz and in an ongoing way to Ellison's thoughts as a mature reader and writer. This connection is more than casual.

The Lost Generation writers epitomized for Ellison the possibilities of prose to shape the way people thought and spoke. Writers associated with the Lost Generation "had not only the comfort of being in the well-advertised advance guard; they were widely read and their characters' way of life was imitated to the extent that several generation of young people stylized their speech and attitudes to the pattern of Fitzgerald's and Hemingway's fiction. . . . With Esquire carrying their work to readers in most of the barbershops throughout the country, these writers were lost in a crowd of admirers, of whom I was one." Lawrence Jackson, in his biography *Ralph Ellison,* goes so far as to observe that Ellison read all the Hemingway he could find in the summer before his return to Tuskegee Institute for his junior year in the fall of 1935.[42] During this time, Ellison was becoming increasingly dissatisfied with sociological explanations of experience and saw in Hemingway's writing an immediacy of emotion in experience.

As his interest in studying music was supplanted by his interest in literature, Ellison used music as a metaphor for the theory of literature and culture that he developed. It was a metaphor that served his thoughts about the relationship between the individual and the collective, between Black culture and white culture, and between the possibilities of democratic liberalism and chaos. In the epilogue to *Invisible Man,* his narrator has reached the conclusion that "Our fate is to become one, and yet many—This is not prophecy, but description."[43]

Ellison constructs a modern literary aesthetic by drawing on a jazz tradition that is at the center of the nation's cultural expression as it simultaneously represents and is relegated to the margins of that tradition. It is a strategy that allows Ellison to invoke an improvisatory ethos that asserts individual and literary agency. That ethos refutes the idea that jazz is inferior and disposable merely because, on the face of things, it privileges spontaneity over the kind of discipline that many recognize as characterizing classical music and literature. This is the process of cultural reconciliation that became so much a part of Ellison's mature work: Black American culture relegated to the periphery even as it defines the mainstream that rejects it, the seamless fluidity between literary art and vernacular expression, and a conception of democracy that is itself fluid and dynamic in literature, in culture, and in music.

When Ellison wrote approvingly about Richard Wright's *Native Son* in his 1941 essay "Recent Negro Fiction," part of that admiration has to do with his observation that Wright has achieved the literary influence he has by understanding and integrating techniques that he assembled from the white writers whose work he had diligently studied: "It is no accident that the two most advanced Negro writers, [Langston] Hughes and [Richard] Wright, have been men who have *experienced freedom of* association with advanced white writers (not because the men from whom they have learned were unique because of their whiteness, but because in the United States even the possession of Western culture is controlled on the basis of color). Nor is it an accident that Hughes and Wright have had, as writers of fiction, the greatest effect upon Negro life [*emphasis in original*]."[44] *Native Son* was, for Ellison, the artistic success it was because Wright had identified and incorporated techniques that he had learned from a disciplined study of writers like Hemingway, Eliot, Dostoyevsky, and Joyce.

Ellison's foregrounding of Hemingway and literary modernism involves attributes easily extended to his thoughts about music. Hemingway clearly contributed to Ellison's thought in relation to modernism and jazz and in an ongoing way to Ellison's thoughts as a mature reader and writer. In 1958, Ellison wrote:

> It is here that he [the jazz musician] learns tradition, group techniques and style. For although since the twenties many jazzmen have had conservatory training and are well grounded in formal theory and instrumental technique,

when we approach jazz we are entering quite a different sphere of training. Here it is more meaningful to speak not of courses of study, of grades and degrees, but of apprenticeship, ordeals, initiation ceremonies, of rebirth. For after the jazzman has learned the fundamentals of his instrument and the traditional techniques of jazz—the intonations, the mute work, manipulation of timbre, the body of traditional styles—he must then "find himself," must be reborn, must find, as it were, his soul. All this through achieving that subtle identification between his instrument and his deepest drives which will allow him to express his own unique ideas and his own unique voice. He must achieve, in short, his self-determined identity.[45]

This passage speaks directly toward the ways the process of education and apprenticeship, culminating in the initiatory process of the jam session, shapes and defines for the jazz musician a place of identification that is simultaneously singular and collective. Technical training is at the heart of the process. That recognition of technique is one of the elements that Ellison drew from the modernists and that contributes to his trajectory from music to literature to something approximating a moral vision.

By the time he published "Hidden Name and Complex Fate" in 1964, Ellison's view of technique had fully synthesized aspects of thinking about technique. Ellison extended technique from simply being a tool that gives one the basic qualification for meaningfully participating in the jam session into the essential meaning of the creative act itself: "[W]hen I say that the novelist is created by the novel, I mean to remind you that fictional techniques are not a mere set of objective tools, but something much more intimate: a way of feeling, of seeing, and of expressing one's sense of life."[46] In Ellison's hands, terms associated with the study of music became intertwined with an archetypal view of human and artistic value. "The process of *acquiring* technique is a process of modifying one's responses, of learning to see and feel, to hear and observe, to evoke and evaluate the images of memory and of summoning up and directing the imagination, of learning to conceive of human values in the ways which have been established by the great writers who have developed and extended the art [*emphasis in original*]."[47] Seen in this way, technique and its acquisition are a process rather than a static objective.

There is also a performative element in what Ellison describes. Materials, often disparate and unrelated, are appropriated, adapted by improvisation, and forged into something new at the moment of performance. By rejecting stasis, jazz reflects the kind of intentionality that Ellison first brought in college to his study of T. S. Eliot and Ernest Hemingway. The jam session musicians who create individuality out of collective experience and the application of technique are, for Ellison, engaged in a symbolic process of democratic ritual. Since many saw jazz and the blues as an undisciplined, dissonant, chaotic music, it is not surprising that many attribute the most negative stereotypes of racialized traits to them.

In short, the least charitable view of jazz reduces it to primitive expression rather than viewing it as a reflection of modernist attributes. This is the same process that circumscribed the work of Black writers by dismissing their approaches to cultural production: "When the white man steps behind the mask of the trickster his freedom is circumscribed by the fear that he is not simply miming a personification of his disorder and chaos, but that he will become in fact that which he intends only to symbolize."[48] Modernism, expressed in the relationship Ellison forms between jazz and literature, seems to be a mode of expression that provides the most "artistic" space for expression. This is particularly true given Ellison's thoughts about the limitations of what naturalism can contribute to the broad category of protest literature.

For Ellison, jazz transcends limitations in the same ways that Black Americans culturally respond to social limitation: "He [the Black American] is a product of the interaction between his racial predicament, his individual will, and the broader American cultural freedom in which he finds his ambiguous existence. That he, too, in a limited way, is his own creation."[49] The working out of the inherent tension that exists between freedom and discipline reflects the ritualized process of the jam session. Ellison views this as a performance of self-identity the musician must undergo in an effort to become integrated with something larger and more consequential: "I don't recognize any white culture.... I recognize no American culture which is not the partial creation of Black culture. I recognize no American style ... which does not bear the mark of the American Negro."[50] Ellison saw the representative qualities of jazz, a form emblematic of Black creativity in the face of limitation and oppression, as reflecting and responding to the chaos of American life in ways that give chaos artistic form, beauty, and meaning. This is a vision that speaks as much to Ellison's view of jazz as it does to the literary modernism that so deeply informed his thought beginning in college.

In speaking of how he understands jazz, Ellison observes that

jazz is an art of individual assertion within and against the group. Each true jazz moment (as distinct from the uninspired commercial performance) springs from a contest in which each artist challenges all the rest; each solo flight, or improvisation, represents (like the successive canvases of a painter) a definition of his identity: as individual, as member of the collectivity, and as a link in the chain of tradition. Thus, because jazz finds its very life in an endless improvisation upon traditional materials, the jazz-man must lose his identity even as he finds it—how often do we see even the most famous of jazz artists being devoured alive by their imitators, and, shamelessly, in the public spotlight.[51]

Ellison's view of jazz, writ small, is remarkably close to his conception of the culture, writ large, that provided the environment in which jazz originated and flourished. The individual has a performative responsibility to respond in collaboration with and in opposition to the collective. There is chaos, but there is also an underlying unity in the face of fragmentation. This is a core principle that Ellison repeats in various ways through his fiction, his essays, and his interviews. Music has its own liturgical function, bordering on a kind of sacredness. In "Living with Music," Ellison claims no particular religious affinity beyond music: "I am not particularly religious, but I am claimed by music"[52] The association that Ellison makes between improvised jazz, American culture, and literary modernism suggests the approach to identity and the democratic ideal that he subsequently developed.

Ellison's adoption of modernism is represented in his admiration of Ernest Hemingway and T. S. Eliot and refined and expanded in the relationship he forged between modernism and Kenneth Burke's ideas. Modernism provides a useful foundation upon which Ellison can position his thoughts on literature and culture and brings with it an artistic distance from the realities of lived experience. This was at the heart of Ellison's angry response to Irving Howe's essay "Black Boys and Native Sons." Their disagreement is often framed, and correctly so, as a disagreement regarding Black literary tradition and its relationship to social protest. This was a generational conflict in which Howe questioned the position of Ellison and James Baldwin as the Black writers most appropriate in their choice of literary form to continue and deepen the work that Wright had begun with *Native Son*. The idea of

Howe's remarks and Ellison's response focused on the idea of "protest" as a viable literary response to oppression. More specifically, Ellison's response vehemently removed him from an overly narrow literary category defined by a series of racialized conventions. Ellison simultaneously rejected Wright's influence on his literary maturation and the Black Power movement's increasing ideological influence on Black culture in America.

In "The World and the Jug: A Reply to Irving Howe," which Ellison published in the *New Leader* in 1963, followed by an additional exchange between Howe and Ellison that was published in the *New Leader* in February 1964, Ellison's pointed response was that Wright was not the ancestor that Howe, and presumably others, claim him to be: "I respected Wright's work and I knew him, but this is not to say that he 'influenced' me as significantly as you assume. Consult the text! I *sought out* Wright because I had read Eliot, Pound, Gertrude Stein and Hemingway, and as early as 1940 Wright viewed me as a potential rival [*emphasis in original*]."[53] One cannot choose relatives, but one can actively choose ancestors. Richard Wright was a relative, Ernest Hemingway an ancestor. Langston Hughes was a relative; T. S. Eliot, André Malraux, Fyodor Dostoevsky, and William Faulkner were ancestors. Ellison argues that Black life in America is a theme worthy of novelistic subjectivity by American writers. Ellison saw this as an important place of difference between how he saw himself relative to the view of Wright, which diminished the expanse of his presence by confining him within the label of Black writer.

Ellison simply sees Hemingway as a better artist, more conscious of craft, than Wright. Ellison further differentiates his literary presence by emphasizing his belief that the power of Black vernacular language and culture allows him to provide representations of race and its implications on multiple registers. But given where he locates his ancestral lineage, the question arises about the depth of his belief in that assertion. The most charitable view of Ellison's assertions here is that the power of craft was a tool that Black writers should wield as assertively as white writers rather than being confined to a restrictive area described as protest literature. The assertion of craft and aesthetics is itself a form of protest as powerful as any other. Less charitable views see modernism as a colorblind, deracinated refuge that obscures the threads of Ellison's ideological alignment. In the essay "Failing Prophet and Falling Stock," Houston A. Baker Jr., for example, sees Ellison's emphasis on modernism as providing a cartoonish representation of Black life in America. Specifically, he paraphrases the conclusion of *Autobiography of an Ex-Colored Man* when he says, "The author of *Invisible Man* pays little studied attention to the intimate horrors of racism in the United States. He relinquishes such analysis for a mess of Eliotian or Hemingwayesque allusions. [Richard] Wright works as an embattled, public, activist, black intellectual. Ellison writes as though intellectualdom is both colorblind and capable of effective, non-engaged, philosophical intervention in the terrors of 'race' in these United States."[54]

This is why Ellison's claims about jazz, blues, and the Black vernacular are so very important to the contours of his thinking. He relegates Black writers to an inherited status but actively chooses white writers as having had the greatest influence on his understanding of the possibilities of craft. But in referencing musical ancestors, the list contains Charlie Christian, Count Basie, Duke Ellington, Mahalia Jackson, and Louis Armstrong. As a musician who claimed to have studied European classical music by day and jazz at night, Ellison recognized an inherent discipline in music that he reflected onto the skills necessary to hone the craft of literature: "It was most confusing; the folk tradition demanded that I play what I heard and felt around me, while those who were seeking to teach the classical tradition in the schools insisted that I play strictly according to the book and express that which I was *supposed* to feel [*emphasis in original*]."[55]

Regardless of the ways Ralph Ellison and his lifelong friend from college and fellow writer Albert Murray invoke a conception of jazz that has implications that extend broadly across music, literature, and culture, the reality is that jazz, in all its manifestations, is notoriously difficult to define with any certainty. Its ambiguity may be the very characteristic that makes it such a useful metaphor for a race and modernity that are themselves characterized by ambiguous applications of critical bias. Most broadly, jazz is a language disruptive of conventional assumptions of form, structure, ideology, and even meaning. So, when critics engage that metaphor, it is important to acknowledge that the jazz aesthetic that permeates Ralph Ellison's work is the result of countless interactions between the music itself, geography, and the historicized cultural environment in which the music existed. Often, jazz and the blues are conflated into a shorthand for something that is improvised, vernacular, and culturally influenced. Though Ellison differentiates the music itself, he often conflates the two terms into something describing Black

American culture in general and the art, music, and literature produced by that culture. Ellison (and his fellow literary traveler Albert Murray) use the terminology to describe the American democratic process itself, and even borrow its terminology.

Albert Murray describes that moment in a jazz performance when the accompaniment retreats to the background or briefly ceases entirely—the break—as being the moment when time ceases and soloists are left alone to succeed or fail on their own merit: "It is on the break that you 'do your thing.' The moment of greatest jeopardy is your moment of greatest opportunity. This is the heroic moment.... It is when you establish your identity; it is when you write your signature on the epidermis of actuality. That is how you come to terms with the void."[56] This assessment certainly resonates with Ellison's vision, particularly as Murray's ideas emphasize the elements of individual creativity, identity, and heroism that are contained at the point where opportunity and unfulfilled possibility meet. The soloist is an individual who must recognize his or her contributions to the composition while simultaneously preparing for the moment of freedom and self-differentiation.

The cultural correlation is as important as the linguistic correlation. If jazz for Ellison suggests democratic possibility, it also represents the cultural exclusion the music and its practitioners experienced in American consumer culture. The distinction that Ellison makes in differentiating jazz from the blues is that the blues, the vernacular sibling of jazz, is the logical outcome of Black struggle in a unrelentingly hostile cultural environment: "The blues is an impulse to keep the painful details and episodes of a brutal experience alive in one's aching consciousness, to finger its jagged grain, and to transcend it, not by the consolation of philosophy but by squeezing from it a near-tragic, near-comic lyricism. As a form, the blues is an autobiographical chronicle of personal catastrophe expressed lyrically."[57] The blues provides Ellison with a form, a structure, and a framework from which to observe and comment. But Ellison relegates the blues and its performance to a kind of primitivism that firmly connects it to the vernacular even as it takes from it any sense of artistic aspiration.

Over the course of the twentieth century, jazz experienced a cultural expansion in the United States and abroad that offered an important counternarrative to the ways Black Americans were described. That counternarrative was an alternative to the ways jazz became transformed from an ephemeral music to the nation's premier example of artistic production. As an art form, jazz has often been identified and defined by the opposition it faced that speaks directly toward race, ethnicity, class, and cultural politics. The jazz tradition has been understood in ways that circumscribe it and its contributors within a series of routinely identified cultural markers that include racism, poverty, capitalist exploitation, otherness, and cultural assimilation that relegated jazz to the margins even as it often claimed the commercial center.

But jazz also generated a cultural meaning that could be mapped, as Ellison so often does, onto a series of social groups. Jazz could easily be seen as an embodiment of the desire for access and recognition. Ellison recognizes the music and its influences as appropriately authentic forms of cultural production that, by association, move Black literature securely into the mainstream with its own series of artistic and historical influences. Since jazz, at least as it existed in American culture through the mid-twentieth century, was very much a modernist undertaking, Ellison's writings that had been influenced by music went a long way toward revising the ways mid-twentieth-century critics considered the world Black American literature described and the ways it located itself in American culture.

Ellison, the musician-turned-writer, exemplifies the ways in which aspects of the musical tradition that he studied and admired could be extended beyond its borders into literature. Music gives voice to experience even as it negotiates and critiques that experience. In Ellison's use of it, literature works to do the work of music. In musical terms, music is transposed into a form that reflects the demands of literature and culture. It serves an emotional function of experience that has the resonances of epistemology. The epistemological anxiety that is inscribed in so much of Ellison's fiction reflects the gulf that he sees between what can simply be told and what can truly be known.

Frederick Douglass traced a similar gulf of understanding in his 1845 *Narrative of the Life of Frederick Douglass*. In it, Douglass describes the songs of the slaves who, on their way to the Great House Farm, "would make the dense old woods, for miles around, reverberate with their wild songs, revealing at once the highest joy and the deepest sadness. They would compose and sing as they went along, consulting neither time nor tune. The thought that came up, came out—if not in the word, in the sound;—and as frequently in the one as in the other. They would sometimes sing the most pathetic sentiment in the most rapturous tone, and the most rapturous sentiment in the most

Frederick Douglass with facsimile signature. Portrait created for the frontispiece of Charles Chesnutt's biography of Frederick Douglass (1899). Library of Congress, Prints and Photographs Division, LC-USZ62-24170.

pathetic tone."[58] This important passage appears early in the *Narrative* and reflects the connection that Douglass registers between words, music, and Black American expressive culture.

Frederick Douglass's *Narrative* explains enslavement by directly describing his experiences to an audience that he knew to lie far beyond his southern readers. Douglass consciously appeals in his writing to a northern reading public who would be receptive to his depictions of a slave system that clearly contradicted the slaveholding master narrative. Douglass was the first to write the explanation *and* offer insight into its significance. And most importantly, Douglass provided his explanation from his position as an enslaved person. The *Narrative* was the literary representation of a social movement organized by the Abolitionists and given voice by enslaved Black Americans. It was protest literature that functioned around a Black interpretation of a Black culture that was hidden in plain sight. Even as he presented this insight into slave culture, Douglass was offering an interpretation of a culture that he knew to be hidden and, when glimpsed, largely misunderstood. It was a call to his white reading audience to recognize the potency of Black cultural subjects and their cultural production.

Douglass hears in the songs of his fellow slaves an expression of anguish and pathos. Song creates meaning that words themselves are ultimately unable to approximate: "I have sometimes thought that the mere hearing of those songs would do more to impress some minds with the horrible character of slavery, than the reading of whole volumes of philosophy on the subject could do."[59] But Douglass, whose *Narrative* focuses on the acquisition of literacy and the consequences of obtaining that knowledge, admits that, although he himself was often brought to tears by their sound, even he "did not, when a slave, understand the deep meaning of those rude and apparently incoherent songs. I was myself within the circle; so that I neither saw nor heard as those without might see and hear."[60] Music has undermined language, and even Douglass, who is himself enslaved and moved by what he has heard, is unable to assign absolute meaning.

In some ways, this place of correspondence between Ellison, Douglass, and the limit of expression is a bit of an anomaly. Ellison had been a student at Frederick Douglass Junior High School, a segregated school in Oklahoma City, and was certainly aware of the influence of Douglass's cultural presence. But he expends far more energy articulating for himself a lineage of

American thought and literature—Emerson, Whitman, Twain, James, Crane, Hemingway, and Faulkner—that largely excludes Douglass. This is not to say that Douglass is entirely absent from Ellison's vision of the nation. In what is perhaps the novel's most significant moment of inclusion, Ellison's invisible narrator encounters Frederick Douglass in the form of an image hung on the wall of a Brotherhood office. In this passage, Douglass, known as much for the impact of his oratory abilities as the invisible narrator, is silent and shadowy. The narrator recognizes but only knows about him by way of the things his grandfather has told him: "Sometimes I sat watching the watery play of light upon Douglass' portrait, thinking how magical it was that he had talked his way from slavery to a government ministry, and so swiftly. Perhaps, I thought, something of the kind is happening to me. Douglass came north to escape and find work in the shipyards; a big fellow in a sailor's suit who, like me, had taken another name. What had his true name been? Whatever it was, it was as *Douglass* that he became himself, defined himself [*emphasis in original*]."[61] Ellison, in kind, defines himself as a writer in relation to the distinction Douglass's *Narrative* makes between word and vernacular production.

By the time Ellison was completing work on *Invisible Man,* he had already encountered the work of T. S. Eliot and Ernest Hemingway in college and the ideas of Kenneth Burke in his association with the radical Left. Ellison had embraced literary modernism as a way of differentiating himself from the limitations he saw encoded in Black protest literature. Frederick Douglass had already done some of that work for him, and Ellison recognized that sonic production was a way of reorienting the possibilities of rhetorical production in an enlarged conception of American cultural history. In "Trumpets, Horns, and Typewriters," David Messmer charts the ways Ellison incorporated Douglass's ideas about music and meaning into *Invisible Man* and, more comprehensively, into his mature thinking about music's relation to the meaning of Black experience in the United States. Specifically, Messmer argues that Ellison's brief but pointed insertion of Frederick Douglass and the *Narrative* into the Brotherhood section of *Invisible Man* represents an important moment in which "Ellison is able to invoke and build upon Douglass's musical subversion of the written word through an act of literary signifying between writers that is, ironically, grounded in the undoing of the written word within both texts."[62] Given that Ellison was sharply critiqued for his focus on craft over political considerations, his attention to craft created a counternarrative to those critical of his decision to distance himself from the Left as well as those critical of the stances he took regarding civil rights and Black nationalist activism.

Ellison's reference to Douglass in *Invisible Man* points toward his awareness of several complimentary aspects of defining literature with reference to music. Jazz and blues provided the opportunity to project meaning from within a culture rather than simply reflect meaning projected on that culture from the outside. Ellison could conceive of agency and self-identification in terms that were very similar to the sorrow songs that Douglass describes in his narrative. Self-expression was the marker of culture, particularly if the production of that self-expression emerged from pain. In "The World and the Jug," Ellison rejected Irving Howe's critique of his literary filiation to Richard Wright. Wright the relative was not Ellison's chosen ancestor. Douglass's description of the sorrow songs projects the core values of Ellison's beliefs about democratic liberalism. The sorrow songs "announced the Negro's willingness to trust his own experience, his own sensibilities as to the definition of reality, rather than allow his masters to define these crucial matters for him."[63]

W. E. B. Du Bois also recognized the ways Black music could provide a glimpse behind the veil of Black double consciousness. In the first chapter of *Souls of Black Folk,* "Of Our Spiritual Strivings," and its final chapter, "Of the Sorrow Songs," DuBois wrestles with the cultural implications of Black vernacular musical culture (as well as the production of other American cultures). In a passage near the conclusion of "Of Our Spiritual Strivings," which echoes Frederick Douglass and anticipates some of Ellison's ideas, Du Bois notes, "We the darker ones come even now not altogether empty-handed: there are to-day no truer exponents of the pure human spirit of the Declaration of Independence than the American Negroes; there is no true American music but the wild sweet melodies of the Negro slave; the American fairy tales and folklore are Indian and African; and, all in all, we black men seem the sole oasis of simple faith and reverence in a dusty desert of dollars and smartness."[64] Like Ellison, Du Bois sees in Black Americans a moral center to a country that has failed to live up to the democratic aspirations of the nation's founding documents or the unrealized possibilities contained in Reconstruction. By virtue of a unique set of experiences and obstacles predating the founding of the republic and memorialized in its founding, Black Americans were the most American of all Americans and their cultural expressions a gift to the nation.

Dr. W. E. B. Du Bois. George Grantham Bain Collection, Library of Congress, Prints and Photographs Division, LC-DIG-ggbain-07435.

Du Bois completes "The Sorrow Songs" by asking the same question that Ellison himself posited seven decades later: "Our song, our toil, our cheer, and warning have been given to this nation in blood-brotherhood. Are not these gifts worth the giving? Is not this work and striving? Would America have been America without her Negro people?"[65] The question goes beyond the cultural legacy of marginalized Black artistic production and speaks to a broader issue of Black subjectivity. For Douglass and Du Bois, the vernacular produces something of cultural value out of a shared gathering of sociohistorical exchange. In modernity, its value could be appropriated, diluted, and made into a cliché by the marketplace. Although Du Bois wrote to the Talented Tenth in distinctly Romantic terms, the underlying anxiety was about the struggle to identify the expression produced by ordinary people who were leading their lives against the threats of assimilation and appropriation imposed by modernity.

The central question, "How does one begin to study the historical formation of modern modes of interpretation if his or her conceptual framework is itself a product or symptom of that history?" that Jon Cruz poses in his study *Culture on the Margins* to Douglass and DuBois has implications for considering Ellison's thoughts about music and culture.[66] The performative aspect of music is important to consider. When Ellison describes his relationship to jazz, particularly in the retrospective descriptions of the music he experienced in Oklahoma City and after his arrival in Harlem, he is often describing the performative aspects as much as the musical aspects of the experience. Often, however, the audiences to whom Ellison wrote interacted with the music in the form of recorded sound rather than in a live, performative context. Ellison's essays often do the work of reconnecting the sound with human production. Both Douglass and Du Bois emphasize the relationship between the Black subject and the music that subject produced. The introduction of recording technology at the beginning of the twentieth century meant that sound was no longer inexorably tied to the cultural practices responsible for its production.

Ellison seemed acutely aware that, while technology could reproduce sound disembodied from the musicians producing it, the relationship between writing and sound was important, especially given the oral nature of Black culture. Modern Black culture is uniquely connected to the music—both the artistic production of the music, reflected in jazz and the vernacular production of the music, which was associated with gospel and the blues—it produced. Furthermore, Black musical production was a central component of the ways in which Black American contributions to democracy could be recognized in the broader context of twentieth-century modernity. The relationship between music and language is not uncomplicated, and Ellison recognized that complexity. This is particularly true since his ultimate focus is on the literary Black American subject rather than exclusively on the influence of music on Black American subjects. His work with music has been to expand the ways in which the cultural significance of the Black American people can be understood.

Ellison's conception of music bridges the gap between performative production and technological reproduction. His essay "Living with Music" describes the significance of the transformation to recorded sound that he experienced when he observes that,

> Between the hi-fi and the ear, I learned, there was a new electronic world.... All this plunge into electronics, mind you, had as its simple end the enjoyment of recorded music as it was intended to be heard. I was obsessed with the idea of reproducing sound with such fidelity that even when using music as a defense behind which I could write, it would reach the unconscious levels of the mind with the least distortion.... Perhaps the enjoyment of music is always suffused with past experiences; for me, at least, this is true.[67]

Ellison was uniquely aware of both the cultural possibilities and cultural limitations of recorded sound. Ellison could appreciate the significance of transmitting music through and across culture because he had grown up with the performative qualities of the music and had subsequently experienced its technological replication. His recognition of its cultural significance was, as he said, a function of his experiences living in music. Without the lived experience, Ellison's concern was that recorded music reduced the depth of its expression to a two-dimensional approximation of its potential.

This is a struggle for self-identification that Ellison and Albert Murray echo in their observations about jazz, improvisation, and the singular interdependency of the individual within the collective. Some of this reflects the ways Ellison internalized his reading of T. S. Eliot's appreciation of ritual expression and Kenneth Burke's example of how to use that expression as a viable means for self-definition. In the context of Black American life and culture, Ellison was able to acknowledge classical myth and ritual and redefine those features, often through the lens of jazz and other vernacular forms. His redefinition magnified the mythic, ritualized qualities of everyday Black American life and culture that were plainly visible without ever really being seen. Ellison's writings about music and his insertions of jazz and blues into his writings, much as Frederick Douglass included the lyrics to slave songs in his *Narrative,* form a kind of call-and-response. Ellison clearly sees in jazz its ability to expand the possibilities of literature and culture. It is a thread connecting that which can be communicated by language and that which could be generated by musical performance. Music takes shape in the ways it occupies its cultural space, and literature is expanded in its relationship with the culture produced by music.

By invoking Frederick Douglass in the way he does, Ellison also invokes unstated questions about how best to present Black American culture to the nation and how best to explain the significance of the culture that existed on the racial margins but was born from the nation's center. When Ellison alludes to Frederick Douglass and the cultural production that Douglass describes, what he is accessing is a musical process that enables collectivity and the cultural transmission of information. The life Ellison describes growing up with jazz and the meaning the music has given to him subsequently emphasizes performance and the ways the music is so intimately connected to Black public spaces.

When Ellison makes his case for the kinds of music he sees relevant to his theory of culture, he is defining an "authentic" art capable of invoking the histories, aspirations, social movements, and struggles of the people who made the music and the people, like Ellison himself, who were sustained by the music. Invoking the idea of authenticity is often problematic in that it suggests characteristics of essentialism and authority and implies a basic anxiety about a kind of erosion into something less true and less genuine. This is certainly a meaningful concern, particularly given the ways Black cultural production has been appropriated, assimilated, and sold for profit in its diluted form, sometimes back to the very people who first produced it. Ellison's concern certainly includes that anxiety. But Ellison's concern more fundamentally emanates from his awareness of the ability of cultural modernism to reflect and create social change. Ellison often observed the ways popular culture was infused with qualities that had their origin squarely in Black culture. His point about this process often has more to do with the circularity of social practice rather than with outright accusations of theft and appropriation.

3

PERSONAL VISION, LIVING CULTURE
Translating Politics into Art

I have no desire to manipulate power. I want to write imaginative books.
RALPH ELLISON, "Five Writers and Their African Ancestors"

TWO WORLDS OF RACE:
THE FLUIDITY OF ART, THE FUNCTION OF POLITICS

I'll be my kind of militant.
RALPH ELLISON, "Ellison"

As Ellison was actively trying to accommodate the transracial ambitions of the Left during his years as an apprentice writer, he was also very consciously creating for himself a language that could contain radicalism and vernacular tradition, protest literature and cultural mythology, the epic and the particular in ways that meaningfully reflected the experiences of Black people in America. That process undoubtedly contributed to his disengagement and isolation from the Left. Radicalism worked to construct a multiracial working-class movement to defeat fascism. Ellison disengaged race from class, even as he formulated a perspective linking race more securely to nation. In the 1960s, Ellison found himself being drawn into a similar battle. Black radicals saw his ideas about American cultural unity as being dangerously backward-looking for a generation intently focused on formulating a new, radical, Black ideology.

In *Ralph Ellison and the Politics of the Novel,* Herbert William Rice argues that Black radicals "did not read Ellison's novel or essays as important political or historical proclamations—they read them as accommodation to a status quo that had too long controlled African-American understanding of the self."[1] This is certainly true, though the radical response to Ellison has as much to do with the stance Ellison took at a time when a new generation of radical Black thinkers was asserting its influence. Their reading of Ellison also has its basis in Ellison's depiction of Ras in *Invisible Man*. By the end of the novel, the invisible narrator has abandoned the politics and ideology that Ras continues to pursue. His brand of nationalism becomes meaningless in its absurdity.[2] The question here is how did Larry Neal, a foundational architect of the Black Arts movement and sharp critic of Ellison in that capacity, come to revise his thinking about Ellison so drastically? Their thinking certainly diverged in crucial ways. Neal's most biting critiques of Ellison look toward a far-reaching theory of oppression and Black separatism that Ellison firmly rejected. Neal's ideas are inconceivable without Ellison's thoughts about the ways the nation's failure to live up to its fundamental principles forms, and subsequently destroys, the subjectivity of Black and white people alike. Unlike Neal, who drew heavily on Frantz Fanon, Ellison is unwilling to consent to the belief that Black people are locked in blackness and white people are locked in whiteness. There is no anti-Black nation for Ellison because, by its very definition, the nation is fundamentally inseparable from the blackness of its whiteness. What Larry Neal came to realize in his reversal of attitude toward Ralph Ellison was that creative artists always bring with them "the accumulated weight of their forebears' experiences."[3] This is what Ellison had been saying since he began distancing himself from the Left two decades earlier. In short, Larry Neal eventually saw the merit of synthesis or, as Ellison preferred to call it, integration. Neal came to see how the new arose from "the accumulated weight of our Western experience" in ways that no singular ideology—philosophical, political, or religious—could adequately replace for understanding experience. Specifically, Neal comes to see the political in Ellison's thinking. But, as he says, "It is just that Ellison's politics are ritualistic as opposed to secular."[4]

Ellison worked to expand the meaning of the Black intellectual beyond the limitations of race. Specifically, art and culture can resist the rubric of a particular racial identity. The Black intellectual is often defined by group loyalty rather than Ellison's attempts to balance multiple claims on that loyalty in the broader service of national complexity. In a remarkably short time after he published *Invisible Man* in 1952, Ellison was catapulted from being a writer relatively unknown to the broad reading public into a prominent novelist and public intellectual who became for many a figure representing the possibilities of Black American intellectualism. This is not to suggest, however, that he had been entirely obscure. Though it may not have seemed particularly clear at the time, Lawrence Jackson shows in the central portion of his examination of Ellison's development as a writer that the public trajectory of Ellison's literary apprenticeship was well over a decade in the making.[5] His body of published work primarily consisted of a broad collection of essays, journalistic writing, and short stories. For four years, beginning in 1938, Ellison had written articles, more than twenty book reviews (some signed, some not), critical articles, and short stories for *New Masses,* followed by a succession of pieces published in a wide variety of places that included *Antioch Review, Horizon, Partisan Review,* and the *New York Times.* His reach extended from *Negro Digest,* the journals *Tomorrow* and *New Challenge,* to the Federal Writers' Project. In short, it is abundantly clear that Ellison's literary apprenticeship was substantial, varied, and deeply influenced by radicalism.[6]

After the publication of *Invisible Man,* Ellison became a public figure regularly called upon to give speeches, teach on college campuses, serve on boards, and contribute to the nation's ongoing discussion of race and American culture. Ellison also became a Black American public intellectual who was perceived by many to be increasingly out of touch with Black Americans. Ellison supported President Lyndon Johnson and the president's policies as they related to the role of the United States in escalating the war in Southeast Asia. This position was particularly relevant since a disproportionate number of Black soldiers served and died in a war that pitted them against other people of color for an unclear objective. Ellison was not involved in the nation's increasing antiwar protests. As antiwar sentiment quickly expanded across the country, and particularly on college campuses, he remained loyal to President Johnson and maintained public silence about opposing the war.

Larry Neal was certainly among those who saw Ellison's work as reflecting an era that was quickly being superseded by a New Breed of artists and activists. Neal's influential 1968 essay "The Black Arts Movement" helped give the movement its name and focus its direction: "The two movements [Blacks Arts and Black Power] postulate that there are in fact and in spirit two Americas—one Black, one white. The Black artist takes this to mean that his primary duty is to speak to the spiritual and cultural needs of Black people. Therefore, the main thrust of this New Breed of contemporary writers is to confront the contradictions arising out of the Black man's experience in the racist West."[7] As the arts editor for the *Liberator,* Neal had been at the vanguard of the development of the movement. He had become a member of the Black Panther Party and the Revolutionary Action movement. He was also one of the founders of the Black Arts Repertory Theater and School in Harlem. He was a prolific writer who produced two volumes of poetry and numerous contributions to *Black Theatre Magazine, Ebony,* the *Journal of Black Poetry,* and a short-lived magazine named *Cricket* that was devoted to Black American music. His work also included writing the introduction to the 1971 edition of Zora Neale Hurston's novel *Jonah's Gourd Vine* and contributing to the publication of her autobiography, *Dust Tracks on a Road.* All of this is to say that his work was expansive and influential for a generation intent on formulating a new vision of the world that asked "[W]hose vision of the world is finally more meaningful, ours or the white oppressors'? What is truth? Or more precisely, whose truth shall we express, that of the oppressed or of the oppressors? These are basic questions. Black intellectuals of previous decades failed to ask them."[8]

In *Black Fire,* Larry Neal argued for a view of Ellison that reduced his work to a kind of literary footnote: "They [the writings of Frantz Fanon and Malcolm X] are especially more pertinent than Ralph Ellison's novel, *Invisible Man,* which is a profound piece of writing but the kind of novel which, nonetheless, has little bearing on the world as the 'New Breed' sees it. The things that concerned Ellison are interesting to read, but contemporary black youth feels another force in the world today. We know who we are, and we are not invisible, *at least not to each other [emphasis in original].* We are not Kafkaesque creatures stumbling through a white light of confusion and absurdity. The light is black (now, get that!) as are most of the meaningful tendencies in the world."[9] The movement that Neal described was at a serious point of transition. The movement had postulated a theory of Black Power but had not yet formulated a workable ideology that could encompass the broad range of experiences throughout the Black community. The movement had accounted for the need to empower separatists and revolutionaries. The movement had begun to disavow Black and white establishment thinking. But the movement had not formulated a consistent theory of social change that was rooted in Black American history.[10]

Ellison was not part of the new construct that the movement was seeking to develop. His thinking, particularly about integration, was part of the old construct that the movement was consciously trying to move beyond. "We must integrate with ourselves."[11] The vision was culturally internal, not external. Black art fulfilled the ritualistic role it had long filled for Black Americans. But for the movement, the role of Black art was to destroy old ideas to affirm the greatest aspirations of the race. "The artist and the political activist are one. They are both shapers of the future reality. Both understand and manipulate the collective myths of the race. Both are warriors, priests, lovers and destroyers"[12] This is the epitome of the self-described "New Breed" of artists and activists.

Larry Neal subsequently revised that assessment. In an essay entitled "Ellison's Zoot Suit" that originally appeared in a 1970 edition of *Black World*, Neal wrote, "Much of the criticism directed against Ellison is personal, oversimplified, and often not based on an analysis of the man's work and ideas. A great deal of the criticism emanates from ideological sources that most of us today reject. To be concise, much of the anti-Ellison criticism springs from a specific of Marxian and black neo-Marxian thought."[13] But the point that Arnold Rampersad, Larry Neal, Amiri Baraka, Toni Morrison, and others make clear is that Ellison clung to a worldview profoundly shaped and overly limited by Jim Crow. Toni Morrison's comment speaks to a broad failure of personal and creative vision: "The contemporary world of late twentieth-century African Americans was largely inaccessible, or simply uninteresting to him as a creator of fiction. For him, in essence, the eye, the gaze of the beholder remained white. But if the ideal white reader made sense for *Invisible Man* in 1952, he or she made less sense for the black writer by the seventies and eighties."[14] Critics note that the foundation of his worldview had been transformed by the contours of American life, beginning in the 1960s and continuing well into the debates about multiculturalism and the canon that continued until Ellison's death in 1994.[15] Specifically, Ellison's ideas about integration—social integration, cultural integration, artistic integration—seemed to cause the most intense critical friction.

Inevitably, the demands of social protest and the writer's responsibility to the world from which his or her work arose were sifted against theories of art, aesthetics, and political value. Near the end of his life, for example, the Reverend Dr. Martin Luther King Jr. began to worry that the work of integration that had been so much a part of the civil rights agenda was misguided. As King's focus had begun to shift to the underclass, he began to fear that integration perpetuated inequality in ways that subverted Black progress by integrating Black people into a burning house. But Ellison strongly believed that Black people could no longer remain outside of American institutions: "Once Negro leaders grasp this fact they will cease to be Negro leaders and be American leaders. Far too often they are provincial in their approach, acting as if all the problems were specifically Negro problems."[16]

In refusing to apologize either for the source of his ideas or for the negative reception they increasingly received on the college campuses on which he taught and lectured, Ellison reaffirmed his belief in American intellectual and cultural pluralism over ethnic particularism: "In other words, we often forget that the only way to be an effective Negro intellectual is by being a most perceptive and responsible *American* intellectual [*emphasis in original*]."[17] The Black intellectual tradition—that is, the *American* intellectual tradition—was under siege by intellectuals driven to the point of separation out of fundamental feelings of frustration: "I believe that the state of black youth points to our failure, and if we have failed them we have failed American youth generally. For all their talk of black separatism—really another version of secessionism, an old American illusion which arises whenever groups reach an explosive point of frustration—and for all their stance of alienation, they are really acting out a state of despair. They are frightened by the existence of opportunities for competing with their white peers on a basis of equality which did not exist for us [those who grew up in a segregated society]."[18]

Ellison's dependence on integration, in word and aspiration, conflates one of the most patently contentious goals of the movement for civil rights with what Ellison saw as his greatest literary aspiration: "I would emphasize my personal affirmation of integration without the surrender of our unique identity as a people to be a viable and, indeed, inescapable goal for black Americans."[19] By invoking "the Negro American idiom" as a vocabulary for interrogating American values, Ellison found cultural segregation an impossible platform from which to do his work. In a conference in May 1965 that had been organized by the American Academy of Arts and Science with the expansive topic "The Negro American," Ellison firmly made the point that "One concept that I wish we would get rid of is the concept of a main stream of American culture—which is an exact mirroring of segregation and second-class citizenship. I do not think that America works that way at all. I would remind us that before there was a United States, a nation, or a form of a state, there were Negroes in the colonies. The interaction among the diversified cultural groups helped to shape whatever it is we are who call ourselves Americans. This, I think, is a very important distinction to make."[20] Ellison was certainly not blind to the fact that the nation at the time was engaged in the movement for civil rights and an escalating war in Southeast Asia. Racial justice was a primary topic in a conference that contained the assumption, ten years after the order to end the nation's practice of legal segregation, that the nation remained firmly separate and decidedly unequal. Ellison's disagreement with this assumption was based on his belief that there was no widespread desire on the part of Black American citizens to enter the American mainstream. There was nothing to which to aspire.

> One thing that is not quite clear to me is the implication that Negroes have come together and decided that we want to lose our identity as quickly as possible. Where does that idea come from? . . . The other thing is that part of the [civil rights] struggle (which I have known now for some fifteen years) has always been not to get away from the Negro community, but to have the right to discover what one wanted on the outside and what one could conveniently get rid of on the inside. . . . The main stream is in oneself. The main stream of American literature is in me, even though I am a Negro, because I possess more of Mark Twain than many white writers do.[21]

The nation was composed of a chaotic, contradictory collection of narratives that each had authority and meaning in the ways Ellison conceptualized democracy and what it means to be American. That was the basis of his thinking about the influence of cultural and artistic integration. No single quality was entirely inseparable from another. In his introduction to *Shadow and Act,* Ellison recognized the inability to isolate one element from another when he noted that "The act of writing requires a constant plunging back into the shadow of the past where time hovers ghostlike. When I began writing in earnest I was forced to relate myself consciously and imaginatively to my mixed background as American, as Negro American, and as a Negro from what in its own belated way was a pioneer background."[22] It was here for Ellison that questions about the relationship between politics and identity merged.

Ellison's disagreement with those whose criticism was most disparaging to him stems from his belief that those associated with the Black Arts movement focused too intently on ideology—"the ideology that has been made of what they call 'Blackness'"[23]—and militant sloganeering rather than on the difficult task of transforming experience into novelistic form. Richard Wright, who died as a French expatriate in 1960, could be claimed in death as an ideological mentor. *Native Son* and *Black Boy* had been read and reread to the point where the ideas they raised had become shorthand ideological references to the nation's turmoil when the character of the civil rights movement changed as its focus moved beyond the issues affecting the South and toward issues concerning an urban population. "But I think much of it was stirred up by the Black Aesthetic people, who are *badly* in need of a hero, and an answer to James Baldwin's criticism of Wright [*emphasis in original*]. Now with Wright safely out of the way they can shape him and his words to their own convenience."[24] The case that Ellison constructed was that, in re-making Richard Wright to fit their ideological needs, those who had adopted Wright as an ideological influence were engaging only a small portion of his thinking: "Thus it's ironic to see these people embracing Wright, because his was anything but such an attitude. In his effort to make some sort of intellectual *Gestalt* for himself, he read all kinds of books, entertained all kinds of ideas. And during the days when I knew him well he certainly didn't allow racial consideration to limit the free play of his intellect. After all, most of his friends, like both of his wives, were white."[25]

Abstracting Black culture from American culture did not distill it into something more powerful, regardless of whatever attempts were made to ground it in the cultural authority of Richard Wright's work. "How can one abstract Afro-American experience from that of the larger culture of which it is so important a part without reducing it, in the name of 'Blackness' to as vapid a collection of stereotypes as those created in the name of whiteness?"[26] What is often lost in discussions is what some see as Ellison's reluctance to merge aesthetic concerns with any public response to racism in American intellectual life. Ellison, however, clearly saw the matter differently. In the "Introduction to the Thirtieth-Anniversary Edition of *Invisible Man*," Ellison notes that the focus his fiction placed on human possibility (and the possibilities contained in social institutions) reflects the best and highest aspiration of politics. "While fiction is but a form of symbolic action, a mere game of 'as if,' therein lies its true function and its potential for effecting change. For at its most serious, just as is true of politics at its best, it is a thrust toward a human ideal."[27] For Ellison, the novel functions best when it functions in direct engagement with democracy: "As I see it, the novel has always been bound up with the idea of nationhood."[28] The novel was not invented by Americans or even for the use of Americans. But Ellison saw in it a form capable of uniting the novelist's imagination with the sense of value contained in the novelist's chosen subjects. Ellison was certainly not blind to the realities contained in the disparities between ideal and reality, principles and practice, aspiration and lived experience, shadow and act, principle and practice. *Invisible Man,* his essays, interviews, public lectures, and even the unfinished second novel are all encircled by his understanding of the tensions framed by these very ideas. But the specter of Ellison's disdain for active political engagement has cast a broad shadow across many of the ways Ellison's ideas are considered.

If Ellison is read in conversation with the very authors with whom he situates his work, perhaps the most compelling critique of the politicism that emerges is that Ellison was not able to provide the kind of clarity and insight about the nation's role—historically and in the nation's ever-emerging present—in defining and maintaining some kind of national ethos of American individualism.[29] One thing that is profoundly clear is that Ellison had no interest in pursuing an agenda—literary or political—of racial solidarity as a viable strategy for obtaining individual self-determination and humanity. In an interview from 1955 entitled "The Art of Fiction," Ellison critiqued his invisible narrator for failing "to run the risk of his own humanity."[30] To some extent, the narrator's shortcomings regarding his reluctance to confront his humanity are a function of the segregated national space in which he lived. That space was predicated on denying Black Americans a full measure of subjectivity, which therefore inhibited the development of identity, particularly as that identity existed in the public sphere.

Much of Ellison's fiction and nonfiction writing is rooted in the foundation of an evolving Black American consciousness and awareness of the effects of segregation that were ultimately bolstered by *Brown v. the Board of Education of Topeka, Kansas,* the movement for civil rights, and the Black Power movement. The sense of possibility that the conclusion of *Invisible Man* ambiguously suggests, and that Ellison presented much more directly in his nonfiction, is that a Black spokesman, on the lower frequencies or otherwise, could speak for all Americans. More specifically, the way in which Ellison constructs his position as a Black public intellectual, perhaps beginning as early as the speech he gave accepting the National Book Award for *Invisible Man* in 1953, suggests his belief in the power of Black American culture to stand on its own terms anywhere throughout the world and to create an understanding of the ways Black culture influenced, as much as it was influenced by, American culture: "Whatever they [America's nineteenth-century novelists] thought of my people per se, in their imaginative economy the Negro symbolized both the man lowest down and the mysterious, underground aspect of human personality. In a sense, the Negro was the gauge of the human condition as it waxed and waned in our democracy."[31]

Thirty years after the publication of *Invisible Man,* Ellison added to the novel's origin story in an extended introduction that was part literary criticism and part memoir combined with a bit of allegory. In appending the essay to the novel's legacy, Ellison returned to a body of ideas that he had long mined. In explaining the origin of the invisible narrator's voice, Ellison notes that "the voice of invisibility issued from deep within our complex American underground."[32] His choice of pronoun—"our"—was not insignificant. It reflected for Ellison something other than W. E. B. Du Bois's influential conceit about double consciousness and the veil in the opening pages of *Souls of Black Folk.* For Ellison, the "our" in "our complex underground" refers as much to Americans in general as it does to Black Americans in particular. Spatializing *Invisible Man* underground and "on the lower frequencies" gave Ellison the opportunity to integrate voices, circumstances, and social and political ideas that anticipated by decades the conflicts that arose in the late 1960s and early 1970s, as well as the rancorous discussions of canon and multiculturalism that consumed the 1980s and 1990s.

Ellison's work relentlessly returns to his understanding of America's past. The crucible that forged the experiences of Black people living in America also forged the attitudes and experiences of white Americans. Slavery and its legacy were not isolated events. Slavery and the failure of Reconstruction shaped the experience of life, and not simply Black life, in America. Many of the accusations of Ellison's reluctance to engage politically with the events that unfolded during his lifetime were based on the belief that art was fundamentally inseparable from politics.[33]

Given the emphasis his fiction placed on a world characterized by chaos, fragmentation, and ambiguity that is ultimately held together by an unseen (and perhaps unknowable) coherence, Ellison is clearly a modernist, albeit one who came to modernism late. His most enduring objective was to fuse the ideals contained in the nation's founding documents with the "social equality" that the invisible narrator stumbles into during his speech following the battle royal. For Ellison, virtually all his public work represented a kind of political action because so much of it contained the crucial element of social critique. To Ellison's way of thinking, his politicism differed from those who criticized him most harshly in form and style, not in commitment.[34]

To put it as directly as possible, Ellison's view of his intellectual and artistic role had virtually nothing to do with preserving and insisting on his Blackness and virtually everything to do with making it clear to the American mainstream that Black experience was synonymous with the nation's experience. This "network of mutual benefaction," in which democratic citizenship necessarily includes an understanding of that mutuality, is precisely the point that political theorist Danielle S. Allen makes about Ellison in *Talking to Strangers*. The relationship between Black Americans and between the racialized political ideologies that involve Black Americans relative to the nation are most often posited in particularly dualistic ways: Integration and assimilation versus separatist nationalism. The question that Ellison raised in *Invisible Man* and quickly reiterated in "Brave Words for a Startling Occasion" has much more to do with how best to acknowledge the pluralistic composition of the nation's past (and the contemporary lived experiences of its citizens) without simultaneously erasing and making invisible the very real differences of its citizens. This, as Timothy Parrish notes in *Ralph Ellison and the Genius of America,* is an area of Ellison's thought that has often been misunderstood or minimized altogether.[35] How can the whole be understood as a place of integration for distinctly unique component parts? Ellison correctly saw the tension that existed between exerting one's individual rights and desires in the context of a larger democratic environment that impaired individual self-determination.

Interpreters of the trajectory of Ellison's role rightfully see the early 1970s as an important point of transition in Ellison's work and its reception. Personally, Ellison experienced a house fire in 1967—however much the extent of what he lost of the additions he had made during the summer to his novel in progress might be contested—and he appears to have restored and revised the unfinished novel in 1972. He managed to publish an excerpt of the novel in 1969 entitled "Night Talk" in *Quarterly Review of Literature* and an excerpt entitled "A Song of Innocence" in 1970. At a time when the relationship between Black politics and Black literary production was changing rapidly and in profound ways, Ellison's attention seemed focused on the completion and publication of the novel that he had begun to work on some twenty years earlier.

He certainly chose against publicly responding to a growing thread of criticism that saw Ellison as an irrelevant race traitor who was more closely aligned to the problems affecting Black Americans than he was to their solution. To some extent, this was a generational changing of the guard as younger writers and political thinkers reassessed their forebears in much the same ways that Ralph Ellison and James Baldwin had attacked the assumptions of literary naturalism and protest literature that had preceded the publication of their own work. Ellison's ideas were about alienation, invisibility, and the consequences of culturally failing to recognize the relationship of Black and white racialized experience on the nation's understanding of itself. Those ideas came to be read as being contrary or even dangerous to a national climate that increasingly saw race as a representation of hypervisibility rather than invisibility. But as Ellison saw it, the democratic ideal functioned around an assimilated multiracial cultural economy rather than racially driven separatism.[36]

By the beginning of the 1970s, the Voting Rights Act of 1965, which had been signed into law by President Lyndon Johnson, faced the possibility of being substantially weakened. The April 6, 1970, edition of *Time* magazine devoted a substantial portion of the issue to the question of race and the condition of Black Americans in the United States. In referring to Black radicalism, *Time* noted in its introduction to the issue entitled "Black America 1970" that "They do not spurn material progress but want a greater share of it—along with freedom and equality. They are indeed faithful dreamers of the American dream—but scandalously hampered in turning that dream into reality for themselves."[37]

By 1970, Ralph Ellison was close to publishing his long-awaited second novel. Though he had experienced a fire in his vacation home that had destroyed some amount of his manuscript-in-progress, Ellison suggested in public and private comments that he was as close to publishing his second novel as he had been. If *Invisible Man* examined the experience of being Black in the age of segregation, the novel in progress seemed intended to confront some of the consequences of segregation and the civil rights movement. In his biography of Ralph Ellison, Arnold Rampersad points out that, as the years went by, Ellison's account of the amount of work he had lost increased dramatically, perhaps as a way of accounting for the novel continuing to fail to appear in publication. Rampersad also saw the period beginning in the mid-1960s and continuing into the 1970s as an important point of transition in which he sees Ellison becoming increasingly disengaged from the cultural changes the country was rapidly experiencing. The point that Rampersad draws from the conflation of these circumstances is that Ellison's estrangement from Black intellectualism was a primary contributing feature of the second novel's ever-extending composition period.

Rampersad's assumption that Ellison somehow failed in achieving his potential as a novelist because of his distance from meaningful Black engagement simply reinforces what Marc Conner, in "Reading Ralph Ellison," sees as more of the cultural reduction that critics had directed toward Ellison since Irving Howe's critique of him in the early 1960s. Timothy Parrish's confrontation with Rampersad's caustic assessment of Ellison's achievement—Parrish firmly faults Rampersad for blaming Ellison's failure to complete his second novel on Ellison's desire to be accepted by white readers at the cost of his own racial identity—raises the question of what Ellison's legacy really is and whether his inability to complete the second novel consigns him to the role of literary failure, particularly in the face of all that he accomplished.[38]

Both novels rely on historical context to provide form and meaning to the idea animating both that history is itself a form of consciousness. Denying the power of historical precedent is a form of physical, spiritual, and intellectual death. Part of the collective burden of Americans is to face the present by retrieving and recovering the past. Hortense Spillers puts it more succinctly in "Ellison's 'Usable Past'" when she conceptualizes *Invisible Man* as "standing on an historical line reaching back and forth" that "embraces history as an act of consciousness."[39]

Invisible Man suggested that the novel's ultimate impact could only be reached through a collaborative process between the reader and the novel's ambiguous narrator. In the novel in progress, that point of cooperation and historical retrieval largely takes place between the Reverend Alonzo Hickman and Senator Adam Sunraider as they engage in an extended call-and-response recitation of their shared history. Though, in many ways, history and the past are protagonists in both novels, Ellison recognized in the novel in progress the difficulty of converting history into a tool for social change. In writing *Invisible Man,* Ellison had created a novel that embodied the effects of segregation on the nation's consciousness. Ellison saw himself as much more than a writer entombed in the sarcophagus of Jim Crow's legacy. His tendency to universalize the meaning of *Invisible Man* is perhaps Ellison's clearest indication of this. Harold Bloom argues as much in *Genius* when he notes that, although *Invisible Man* furnished an incisive vision into Black American consciousness, "So much has changed, in the American half-century, that *Invisible Man* might be reduced to a period piece if it were primarily a vision of African-American dilemmas. The novel's permanence stems from its universality: it is one of the major American visions of what Emerson and Whitman regarded as the infinite possibilities of life in the United States"[40]

Ellison's worldview clearly conflated race and the nation. Black Americans were more American than many chose to acknowledge. This is particularly relevant in the late 1960s and early 1970s. Medgar Evers had been murdered, followed by Freedom Summer workers James Chaney, Michael Schwerner, and Andrew Goodman. After the murder of the Reverend Dr. Martin Luther King Jr. and the rise of conservative Republican leadership like Richard Nixon, many in the nation turned away from the civil rights era's strategy of nonviolence and began to embrace the strategies of active confrontation that characterized Black Power movement ideology. In Ellison's assessment, white Americans owed far more to the contributions of Black Americans than they were willing to acknowledge. Consequently, Black contributions were often made culturally invisible. The problem, particularly during the turbulence surrounding this period, was that obscuring the ragged edge between Black and American was often unwelcome by those on both sides of the color line.

As one of the nation's most recognized cultural thinkers on the intersection of race and nation, Ralph Ellison had placed himself in the untenable position of being expected to speak for a cultural reality increasingly composed of the kinds of confrontation and social turbulence that he had conceptualized and articulated in the late 1940s and early 1950s. Ellison had integrated the world of arts and letters with the publication of a novel that itself insinuated that the nation and the Black people who constituted a portion of the nation were already far more integrated than many thought possible. But in doing so, Ellison integrated himself into a world that accepted him as a singular representative figure. Rampersad, among others, saw Ellison as using his unique position in the literary community to preserve his stature and to distance himself from other promising Black writers. Ellison was accused of replicating what many saw as a kind of singularity, even though the lectures he presented and the essays he published seem to suggest that he remained deeply engaged with the nation's changes in the ways that he thought most important.[41]

Ellison grew up in a Black community in Oklahoma City. For three years, he attended Tuskegee Institute, a historically Black university located in Tuskegee, Alabama, that was founded in 1881 as the Tuskegee Normal School for Colored Teachers by Booker T. Washington. In 1933, the same year the Scottsboro boys were being retried, Ellison arrived at Tuskegee Institute after having survived being thrown from a freight train in Macon County, Alabama. After leaving college, Ellison migrated to New York City where he lived, in Harlem, for the rest of his life. His work, beginning with the earliest essays and experiments with fiction that he produced with Richard Wright's encouragement, largely focused on race and class in the United States. None of this suggests someone who had the kind of ambivalent attitude to questions of race that his detractors accused him of having a generation later. Ellison never stopped advocating for a position that recognized the shared, intertwined history of Black and white Americans. The history of the United States was particularly distinctive because of its unique trajectory through slavery, segregation, and a cultural fluidity that securely bound Black experience to the nation's democratic aspirations.

That is not to say that Ellison saw the experience of that shared history to be the same for Black people as it was for white people. Ellison never used his ideas about cultural pluralism as a point of departure for his own racial denial or as a justification for any kind of racial ambivalence whatsoever. His point of view as a racialized subject informed the way he conceptualized himself as an intellectual and literary artist. Ellison's ideas about cultural permeability should not be taken to mean that racial difference was inconsequential or simply did not exist. He had found segregation profoundly troubling. He found the discrimination spawned by the legacy of segregation to be deplorable. But the fact that Ellison's work compellingly identified the shortcomings of the nation's attitudes about race also meant that Ellison himself became identified with those shortcomings and, by extension, responsible for the formulation of solutions—or at least viable responses—to those shortcomings. While Ellison certainly recognized and accepted that responsibility, he firmly resisted any pressure to formulate a response purely based on ideology. Though he valued his racial membership, Ellison also realized that race alone put him in the position of being one voice among many: "I am, after all, only a minor member, not the whole damned tribe; in fact, most Negroes have never heard of me. I could shake the nation for a while with a crime or with indecent disclosures, but my pride lies in earning the right to call myself quite simply 'writer.'"[42]

Ellison seemed to understand and accept the uncomfortable relationship that existed between being a writer with universalizing literary impulses and being a writer intent on practicing his craft. In the literary conversation Ellison had with Irving Howe, published as "The World and the Jug," Ellison noted:

> But as to answering his [Irving Howe's] question concerning the "ways a Negro writer can achieve personal realization apart from the common effort of his people to win their full freedom," I suggest that he ask himself in what way a Negro writer will achieve personal realization (as a writer) *after* his people shall have won their full freedom [*emphasis in original*]. The answer appears to be the same in both instances: he will have to go it alone! He must suffer alone even as he shows the suffering of his group, and he must write alone and pit his talents against the standards set by the best practitioners of the craft, both past and present, in any case. For the writer's real way of showing the experience of his group is to convert its mutual suffering into lasting value.[43]

Ellison clearly disliked Howe's insinuation that he was in any way incapable (that is, somehow not Black enough or not the right kind of Black voice) of putting words to the experiences Black people faced across the nation. Numerous perspectives were competing for recognition and influence in the nation's discussion of race. In an uncanny reference to the primary conceit of his first novel, Ellison may have come to realize that many had moved beyond his thoughts about what constituted the battle in which the nation was engaged. In doing so, they had consigned Ellison's ideas about Black cultural invisibility to its own place of cultural insignificance.

While the legacy of a segregated nation informed all aspects of civil rights and the nation's response to the movement, Ellison tenaciously clung to his beliefs that the only way to begin a discussion about race in the United States was to acknowledge the nation's racial interconnectedness. On December 1, 1973, Ellison spoke, along with Nathan Huggins, Harold Cruse, and his longtime friend Albert Murray, at Harvard University on the occasion of the Alain L. Locke Symposium. Early in his tribute, Ellison articulated his position as clearly as he ever had: "Al Murray has said that all blacks are part white, and all whites part black. If we can deal with that dilemma—and it is a dilemma—then we can begin to deal with the problem of defining the American experience as we create it. You cannot have an American experience without having a black experience. Thus it seems amazing to me that we can have moved away from that complex, mysterious, perplexing sense of our role in this country to something which is much too simplistic."[44] One thing that his comments seem to emphasize is that the area of intellectual territory upon which Ellison grounded his thinking is significantly more expansive than the intellectual, political, and artistic territory from which he was most often critiqued.

FROM ANOTHER SPACE AND ANOTHER TIME

[A] writer learns (and quite early, if he's lucky) to depend upon the authority of his own experience and intuition.

    RALPH ELLISON, "Study and Experience"

Part of the cause for the ways Ellison's intellectual eclecticism was misread may have as much to do with a combination of the nation's political changes as it did with the convergence of published writing that shaped the spirit of the age. Ellison frequently insisted that he was not interested in writing about politics. This is not to suggest that his writing was not political, however. Like Frantz Fanon, Ellison's personal biography is often read as a way of understanding his published work. And, like Fanon's, Ellison's ideas are often recognized as exploring the relationship between race and political ideology. But this is a point of divergence between the two. Fanon argued for the necessity of a violent response to oppression, particularly in *The Wretched of the Earth* (1961, *Les damnés de la terre*), which Ellison categorically dismissed, just as he dismissed the thought of rebuilding national culture in the aftermath of violent confrontation. Equally important for Ellison was his categorical rejection of seeing the oppression of Black people throughout the diaspora through the lens of internationalist politics. Fanon's thinking shifted away from theorizing race to a series of ambitious considerations of radical anticolonial struggle and visions of the possibilities of postcolonial society. Conversely, Ellison's thinking can be seen as becoming increasingly insular in its insistence on American cultural integration. The significance here is that Ellison's rejection of a Black collective identity driven by ideology was seen by Black nationalists as nothing less than an overtly bourgeois political stance. Much was at stake in the disagreement between Ellison and the New Breed of activists and artists who were looking to supersede what Ellison represented.

Ellison's literary stature continued to expand, and his influence continued to deepen on the reputation of *Invisible Man,* the essays he published (some of which he eventually collected in *Shadow and Act,* which he published in 1964), and the public's anticipation for his second novel, from which he had excerpted "And Hickman Arrives" in 1960, "Juneteenth" in 1965, and "Cadillac Flambé" in 1973. All told, Ellison published eight excerpted passages from the novel in progress between 1960 and 1977, which further fueled what was already keen anticipation for the follow-up to *Invisible Man.* But while Ellison continued to work, his writings and public lectures increasingly became seen as backward looking, disengaged from the changes American society was rapidly undergoing, and overly integrationist in their focus on culture and literary craft.

To some extent, this view was reinforced by the publication of *Shadow and Act,* which traced the impact of growing up in the former Oklahoma territories on Ellison's conception of race, nation, music, and literary art. But many of those ideas were directly formed by the literary conversations with Stanley Hyman, Irving Howe, and Ellison's indirect responses to the flow of ideas in which he had sought to situate himself—and differentiate himself from—during the decade surrounding the publication of *Invisible Man. Shadow and Act* consciously lacks the kind of "black fire" of violent politicized racial confrontation that the concluding chapter of *Invisible Man* seemed to foretell. The impending race war that is on the verge of engulfing Harlem is the confrontation that the invisible narrator goes underground to avoid. Though the narrator concludes his narrative by insisting, and unconvincingly so to some readers, that his period of hibernation is ending, the fact is that his final act of any substance was to escape underground to avoid the frenzy and chaos of the street gangs. Their ill-conceived, ideologically weak uprising threatened to unstick the glue of historical cohesion that bound the nation together in a shared cultural system.

In the larger context of increasingly incendiary ideology and revolutionary rhetoric, Ellison's writing seemed, as it was intended, to tread a path of intellectual continuity. *Shadow and Act* looked backward to Ellison's passionately nuanced contemplations about his relationship to American culture. "That Same Pain, That Same Pleasure," originally published in 1961, opens the collection with an interview about the ways he, "as a Negro writer," had "vaulted the parochial limitations of most Negro fiction."[45] "Twentieth-Century Fiction and the Black Mask of Humanity" was originally written just after the Second World War but was not published until 1953. In preparing the piece for its original publication, Ellison decided that "When I started rewriting this essay it occurred to me that its value might be somewhat increased if it remained very much as I wrote it during 1946. For in that form it is what a young member of a minority felt about much of race writing. Thus I've left in much of the bias and shortsightedness, for it says perhaps as much about me as a member of a minority as it does about literature."[46] "Change the Joke and Slip the Yoke," a piece originally published in *Partisan Review* during the spring of 1958, was Ellison's portion of a dialogue that he had with Stanley Edgar Hyman, a longstanding personal and intellectual friend with whom Ellison enjoyed the spirit of debate. "Richard Wright's Blues" reached back to an essay he had published in the *Antioch Review* in 1945 to discuss the influence of Jim Crow on his mentor's development and to argue that "All of this makes the American Negro far different from the 'simple' specimen for which he is taken."[47]

The central portion of the collection, which was oriented around discussions of Mahalia Jackson, Charlie Parker, Charlie Christian, and Jimmy Rushing, pointed to a golden age of Black music and culture that time was threatening to leave behind. These essays address the difficulty of living with a music whose meaning and coherence had been supplanted by the chaos and fragmentation of the bebop revolution pioneered by Dizzy Gillespie and Charlie Parker. Ellison saw bebop as creating a new musical vocabulary that unnecessarily distanced people from the cohesion of swing-era music, its musicians, and the territory bands that had meant so much to Ellison's conception of himself and to the ways he saw himself reflected in American culture. "Perhaps in the swift change of American society in which the meanings of one's origins are so quickly lost, one of the chief values of living with music lies in its power to give us an orientation in time. In doing so, it gives significance to all those indefinable aspects of experience which nevertheless help to make us what we are." Ellison's thoughts about Charlie Parker, Dizzy Gillespie, and the ways their music had supplanted, to the detriment of American culture, the swing-era music from which bebop grew were far less than charitable. Much of this is echoed in his essays "On Bird, Bird-Watching," and "Blues People."[48]

The final portion of the volume discusses William Faulkner, D. W. Griffith, and the portrayal of Black people in "The Shadow and the Act." "The Way It Is" presents a portrait of Harlem from the perspective of a longtime resident to argue that here is "one of the best arguments for the stabilization of prices and the freezing of rents." Ellison had previously published the essay in *New Masses,* late in 1942.[49] *Shadow and Act* concluded with "An American Dilemma," a review originally published in 1944 in the *Antioch Review* in which Ellison takes Gunnar Myrdal to task for the assumptions about social science and American Negro destiny that Myrdal presents in *An American Dilemma.* Ellison's concluding thoughts in his review, and to *Shadow and Act* itself, are that "what is needed in our country is not an exchange of pathologies, but a change of the basis of society. This is a job which both Negroes and whites must perform together. In Negro culture there is much of value for America as a whole. What is needed are Negroes to take it and create of it 'the uncreated consciousness' of their race. In doing so they will do far more; they will help create a more human American."[50]

Shadow and Act spoke volumes about the circumstances that had shaped the trajectory of Ellison's artistic development as profoundly as it had shaped the fundamental aspects of what defined how he saw himself as an American Negro. But at a time when activists and writers like Amiri Baraka (who had previously written as LeRoi Jones), Haki R. Madhubuti (formerly Don L. Lee), and Larry Neal were abandoning a pluralist American Negro identity in favor of a more singular, ideologically driven Black identity, Ellison's brand of racial identification became far more than a place of departure. It became representative of a pathology of internalized self-hatred that inhibited the progress of an authentic Black identity. That identity had been repressed in the nation's consciousness since the expansion of the Atlantic slave trade and the ideologies associated with the systemic institutionalism of white supremacy.

Separatism, for Ellison, was empty rhetoric that had nothing to do with the nation's realities. Conversely, the culturally pluralistic high ground from which Ellison's views emanated became for Black nationalists an example of the bourgeoisie political stance. It illustrated Ellison's profound discomfort with the Black lower class that was revealed most tellingly in Jim Trueblood's incestuous, blues-tinged sharecropping. The narrator's brief and disgusted interaction with Trueblood serves as the catalyst that propels the invisible narrator from the idyllic coherence of college into the chaotic fragmentation that ultimately sends him underground. While underground, the invisible narrator confronts and tries to reconcile the metaphor that Ellison devised to represent the continuity—past, present, and future—of Black citizenship. That continuity was represented by the constraints created and maintained by both Black and white people alike for managing and hindering Black social advancement.

Ellison never exhibited any inclination to publish an autobiography, but his essays, taken collectively, provide a useful autobiographical counternarrative to his published fiction. In the mid-1960s when *Shadow and Act* was published, Ellison's readers knew remarkably little about him. Until the arrival of *Shadow and Act,* the reading public knew of the geographic trajectory his life had taken and knew something of his ideas by way of his National Book Award acceptance speech, a handful of interviews, and several sections of what everyone assumed to be his forthcoming novel. The collection's retrospective focus essentially separated Ellison from much of what was going on around him and relegated him to a position of urbane intellectual commentator whose work did not meaningfully engage the implications of being a Black writer in a nation defined by race. It also served as a potent response both to an older generation of critics, some of whom had supported and encouraged his work soon after the publication of *Invisible Man,* and to a younger generation of New Breed artists and activists whose outlook was increasingly becoming nationalist and Pan-African.

What became lost in translation was Ellison's insistence on recognizing the autonomous Black core that was contained in the nation's pluralism. Ellison's work did not reflect the consciously political engagement of James Baldwin, John A. Williams, or Amiri Baraka. But neither did his work reflect the kind of southern paternalism contained in the work of William Faulkner.

Ellison regularly referred to the influence jazz played on his conception of himself and his work. The reference is a useful metaphor for his sense of what is truly at stake in the struggle between self-assertion and group dynamic. Neither freedom nor repression is absolute. As a matter of fact, the perception and recognition of one can only be seen in relation to the other. Understanding that paradox means understanding the basis of the human condition. Unlike the radicals who stood in opposition to him, Ellison saw the world in the context of its restriction rather than in the context of the possibilities it presents for absolute, unambiguous freedom and autonomy: "The blues is an art of ambiguity, an assertion of the irrepressibly human over all circumstance whether created by others or by one's own human failings. They are the only consistent art in the United States which consistently reminds us of our limitations while encouraging us to see how far we can actually go."[51] Chaos and fragmentation are at the heart of coherence; tragedy is embedded in comedy; illusion is a component of reality.

Invisible Man had been read very differently by Black and white reviewers when it was published. That disparity only increased as Black activists relegated the usefulness of Ellison's ideas to the margins. *Invisible Man* was recognized in mainstream reviews like the one contained in the book review of the *New York Times* on April 13, 1952, for the risks contained in its writing style, or the book review of the *New York Herald Tribune* on April 13, 1952, which recommends it to those "interested in Negro-white relations in the depression decade." Ultimately, the universality to which Ellison aspired diffuses Ellison's deconstruction of the myths of American possibility and Black uplift. Perhaps unsurprisingly, Irving Howe's review in the *Nation* on May 10, 1952, confronts the fact that prevailing national social conditions provide relatively few alternatives to Ellison's conception of invisibility.[52] Black responses to the novel, largely relegated to Black or leftist publications, were considerably less enthusiastic about what, if anything, Ellison had truly achieved. The March 1953 issue of the *Crisis* and the May 1953 issue of *Negro History* each did little more than point to the positive reception the novel had achieved in the mainstream press. Black critics associated with the Left like Abner Berry in the June 1, 1952, issue of the *Worker,* Lloyd L. Brown in the June 1952 issue of *Masses and Mainstream,* and John Oliver Killens in the June 1952 issue of *Freedom* noted what they saw as Ellison's apparent disdain for the Black masses, his distortions of the Left, the blame he places on Black characters for circumstances they cannot control, and his pretentiously artistic literary experimentation. The novelist John Oliver Killens contributed a review to the June 1952 issue of Paul Robeson's *Freedom* newspaper that saw little in the novel worthy of approval:

> The thousands of exploited Negro farmers in the South are represented by a sharecropper who has made both his wife and daughter pregnant. The main character of the book is a young Uncle Tom who is obsessed with getting to the "top" on the basis of pleasing the Big-Rich-White Folks. A million Negro veterans who fought against fascism in World War II are rewarded with a maddening chapter of crazy vets running hog-wild in a downhome tavern. The Negro ministry is depicted by an Ellison character who is a Harlem pastor and at the same time a pimp and numbers racketeer.... The Negro people need Ralph Ellison's *Invisible Man* like we need a hole in the head or a stab in the back.[53]

Not surprisingly, Langston Hughes in *New York Age*, February 28, 1953, and Alain Locke in *Phylon* 1953 both acknowledged weaknesses while offering continued unwavering support for Ellison's accomplishment. Alain Locke even went so far as to rank the novel just behind *Cane* (1923) and *Native Son* (1940) in the ways it advanced the possibilities of Black literature in the United States.

The disparity in the orientation of Black and white response is even more apparent in the reception of *Shadow and Act*. While the overall response to the collection was considerably more muted than how *Invisible Man* was received twelve years earlier, the relative silence surrounding the collection from the Black press is striking.[54] In many ways, this is emblematic of the fact that many Black readers simply did not see themselves as representing Ellison's audience. Accusations of Ellison's inaccessibility to Black readers only increased in the following years, along with the acknowledgments that Ellison's reputation produced. For his detractors, the paradox is that his reputation deepened precisely because of his unwillingness to engage in polemics that were based in ideology. Because of that, Ellison's voice became an unwelcome counterbalance to those advocating a Black nationalist agenda.

In many instances, the acknowledgments that Ellison received were given by those least interested in or supportive of Black nationalism. In September 1965, Ellison was ranked sixth (one place above Norman Mailer and two places above Ernest Hemingway) in a poll conducted by New York Herald Book Week. The poll asked scholars and intellectuals to suggest the names of authors who had made the most distinguished contribution to literary fiction in the post–World War II period. Since no Black scholars or intellectuals were invited to respond to the poll, Ellison's inclusion reflects a much broader acceptance of his intellectually serious approach to the conversations of race and nation that were playing out in all strata of intellectual, political, and popular culture. The poll ranked *Invisible Man* as the most distinguished novel of the postwar era.

Writers have no control over how their work is understood and discussed after it is published. The context in which a work is consumed can be as significant as what the work itself is understood to mean. This is certainly the case with a novel as resolutely ambiguous as *Invisible Man*. The interests of Black and white people were often diametrically opposed. Even intragroup beliefs about the definition of the issues they faced and how best to address them varied widely. All sides needed a lens to focus their thoughts, and Ellison, particularly due to the ways his work and cultural presence resonated through the post–civil rights years, provided a unique place in which to locate that discussion. What is not included in many of those discussions is the idea that makes it possible for so many of those discussions to be in conversation with each other: the idea that the United States exists as the nation it does because of an autonomous Black culture that exists within the framework of the nation's every-changing pluralism.

Ellison's attempt to see Black experience in the context of something much greater may have given white readers the very tool that allowed them to substitute their engagement with Ellison for a more direct confrontation with race and its complexities. Ellison's personal bearing, coupled with his fascination with folklore, may also have made his work particularly attractive to scholars interested in exploring the possibilities of New Criticism. In a special issue of *Black World* devoted entirely to Ellison, Larry Neal in his role as arts editor recognized the inherent difficulty of critiquing Ellison. Though he declined to offer the kind of engagement that many had come to expect, "His creative works are for the most part grounded in a kind of Afro-American folk tradition, especially in the linguistic sense."[55] But his critical ideas are firmly grounded in the thinking of New Critics "like T. S. Eliot, Kenneth Burke, Ezra Pound, and Andre Malraux."[56] In response to the criticism he received in the issue, Ellison chose to disengage: "Hell, man, what would you expect? It was obvious that I couldn't have a fair exchange of opinion with those who used the issue to tee off on me, so there was nothing to do but treat them as I had bad dogs and bigoted whites down South: Mentally, I walked away from it. Long before that issue was published they had been banging away at a hateful straw man who they'd labeled 'Ellison' and were using it as a scapegoat for their discontents and disappointments, and it appeared that the more I refused to be provoked the more strident they became."[57]

But Ellison was not attempting to escape a Black culture that had formed him as a writer and that had supplied the foundation of so much of his work. Larry Neal realized this when he acknowledged what he referred to as Ellison's "cultural nationalism."[58] Ellison's sources were not the issue. Neither were his techniques or even his ideas about protest. The issue was that Ellison's unwavering acceptance of New Criticism left him unable to function as a literary artist in the Black community from which his work ostensibly emanated: "Ellison's work, for all its beauty of style and depth of perception, is read by more whites than Blacks. To what extent is the writer responsible for the situation? The artist must be a part of the condition in which he exists. If that condition is an oppressive one, he must use his work not only to transcend that condition, but to destroy it. If he is interested in his people, he will place his work where it can reach them. If not, he will continually beg the question by resorting to nice sounding literary chit-chat."[59]

The influence of New Criticism on Ellison's literary outlook should not be minimized. While it was most deeply influential from the 1940s through the 1960s, its origins and contributions to literary theory are substantially broader. They may not have necessarily thought of themselves as New Critics or even as part of a cohesively organized literary movement. Some of the most influential New Critical works included T. S. Elliot's "Tradition and the Individual Talent" (1917) and "Hamlet and His Problems" (1919), William Empson's *Seven Types of Ambiguity* (1930), Cleanth Brooks's *Well Wrought Urn* (1947), as well as the *Southern Review* journal, which Brooks edited in collaboration with the poet Robert Penn Warren. The *Southern Review* served as a literary journal important for publishing Southern writers and New Critical articles. The movement relied on close readings that emphasized language, structural textual analysis, objectivity, and the complete elimination of historical considerations or biographical concerns.[60]

At its heart, New Criticism functions around the understanding that textual meaning is created by interweaving elements that simultaneously work in relation to and in opposition to each other. What New Criticism particularly valued was a plurality of perspective. Meaning could never be uniquely singular. With the text itself serving as the best source of its own interpretation, the author's beliefs about the meaning of the text he or she created become irrelevant. Intentional fallacy, or the mistaken belief that authorial meaning is synonymous with textual meaning, focuses attention back on the text itself. Perhaps more importantly for the way Ellison's work was understood, Ellison's race would have been largely irrelevant to the ways New Critics would have understood the underlying unity and universalism of the text he produced.

The contradiction, of which Black nationalist writers were particularly aware, is that the significance of a novel like *Invisible Man* simply could not be addressed without focusing considerable attention on the historical context in which it was produced and from which Ellison himself drew his understanding of how literature functioned in the world. Ellison was particularly inclined to think about his work in aesthetic rather than political terms. But his work, with its psychological, sociological, and historical dimensions, was certainly not an isolated aesthetic textual object from which a single meaning could be discerned by employing a single method. The New Critics wanted to link an interpretation to the discovery of the text's organic unity in a way that so much of Ellison's literary ideas actively resist. But Ellison's attraction to an underlying sense of unity within chaos and fragmentation would certainly make a critical approach focusing on timelessness and aesthetics, coupled with an understanding of literature as an artistic production worthy of consideration for its own sake, particularly attractive.

The critique of Ellison as an establishment writer who pandered to a white audience with allegorical fiction and essays about his views of art and his development as a writer was nothing new. Amiri Baraka, writing at the time as LeRoi Jones, had as early as 1962 in "The Myth of a 'Negro Literature'" made this very point about all Black writing that failed to adopt a nationalist point of origin.[61] In the essay, which was originally presented as an address given at the American Society of African Culture in March of 1962, the central point of what Jones has to say is that "The Negro writer on Negro life in America postures, and invents a Negro life, and an America to contain it. And even most of those who tried to rebel against that *invented* America were trapped because they had lost all touch with the reality of their experience within the *real* America, either because of the hidden emotional allegiance to the white middle class, or because they did not realize there the reality of their experience lay [*emphasis in original*]."[62]

In what seems to be a direct attack on Ellison's insistence on cultural integration, Jones argued that Black culture would always remain a distinct entity within American culture because Black culture remained *in* but not truly *of* the culture that surrounded it. For Jones, integrationist thinking would remain as unsuccessful as the creoles who "thought they had found a place within the white society which would preclude their being Negroes. But they were unsuccessful in their attempts to 'disappear' because the whites themselves reminded them that they were still, for all their assimilation, 'just coons.'"[63] Black American artists like Ellison, for all their desire to integrate the nation with its blackened origins, simply could not pursue mainstream acceptance—artistic or otherwise—without becoming little more than observers to the society in which they lived.

What is at stake in the disagreement between Ellison and the New Breed of artists and activists is a reassessment of a series of fundamental assumptions about the nation's political, artistic, and social values. The conflict occurred as much within Black America as it did between the nation's mainstream and the often-competing beliefs that were present within various Black political and social ideologies. The New Breed, at least as Larry Neal saw it in his afterword to *Black Fire,* the movement's manifesto, could only define itself through its actions, and its actions could only be rendered through a synthesis of all the nationalistic movements that had preceded it. In doing so, Black Power recognized the need for an inherent separation—even in literature—between Black writing and the nation that produced it: "Every black writer in America has had to react to this history, either to make peace with it, or make war with it. It cannot be ignored. Every black writer has chosen a particular stance towards it."[64] Black nationalist writing saw itself as engaged in the elimination of double consciousness, not in the artistic integration of double consciousness.

Ellison's writing felt particularly irrelevant for some because the trope of invisibility that made Ellison's narrator invisible to both white and Black people was antithetical to a movement that established itself on the premise that Black people were not invisible to other Black people.[65] At a time when New Breed writers and activists were interested in looking backward toward Jim Crow and beyond to justify their thoughts about a separate Black nation, Ellison was using the legacy of segregation to argue against the viability of any cultural or artistic assessment that could not embrace the necessity of plurality and integration. Black nationalist writers and activists increasingly turned toward Pan-Africanism as a way of empowering Africans and people of African descent throughout the diaspora. Ellison refused to consider his thoughts about American democracy in a broader framework. Black American identity was, for him, firmly attached to, and completely inseparable from, American history: "The African content of American Negro life is more fanciful than actual.... As long as Negroes are confused as to how they relate to American culture, ... they will be confused about their relationship to places like Africa."[66] He firmly valued cultural cohesion over political affiliation. The Black presence in America was entirely shaped by its relationship to the nation, even if the depth of that history was largely unacknowledged.

BLUES PEOPLE, BIRD FLIGHTS, AND BLACK NATIONALISM

I don't fight the race problem in matters of culture but anyone should know the source of their tradition before they start shooting off their mouth about where jazz comes from.

Letter from **RALPH ELLISON** to **ALBERT MURRAY**, September 28, 1958

What does Ellison's scathing review of *Blues People* tell us about the significance of his thoughts on the formation of national culture, particularly as that formation relates to the influences of Black vernacular culture? In his perceptive reading of Ellison's contentious intellectual relationship with Amiri Baraka, James Smethurst amplifies Baraka's importance as a cultural critic when he observes in *Brick City Vanguard* that, "While Baraka established his reputation as a critic writing in *Downbeat, Metronome, Kulchur,* and other jazz and arts journals, it was the publication of his historicist study of the social meaning of jazz, *Blues People* (1963), that clearly marked him as the leading proponent of a new sort of black cultural studies."[67] Smethurst goes on to argue that Ellison's unfavorable review of *Blues People* was as much about his antipathy to Baraka's sociological approach as it was his attempt to revise the lens through which *Invisible Man* could be read when he writes, "Ellison reimagines the place and meaning of African Americans and African American culture, especially music, in U.S. culture and politics, offering also a new ideological vantage point from which to read *Invisible Man*."[68]

While it is Smethurst's intention to foreground Baraka and *Blues People,* his thinking about Ellison's desire to reframe critical interpretations of *Invisible Man* is an important observation, particularly in the context of a younger generation of activists like Baraka who favorably cited aspects of *Invisible Man* even as they recontextualized the novel in the evolving radicalism of their own ideologies. Their thoughts about Ellison were far less favorable when they considered him as a person, a literary figure, and a representative of the kind of revolutionary politics that the chapters of *Invisible Man* preceding the epilogue suggest. The epilogue turns away from the race riots that consume Harlem at the end of the novel and turns instead toward the narrator's universalist message that concludes the novel. But the point here, as Smethurst signals in *Brick City Vanguard,* is that the review also signaled a major disparity between the way Black music could, and should, be used in the more fundamental discussion of understanding the relationship between Black people and the nation.

Ellison and Baraka are central to this discussion, particularly since *Blues People* markedly diverged from Ellison's thoughts about the cultural presence of Black people in the nation. Although Baraka had not yet fully embraced Marxism and Black nationalism, *Blues People* sees Black people as having been colonized and thereafter embarking, through sacred and secular music, on a cultural passage from African to African American. In an assessment of *Blues People* that was published in 1978, Nathaniel Mackey wrote approvingly that "The book thus has to do with the various transformations—from African to Afro-America, slave to citizen, rural to urban—undergone by black people in the United States and the attendant transformations of Afro-American music."[69]

In the February 6, 1964, edition of the *New York Review of Books,* Ralph Ellison published a biting review *Blues People: Negro Music in White America* by LeRoi Jones, several years before he became widely known as Amiri Baraka. The review was as much about Ellison's thoughts on the relationship of the blues to Black American culture as it was a review of Jones's book. Jones, in what can be seen as a foundational contribution to the field of American cultural studies, wanted to use the blues as a conduit through which to explore "the *path* the slave took to 'citizenship'" and to use the blues as a way most broadly of understanding the social configuration of the United States and most particularly of understanding the trajectory of Black Africans beginning with their arrival in colonial America [*emphasis in original*].[70]

The publication of *Blues People* preceded the publication of *Shadow and Act* by about a year and, appearing as it did around the time of the 1963 March on Washington, introduced its readers to the thinking of an emerging Black activist and intellectual who was putting forth a counternarrative to the predominant civil rights narrative of equality and assimilation. Jones's assessment linked Black writing to activist Black liberation. That vision of engaged artistic activism remained largely unchanged for the remainder of his creative and intellectual life. Jones's opinions about Ellison were certainly not softened in any way by Ellison's critical review of *Blues People*. What perhaps made Ellison's review of the book seem particularly harsh was that, at its center, Ellison's critique was essentially a denunciation of Jones's assumptions about race and culture. In return, *Black World* offered a review of *Shadow and Act* that called into question Ellison's optimistic cultural assumptions about the power and willingness of American democracy to remediate its relationship to the nation's Black population. This, coupled with Ellison's public pronouncements about the nation's racial conflict and his obvious dislike for the quality of writing the movement was producing, led to what Ellison saw as nothing more than a retaliation that was much more about ideology rather than art.

For Jones, blues and the jazz it helped create are transhistorical cultural expressions that are inscribed by their very otherness rather than by their assimilation. It is precisely its marginalization that gives Black culture the opportunity to separate from the mainstream and actively respond to its own otherness. That is precisely what made bebop such a powerful form for Jones. Bebop was a return to a position of separateness because it reinforced alienation, but "on the Negro's terms."[71] By the time *Blues People* turns its attention to 1940s bebop, Jones has laid the foundation for pronouncing bebop to be a crowning achievement for jazz and Charlie Parker "the soul and fire of the bebop era."[72] What makes Charlie Parker such a powerful figure in Jones's formulation is that Parker's emphasis on theme and the variation of improvisation echoed throughout bebop and linked bebop to the call-and-response elements of the blues tradition. By 1963, Charlie Parker had been dead for eight years and his revolutionary musical form superseded by the cool jazz and hard bop that characterized the sound of late-1950s jazz. Jones denigrated the jazz that emerged after Parker's death as being a series of stylistic modifications that contained little authentic emotional content. Parker's improvisations had connected him to the blues while simultaneously creating for his music a unique counterpoint to Western music's emphasis on composition and notation. Miles Davis's assessment of Charlie Parker was that "Bird was a great improviser.... His concept was 'fuck what's written down,'... just the opposite of the Western concept of notated music."[73]

Though Ellison's review of *Blues People* was particularly biting, his thoughts about the book (and about the larger body of writing associated with Black Arts) should be placed into a broader context. While Black Arts writers often repudiated Ellison, they often used his work as a point of departure for their own. Though the focus is most often on the ways the movement's ideas and objectives diverged from Ellison's, his work certainly influenced some of the era's most inventive work. For example, Jones's play *Dutchman,* which was first produced in 1964, was an important example of 1960s revolutionary Black theater. It was subsequently produced as a film in 1967. It was intended allegorically to depict the nation's race relations by drawing on the image of a naive protagonist in a subway underground in Harlem. He is a middle-class, twenty-year-old Black man who is college educated and eventually brought to a breaking point at the end by the racism contained in the action of the play. Toni Morrison also drew on Ellison in her rewriting of the Jim Trueblood episode from *Invisible Man* in her first novel, *The Bluest Eye,* which was published in 1970.[74] In fact, though, Ellison's review of *Blues People* was as much about Ellison himself as it was about Jones's book: "*Blues People,* like much that is written by Negro Americans at the present moment, takes on an inevitable resonance from the Freedom Movement, but it is in itself characterized by a straining for a note of militancy which is, to say the least, distracting."[75] Ellison is particularly bothered by Jones's reliance on sociology as the organizing principle to situate his thoughts about the influence of the blues on Black culture when he sardonically notes that "The tremendous burden of sociology which Jones would place upon this body of music is enough to give even the blues the blues."[76] More tellingly, Ellison firmly rejects Jones's assertion that bebop was a music of rebellion. Instead, he characterizes its practitioners as nothing more than entertainers who, in formulating a new musical language, were reaching for a level of musicality that Louis Armstrong, Coleman Hawkins, Count Basie, and Duke Ellington had already achieved by mastering the traditions of blues and jazz that define their music.

Unsurprisingly, Ellison located the true power of the blues in its artistic and technical qualities rather than in its political implications. Ellison's view is hardly provocative. While guided by propriety and a sense of tasteful musical decorum rather than political expression, Ellison reiterated the same lesson that he had learned growing up in the former Oklahoma territories and that he recalled in *Shadow and Act*. Jazz and the blues do not gain their power from their political assertions but rather from their process of accessing the vernacular. Far from representing otherness and reinforcing alienation (even if it was an otherness configured and maintained on Black Americans' terms), Ellison's vision of the vernacular influence of jazz and blues infiltrated all aspects of American life in a pluralistic expression of social democracy. The result is the reconciliation of fragmentary, diffused chaos into something both new and independent from its origins.

For Ellison, *Blues People* dilutes cultural complexity in favor of an ideological agenda that ignores the vitality "of enslaved and politically weak men successfully imposing their values upon a powerful society through song and dance."[77] The failure of *Blues People* is a failure to recognize the vernacular impulse toward synthesis, aesthetics over ideology, and art over politics. By extension, the failure of Jones's analysis is a direct reflection of Ellison's perception of the inability of New Breed writers and activists to recognize the same distinctions.

To some extent, the publication of *Blues People* was an opportunity for Ellison to reconnect with a topic that was a cornerstone of his ideas about art and culture. He had already written widely about the subject. This was a book that Ellison himself could have written. The bitterness that his review provoked, combined with the publication of *Shadow and Act*, implicitly repudiated the literary and social climate in which it appeared by simply refusing to acknowledge the existence of that environment. Instead, Ellison focused on publishing a gathering of essays and assorted pieces written for various occasions that collectively pointed to the Oklahoma of his youth. It was for him a place as defined by race as anywhere else in the United States. It was also a place on the margins of cultured civilization that was characterized by the expansiveness of frontier opportunity. Meanwhile, *Blues People* was situated on the vanguard of a collection of ideas that eventually coalesced into a movement of Black Arts with its own publications. These publications included *Black World,* for example, which spoke to a readership that had grown beyond the ideological confines of *Negro Digest* (the original title of the magazine that was renamed *Black World*), *Liberator,* and influential anthologies like *Black Fire.* Collectively, the ideas these publications contained had replaced the idea of being "Negro" with uncompromising assertions of what it meant to be "Black."

But these New Breed writers were not alone in their forward-looking revision of the cultural landscape. The cultural conversation about race and the effects of race on Black Americans and the nation's psyche was being driven by James Baldwin in *The Fire Next Time* (1963), Adrienne Kennedy's one-act play *Funnyhouse of a Negro* (1964), *The Autobiography of Malcolm X* (1965), John A. Williams in *The Man Who Cried I Am* (1967), and John Oliver Killens's *The Cotillion; or, One Good Bull Is Half the Herd* (1971). Ellison was seemingly preoccupied with recasting his past into a frontier-born evocation of Black folklore that culminated in his own artistic maturation.

In a collaborative essay between Ralph Ellison and James Alan McPherson that took place in July 1969 and was published in the December 1970 issue of the *Atlantic,* Ellison addressed the disparity between his self-identification as a Negro American at a time when many younger Black activists were consciously separating themselves from the influences of American culture. Ellison, in 1969, had written a promotional jacket advertisement for McPherson's new short-story collection *Hue and Cry* in which he pointedly observed, to the displeasure of radical writers, McPherson's decision to pursue craft over argumentative assertion. Ellison's comments, distilled into the short promotional paragraph that appeared on the book's jacket, speak to the uncomfortable relationship between the implications of being a writer who is Black and a writer who is American. A generation earlier, Ralph Ellison had been forced to reconcile and come to terms with many of the exact same issues that a younger generation of Black writers were facing. James Alan McPherson recognized that irony as well as he recognized that Ellison's refusal to become part of an ideologically based "movement" had consigned him to a point of departure from which radical Black writers could differentiate their ideas.

Ellison, in life, had become as much a symbol of assimilation and political stasis as Richard Wright, in death, had become a representative figure of authentic Black radicalism. As McPherson observes in the essay, a work like Wright's *Native Son,* which was published in 1940, is most often compared to the work subsequently produced by Ralph Ellison and James Baldwin rather than to the writers and their works—John Steinbeck's *Grapes of Wrath* (1939), Ernest Hemingway's *For Whom the Bell Tolls* (1940), Willa Cather's *Sapphira and the Slave Girl* (1940), and Carson McCullers's southern gothic novel *The Heart is a Lonely Hunter* (1940)—that were Wright's true contemporaries.[78] "I think that now a very articulate group of young writers doesn't quite know what to make of me.... I think that since I have not embraced some of their literary theories, they feel that I am the enemy. My position has always been that ideology is one thing. Show me what you make of it. If you make art out of it, I will praise the art even while I argue with the ideology. But I haven't seen enough of the art. I suspect that I have annoyed a few people by insisting upon the mastery of craft."[79]

Though it took five years, one of the people whom Ellison had indeed annoyed rethought his position and said so publicly in 1970. Larry Neal wrote a series of essays published in *Liberator* in 1965 and 1966 that examined the work of Richard Wright, James Baldwin, and Ralph Ellison. His goal was to consider "The Black Writer's Role" in contemporary society. The essay focusing on Ellison, as well as the inflammatory comments he made about Ellison in the afterword he contributed to *Black Fire,* were relentlessly anti-Ellison. That antipathy made his turnabout in a 1970 essay he published in *Black World* entitled "Ellison's Zoot Suit" particularly compelling. Much of the criticism leveled against Ellison had a political basis that often overwhelmed other areas of critique. Neal's realization five years after the critique he initially published was that Ellison's work had produced a "fantastic impression."[80] Neal came to recognize that some of the most outspoken criticism of Ellison's work had far more to do with ideology and political activism than with creative vision and the craft of writing.

In an interview conducted by Charles Rowell that appeared in a 1985 edition of *Callaloo* devoted to him, Neal indicated the ways he came to recognize the importance of articulating an aesthetic language that was firmly rooted in culture. Neal had long considered Ellison's embrace of craft and European culture disruptive of the obligation writers had to reach for specific cultural referents to unify them more effectively with their audience. But this interview indicates that, in his reassessment of Ellison, Neal had moved beyond viewing literature exclusively based on function: "'What is our relationship to the literary heritage of the West?' Ralph Ellison had to ask himself this question.... All black writers that were conscious of critical problems asked themselves this question.... They have to ask themselves: 'What is my relationship to the established literary tradition in which I find myself?'... What parts of the literary tradition do I claim, and what parts do I reject? Where do I add my own voice, and where do I propose another way, another direction?" These are the questions, far beyond ideology and far beyond function, that Neal recognized Ellison to be grappling with and that fundamentally changed Neal's assessment of Ellison and his work.[81]

By the 1970s, Neal could reclaim Ellison because, as Houston Baker argues in "Critical Change and Blues Continuity," Neal had abandoned militant separatism for what he refers to as "establishment theater." In his 1972 essay "Into Nationalism, Out of Parochialism," Neal concedes the need for Black artists to "take on the American theater sensibility and replace it with ours. Or, at least, place our statement in the arena."[82] Who had argued more persuasively than Ralph Ellison for the need to confront rather than withdraw from Western art? While Neal's initial criticism took Ellison to task for his belief that Ellison was seduced by the siren song of literary and cultural criticism, his reassessment places Ellison squarely at the center of the literary and cultural "others" who drew upon and amplified his work. Perhaps, by the 1970s, Neal came to see Ellison as a metaphor for his own critical and artistic evolution.

Ellison's ties to the Left are undeniable. His introduction to Langston Hughes in 1936 when Ellison arrived in Harlem quickly led to Ellison's introduction to others with leftist political leanings. It was through Hughes, for example, that Ellison met Richard Wright, who had moved to Harlem from Chicago to coordinate the *Daily Worker* for the Communist Party USA. Though Ellison declined party membership, he remained in close proximity to the Communist Party USA's agenda. Precisely how close and for how long is unclear. But what is clear is that Ellison had a serious interest in leftist ideas, published his earliest work in leftist publications, and befriended (and was befriended by) people active on the Left.

His trajectory was anything but singular. The Communist Party USA had shown itself to be an attractive place for Black writers to pursue their art. In the March 1967 issue of *Harper's Magazine,* later republished as "A Stern Discipline," Ellison discussed the limitations of Communist ideology relative to

Black Americans. Black people were incidental to the Communist Party USA's interests as Ellison came to see the party as little more than an American wing of Soviet foreign policy. Black people were simply cogs in the wheel of a strategy that was unwilling to acknowledge any plurality of interests: "They fostered the myth that Communism was twentieth-century Americanism, but to be a twentieth-century American meant, in their thinking, that you had to be more Russian than American and less Negro than either."[83] In short, Ellison could not see a way in which the Black intellectuals during his closest association with leftist ideology could formulate a robust radical political stance that was developed by Black people for the benefit of Black Americans that would not ultimately get co-opted by white Marxists who thought of America's "Negro Problem" as a piece of an international Marxist perspective. His warning to the younger generation of activists was unequivocal: "[W]hen the war came, Negroes got caught and were made expedient in the shifting of policy, just as Negroes who fool around with them today are going to get caught in the next turn of the screw."[84]

Ellison's association with radical politics may be seen as a place in which Ellison struggled to reconcile leftist ideology with the presence of Black Americans, who had a very particular, systemic history of oppression and discrimination in the United States. Part of what Ellison was struggling to reconcile in the late 1930s and early 1940s was what Black culture meant in the larger context of an ideological stance whose focus was on class inequality and the unequal distribution of resources. The meaning of the "Negro Question" disappeared in (or, less charitably, was simply co-opted by) a much broader social and political agenda.

Though Ellison contributed to radical publications and attended Communist Party events like the League of American Writers' Congress, which were sponsored in 1935, 1937, 1939, and 1941, Ellison was less driven by propagandistic conceptions about the Negro struggle and the Black proletariat. He was far more interested in the influence, and the potential threat of dissolution, of Black social, cultural, and political agency. In dissenting from fully embracing leftist thought, Ellison creates a nationalist vision that predates by some thirty years the nationalism that subsequently rejected him.

What Neal had belatedly recognized was that Ellison's sleight of hand had substituted cultural inequality for Marxism's focus on class-based inequality. This is the idea that resurfaces in Ellison's disparaging response to *Blues People*.[85]

Neal locates Ellison's earliest attempts to wrestle the often competing (sometimes mutually exclusive) claims of culture and politics in an unsigned editorial that appeared in the pages of *Negro Quarterly* in 1943. Given the editorial's subject matter, its approach to the theme, its tone, and the development of its ideas, it is entirely plausible to ascribe authorship to Ellison. As such, Ellison at this early stage of his writing life had already found himself stuck between two incompatible positions that remained in some form or other in his writing consciousness for the remainder of his life: how to articulate a meaningfully sustainable vision of identity and self-definition that is entirely distinct from the white cultural space in which it exists while simultaneously immersing itself in the chaos of competing impulses that define the American democratic process.[86]

In 1943, Ellison was trying to make these connections within the framework of a Marxist ideology that he certainly had a proximate relation to without being able to give it his complete support. His engagement with a political frame is nothing more than a lens through which to examine the artistic. Ellison's eventual decision was to disavow the political in favor of the artistic. Politics hindered the production of true art rather than encouraging its creation. Neal recognized what Ellison had begun working through a generation earlier and saw that the political confines imposed by a movement seemingly committed to Black advancement in the 1960s and early 1970s could be as artistically confining as the leftist politics through which Ellison first began to find his voice.

Not everyone was as willing as Neal to reevaluate their thinking about Ellison's body of work relative to the New Breed writers and political activists. The New Breed were actively working to leave behind Negroness in favor of a political and economic expression of Blackness that recognized diasporic movements worldwide and brought these international communities in conversation with each other under a broad, Marxist-inspired umbrella. This, for Ellison, was a definition of pigmentation rather than culture: "What makes you a Negro is having grown up under certain cultural conditions, of having undergone an experience that shapes your culture. There is a body of folklore, a certain sense of American history. There is our psychology and the peculiar circumstances under which we have lived."[87] The shadow of *Invisible Man,* with an antihero unable to come to terms with the various visible and invisible political agendas competing for his acceptance, loomed over 1960s Black radical writers and activists as fully as the specter of shifting ideology and political agendas that had loomed over the Black Left in the 1930s and 1940s.

While Ellison was reluctant to draw a direct line of connection between his experiences with the Left and 1960s Black radical writing, he remained very conscious of the dangers of sublimating art to politics. Folklore, not political ideology, reaches to the most profound areas of the Black presence in the United States. "In folklore we tell what Negro experience really is."[88] That is the element toward which Ellison was reaching even during the Marxist phase of his writing life. Ellison, during the 1960s and 1970s, claimed a certain double consciousness that alternated between the leftist propaganda he had been asked to write and the fiction he chose to write. "I never wrote the official type of fiction. I write what might be called propaganda having to do with the Negro struggle, but my fiction was always trying to do something else, something different even from Wright's fiction. I never accepted the ideology which *New Masses* attempted to impose on writers."[89]

Though Ellison's sensibility is far from the neo-Marxist sensibilities contained in Black Arts–influenced writing, Neal's recognition of an incipient form of nationalism, which Ellison would have most certainly disavowed, radically alters the ways Ellison's insistence on Black American folklore, ritual, blues culture, and synthesis was read. This was particularly true by the mid-1970s when the tone of literary and political partisanship had shifted focus. Some of the writers who had been least supportive of Ellison were asserting their literary presence in the shadow of ideas that Ellison himself had presented in *Invisible Man* and *Shadow and Act*. Ellison's ideas, which had seemed isolated and almost irrelevant a decade earlier, were now reclaimed, sometimes fragmentarily, as places where younger writers located their own origin narratives.

Ellison's ideas have significant consequences when read beyond the confines of the cultural moment. While Larry Neal's reassessment of Ellison's work connected Ellison more directly to the New Breed writers eager to assert their own influence and cultural relevance, perhaps the true point of connection is Ellison's contribution to the American intellectual tradition. Radicalism for Ellison, influenced by his association with the Left, had far more to do with deepening the ideas that Alain Locke proposed in *The New Negro* than with Black nationalist social and political ideology. Ellison remarked during the Alain Locke symposium held at Harvard University on December 1, 1973, that Locke was a "guide" who "stood for a conscious approach to *American* culture [*emphasis in original*]."[90] It was through Locke's ideas of cultural pluralism that Ellison sought to develop his own. Ellison was most certainly no intellectual disciple of Locke, and he said as much as he neared the conclusion of his remarks. But he most certainly recognized that Locke was very consciously grappling with the idea of what it meant to be Black and American in a country unable to come to terms with the true meaning of its cultural pluralism.

Though Ellison saw in Locke's thinking a pathway for articulating his own, he had, even in the 1930s, differentiated his thinking by refusing to accept the New Negro movement's fascination with African primitivism. In the mid-1970s, he disparaged without qualification a similar impulse to link Black people in America to an African influence that he thought at best to have been filtered to the United States via Europe. Ellison further saw Africa's influence as having touched all Western culture rather than exclusively touching the cultural trajectory of Black American citizens. This is at the heart of what separates Ellison from a vision of society defined by political ideology and a society defined by the expansion of its cultural influence.

For Ellison, arguments that make the case for any direct lines of cause and effect rooted in political ideology are unconvincing. Applying a similar metric to cultural influence was an exercise in futility. Cultural influence was non-linear and indirect and circulated in ways that politics could not approach. While political ideology was often too rigid to survive in inhospitable circumstances, the hallmark of cultural influence was its ability to be consumed and to reemerge in ways that are as unexpected as they are influential. Ellison, much to the derision of Black people across the spectrum of radical thought, had long argued in favor of cultural and racial integration. Ellison's impulse was to privilege human initiative over the external requirements of politics. It most likely has its roots in the assumption that political constructions inevitably become hierarchal structures that unevenly distribute the costs of creating and maintaining its system.[91] Ellison had created a counternarrative in which art contextualizes politics, rather than an ideology in which politics provides the textual space for the creation of art. The success of the democratic ideal functioned on imagination rather than political intention. Ellison's democratic ideal envisioned the multiracial possibilities to which the nation's founding documents ostensibly aspired, even as fulfillment of that multiracial possibility remained enigmatic and evasive. "When I write, I am trying to make sense out of chaos. To think that a writer must think about his Negroness is to fall into a trap."[92] At the heart of that counternarrative, writing itself became the political act, particularly as that act of imagination remained fundamentally distinct from ideology.

4

IN THE SHADOW OF DEMOCRACY

Perhaps the most insidious and least understood form of segregation is that of the word.

RALPH ELLISON, "Twentieth-Century Fiction and the Black Mask of Humanity"

SOME QUESTIONS AND SOME ANSWERS

We must learn to wear our names within all the noise and confusion of the environment in which we find ourselves, make them the center of our associations with the world, with man and with nature.

RALPH ELLISON, "Hidden Name and Complex Fate"

In *Invisible Man,* Ralph Ellison presents a confrontation with democratic individualism that is decidedly Black. The novel addresses the fundamental cultural question embedded in the national ethos of the United States: How could Black people in America achieve the possibility contained in the promise of democracy in a nation that hovered between an open hostility to Black people and a basic inability to see the fullness of Black American culture and its contributions to the nation? Ellison's complicated assessment of his namesake, Ralph Waldo Emerson, is central to the ways the relationship and influence of race in the formation of national culture is presented and understood in the novel.

Even with his outsized emphasis on democracy, this is not to say that Ellison saw the nation's performance of democracy as being a representative model of what democracy could, or should, be. This is particularly true when it came to the Black presence in America. Ellison's critique calls into question the possibility of a functional democracy for Black people in America. Democracy has, from its inception at the founding of the nation, misrepresented the influence of, and its responsibility to, Black America. Ellison's critique redistributes Emerson's ideas about individualism across a much broader conception of American identity. Perhaps Ellison's most dramatic revision is to transform the homogeneity of Emerson's conception into an application that embraces an acceptance of the nation's plurality. Emerson certainly would not have accepted that formulation. White critics rejected Ellison's revision, particularly as it related to the ways culturally Black experiences contributed to his thinking. And Black nationalists like Amiri Baraka and Larry Neal likewise rejected the terms of his revision. But the ongoing significance of Ellison's revision should be examined in context.

In his essay "Hidden Name and Complex Fate," Ellison admits to the discomfort he felt from being named after Emerson and the pressure it brought to understand his namesake while simultaneously exerting his own place in the world. Ellison addressed the tension inscribed in his relationship to his namesake by quoting his good friend Albert Murray: "A small brown bow-legged Negro with the name 'Franklin D. Roosevelt Jones' might sound like a clown to someone who looks at him from the outside,"... "but on the other hand he just might turn out to be a fireside operator. He might just lie back in all of that coming juxtaposition of names and manipulate you deaf, dumb and blind—and you not even suspecting it, because you're thrown out of stance by his name! There you are, so dazzled by the F.D.R. image—which you *know* you can't see—and so delighted with your own superior position that you don't realize that it is *Jones* who must be confronted [*emphasis in original*]."[1]

By consciously inserting Emerson's thoughts on democracy into the novel, Ellison offers a redefined vision of democratic American liberalism that critiques it even as Ellison embraces it and claims an enlarged version of it as his own. Black people are not simply contributors to American literature; Black people are at the very core of America and its literature. As Lucas Morel reminds in "In a Strange Country," "to be included, and not merely assimilated, presumed an agency and initiative, thereby according a greater respect for the capacity of 'the included' to observe, weigh, sift, and determine for themselves what it means to live in America—which is to say, what it means to live as Americans."[2] What makes Ellison's presentation of race so compelling is that it confronts and redefines the nation's conception of racial justice. Democratic individuality is impossible without casting aside normative whiteness in favor of historically contextualized, color-conscious interventions.

Ralph Waldo Emerson. Lithograph by L. Grozelier, 1859. Library of Congress, Prints and Photographs Division, LC-DIG-pga-01425.

Though Ellison's relationship to his namesake remained an important component of the ways he conceived himself as a writer and public intellectual, Ellison's actual relationship to Emerson's ideas—and the implications of those ideas for Black Americans—is considerably more difficult to specify. *Invisible Man* is the text in which Ellison most fully examines Emerson's ideas, but Ellison regularly returns to considerations of the democratic significance of what it means to be a writer. In a consideration of what is Ellison's true Emersonian project, Jack Turner observes in "Awakening to Race" that "Ellison gives us a picture of democratic individuality in black, and in his essays, displays a democratic individualist sensibility that confronts rather than evades race."[3] In confronting race, as Turner asserts, Ellison considers Emerson in ways that challenge the context of social and historical structures in which race is lived and understood. Emerson believed that democracy endows everyone with the ability to shape their own lives through self-reliant thinking. This is at the center of Emerson's thoughts about the individual and the individual's relationship to the public sphere. Individuals could then extend the power of that self-reliance through meaningful participation in the realm of the governing process and public life. Everyone has the potential to be a representative figure.

The public sphere is essential to the democratic process. The very act of living in a democracy means that individuals must have some meaningful relationship to the public realm as either author or audience. Emerson's interest in the relationship between individuals and the world in which they lived remained central to his thinking from his earliest addresses in the 1830s through *Society and Solitude,* which he published in 1870. Scholars who see Emerson as truly individualist argue that moral equality between individuals is the most important component of his thinking and that the role of democracy is to ensure and maintain that equality.[4] In "Thinking for Thousands," Hans von Rautenfeld observes of Emerson's thoughts on the author's role in a democratic society that, "Just as representatives mediate participation in the branches of government, so too does public discourse center around representative individuals who stake out positions and provide focal points for public debate and deliberation." But there are moments when Emerson's thoughts on the relationship between the individual and democracy can be difficult to untangle. In his 1841 essay "Self-Reliance," Emerson seems to suggest that individuals and the social communities in which they live can descend into opposition when he notes that "The objection to conforming to usages that have become dead to you is that it scatters your force. It loses your time and blurs the impression of your character.... For nonconformity the world whips you with its displeasure." So, as Judith Shklar questions in "Emerson and the Inhibitions of Democracy," "What, then, is self-reliance to achieve?"[5] Seen from this perspective, the individual is inherently apolitical. But the individual still embodies the world of which they are a part. In "Uses of Great Men" in *Representative Men,* Emerson goes so far as to say that "Other men are lenses through which we read our own minds."[6] These ideas are not entirely contradictory. Representative figures simply consider a broad range of ideas that are reflected in the collective identity of the communities for which they speak. The ideas these representative figures present are nothing more than the arrangement of ideas that comprise the identity of the community itself.[7]

The relationship of an individual to the community is the central aspect of a democratic society: "He [the individual] cleaves to one person, and avoids another, according to their likeness or unlikeness, to himself, truly seeking himself in his associate, and moreover in his trade, and habits, and gestures, and meats, and drinks; and comes at last to be faithfully represented by every view you take of his circumstances."[8] The connection between Emerson and individualism has become a widely considered framework for understanding his work. Emerson's idealized, utopian appropriation of individualism, based on his critique of Enlightenment thought, marks a uniquely American model.

In his 1835 assessment of New World egalitarianism published in *Democracy in America,* Alexis de Tocqueville saw dangers inherent in the concept of individuality. In "Political Consequences of the Social State of the Anglo-Americans," he argues, "But in the human heart a depraved taste for equality is also found that leads the weak to want to bring the strong down to their level and that reduces men to preferring equality in servitude to inequality in liberty."[9] A truly democratic state had to balance individual impulses with the needs of civil society. For Tocqueville, ordinary citizens who failed to yield to their more talented counterparts in society did nothing but cause mediocrity: "'Individualism' is a word recently coined to express a new idea. Our fathers only knew about egoism."[10]

In "Of Individualism in Democratic Countries," during a critique of democracy that eerily foreshadows the narrator's experiences in *Invisible Man*, Tocqueville goes so far as to say that, unlike aristocracy, which creates an unbroken connection reaching from peasant to king,

> [D]emocracy breaks the chain and sets each link apart. As conditions become equal, a greater number of individuals will be found who, no longer rich enough or powerful enough to exercise a great influence over the fate of their fellows, have nonetheless acquired or preserved enough enlightenment and wealth to be able to be sufficient for themselves. The latter owe nothing to anyone, they expect nothing so to speak from anyone; they are always accustomed to consider themselves in isolation, and they readily imagine that their entire destiny is in their hands. Thus, not only does democracy make each man forget his ancestors, but it hides his descendants from him and separates him from his contemporaries; it constantly leads him back toward himself alone and threatens finally to enclose him entirely within the solitude of his own heart.[11]

This brief, often-quoted passage, contained in more than seven hundred pages of critique about democracy, is perhaps Tocqueville's most penetrating and extended discussion linking individualism with self-isolation.

As Tocqueville noted, "individualism" was a relatively new idea when he published the first volume of *Democracy in America* in 1835 and the second in 1840. For all of the attention Emerson gives to the individual in his 1841 essay "Self-Reliance," the word "individualism" does not appear in the essay, and he does not actually use the term until the lecture "New England Reformers" that he delivered to "The Society" in Armory Hall on March 3, 1844, and that appears in *Essays: Second Series*. At the time, the idea of "individualism" was at the center of an ongoing debate in Europe and the United States about how societies should best be organized. Though there were profound differences of opinion about the distinctions between "individuality" and "individualism," the point here is that Emerson confronts "individualism" and unites it with core principles of the nation itself: "The union is only perfect, when all the uniters are isolated.... Each man, if he attempts to join himself to others, is on all sides cramped and diminished of his proportion; and the stricter the union, the smaller and the more pitiful he is.... The union must be ideal in actual individualism."[12]

For Emerson, the Over-Soul, the Universal Mind, the Life Force, God, the Universal Soul, the One, or simply Unity lies within everyone and is the origin of all natural law. According to this line of thought, individuals, who are fragmented and limited by the very circumstance of being human, all deserve equal respect because each contains a portion of the Universal. This kind of radical egalitarianism was ridiculed by some as a kind of idealistically abstract "transcendental selfishness" because of the ways it subordinates all things in the universe to the individual soul. But these ideas had the potential to speak very directly to the issues of slavery and abolition that divided the nation in the first half of the nineteenth century. Though espousing a system of unity, Emerson fundamentally found it impossible to see race as anything other than an essential, unambiguous quality that ultimately places the white race above all others. Emersonian Transcendentalism has been criticized for containing the seeds of atheism in its insistence on worshiping the self over worshiping God. Its theories of the self also contained profoundly regressive beliefs about race.[13]

This seems to be an issue to which Emerson returned in both his private ruminations and his public pronouncements. Publicly, Emerson took an abolitionist stance and was a staunch adversary of the removal of native people from their ancestral homelands. But his public opinions often obscure deeply held private reservations, usually reserved for expression in the pages of his journal, about race, gender, and democratic possibility. In much the same way that the framers of the nation's constitution failed to reconcile the contradictions between democratic possibility and the limits imposed by systemic, institutionalized bias, Emerson found himself in a position in which he minimized his deepest concerns about the ability of all who are non-white to understand and embody the kind of self-reliance in which he believed. Emerson's private writing shows him wrestling with race and true equality:

I believe that nobody now regards the maxim "that all men are born equal," as anything more than a convenient hypothesis or an extravagant declamation. For the reverse is true—that all men are born unequal in personal powers and in those essential circumstances, of time, parentage, country, fortune. The least knowledge of the natural history of man adds another important particular to these; namely, what class of men he belongs to—European, Moor, Tartar, African? Because Nature has plainly assigned different degrees of intellect to these different races, and the barriers between are insurmountable. This inequality is an indication of the design of Providence that some should lead, and some should serve....[14]

Emerson was most certainly a man of his times, and his writing, particularly the private record of his thought contained in his journals, suggests a man grappling with his own ideas about race, forward-looking as they might be, in a larger cultural context that was simultaneously struggling to make practical sense of egalitarianism and individualism.

In the context of the ideological conversation about individualism that went on between Ralph Ellison and thinkers like Emerson, Henry David Thoreau, Walt Whitman, and perhaps even Abraham Lincoln, it is important to recognize the differences between the individualism defined by an emphasis on personal and political rights and the individualism defined by the democratic cultural environment in which those personal and political rights are recognized and nurtured. Though Emerson and those who shared his views focused largely on the former, Ellison uses his conception of personal individualism to speak to the abstractions that define and complicate the social contract. Unlike Emerson's, however, there is no reasonable conception of individualism—personal or democratic—that can be proposed without including a consideration of the racial anxieties encoded in American culture and the historical conceptions of race that have touched all facets of American experience.[15]

Neither the invisible narrator nor, most likely, Ralph Ellison himself would have found himself to be considered by Emerson as being part of the audience to whom Emerson spoke. For Emerson, disparities in society were not necessarily antithetical to the concept of society. As a matter of fact, the very definition of society includes for Emerson inequality and its implications. It is, for Emerson, "the design of Providence that some should lead and some should serve." Racial differences, for example, are intrinsic to social hierarchy rather than externally imposed upon it. Put differently, because of intellect and moral attainments, Emerson saw the Saxon race, as he referred to white people, as being the dominant race. It is the destiny of all other races to serve the Saxons.[16]

The crucial element of the heavily conflicted ideas that Emerson puts forth in his public and private writings about the relationship of individuals in society is that he neither sees nor acknowledges Black people as individual, unique subjects. But Emerson's inability to conceptualize independent Black subjectivity should not lead to the conclusion, as Cornell West has argued in *The American Evasion of Philosophy,* that race is anything but a central component of Emerson's thinking.[17] Emerson's thinking, particularly as it related to race, was as fractured as the nation upon which he tried to affix his idealized conception of a distinctly American ethos. During Emerson's lifetime, the nation wrestled with the consequences of Jacksonian democracy, its conception of itself in the decades preceding the Civil War, and its conception of how to rebuild itself in the decades following Reconstruction. Ralph Ellison particularly engages with Emerson in the area of *Invisible Man* that focuses on the narrator's experiences in college and in New York before his association with the Brotherhood. That engagement is nothing less than a repudiation of Emersonian universalism rather than an assertion of its potential. Like so many of the characters depicted in *Invisible Man,* Emerson's expansive vision of idealized radical democracy is profoundly diminished by radical shortsightedness.

To say that Ellison was not at all representative of the audience to whom Emerson wrote and spoke understates the important subtext of audience that is so central to *Invisible Man.* Alan Nadel argues in *Invisible Criticism* that "Ellison's final position on Emerson is thus filled with ambivalence. Without fully rejecting him, Ellison suggests, through his allusions, great problems with either the pragmatic approach to Emerson or the idealistic."[18] While Emerson seems limited in the ways in which he conceives his potential audience, Ellison is profoundly aware that Emerson's universalized vision means different things to different audiences. That is at the very heart of Ellison's repudiation of Emerson's ideas.

Ellison's appropriation of Emerson's ideas ultimately gave Ellison the usable past that he needs to contextualize his own vision of the world. In "Twentieth-Century Fiction and the Mask of Humanity," Ellison argues that "This conception of the Negro as a symbol of Man [Twain's depiction of Jim in *The Adventure of Huckleberry Finn*]—the reversal of what he represents in most contemporary thought—was organic to nineteenth-century literature. It occurs not only in Twain but in Emerson, Thoreau, Whitman and Melville (whose symbol of evil, incidentally, was white), all of whom were men publicly involved in various forms of deeply personal rebellion."[19]

The racial obstructions encoded in the writing that emerged from the American Renaissance are the targets of the critique contained in *Invisible Man*. The ambitions contained in nineteenth-century American literature are the goals, initially at least, to which the narrator aspires until his complete disillusionment following his encounter with Mr. Emerson Jr. The narrator is an intellectual, though his intellectualism is shallow, ambiguously unstable, and largely underdeveloped. When he first meets Mr. Norton, he responds to Mr. Norton's query about his knowledge of Ralph Waldo Emerson by saying "We haven't come to him yet."[20] One of the consequences of his careless appropriation of the ideas around him is that the ideals to which he aspires so passionately are thoughtlessly idealistic relative to the world in which he lives. The narrator's aspirations are undeniably admirable. He intends to work hard and ascend to a position of Black leadership in a society without adequate Black leadership. But just as the blindness of others renders him invisible, his own social blindness renders the thoughtlessness of his abstractly idealized aspirations invisible to him. He cannot recognize the absurdity of his aspiration for Black subjectivity in a cultural context that has failed, from the roots of its renaissance, to acknowledge and reconcile Black subjects. Ellison's critique is that success in a world based on doubleness—not simply a reworking of W. E. B. Du Bois's double consciousness but an actual realization of egocentric, self-advantaging duplicity—requires the ability to recognize duplicity and to recognize the kind of duplicity that actively undermines one's own personal interests.

Emerson's assertion from *Nature* that "Standing on the bare ground,— my head bathed by the blithe air, and uplifted into infinite space,—all mean egotism vanishes. I become a transparent eye-ball; I am nothing; I see all" anticipates Ellison's central images of disembodied blindness and invisibility. Once the eye can release itself from the constraints of its body, it becomes transparent and merges with all that it sees. In this state of disembodiment, the thinking self achieves unity between human spirit and the natural world beyond. But Ellison's ironic use of this elaborate metaphor serves as a critique of the simplistic, idealized distortions of Emerson's ideas and the fundamental inability of American culture to be able to make practical use of Transcendentalist thought.

Ellison's critique rests on invisibility and blindness and, more generally, on the fact that vision itself is not necessarily very good at distinguishing reality from illusion. As the invisible narrator learns, vision is limited. In a very modernist sense, the power of vision is very much a function of its perspective. The social, temporal, spatial, and political boundaries the narrator experiences are, at best, inconsistent. The process he uses to recognize his own individuality is as much a process of socialization as anything else, even in the framework of his own voluntary withdrawal underground from society.

One of the limitations of Transcendentalism is its reluctance to acknowledge and reconcile the existence of evil. Emerson's most direct thoughts on the issue even go so far as arguing against the very existence of evil. He saw individuals as possessing a level of individual agency that ignores the realities of human existence. In a worldview broadly satirized by Nathaniel Hawthorne in "The Celestial Railroad" and by Herman Melville in *The Confidence Man*, evil was simply the absence of good. Melville and Twain, as Ellison understood their work, realized that goodness is only a veneer covering something decidedly less optimistic and often rather unsavory. Later in his life, the celebration of naive idealism transformed into a far less optimistic fatalism that recognizes the influence of nature on determining and limiting the boundaries of individual agency. In Ellison's understanding of American society, it was race and the manifestation of racial inequality that was covered over, ignored, and made invisible. Slavery became symbolic of darkness obscured by the facade of Emersonian optimism and democratic individualism. The Black people represented in works like Melville's *Benito Cereno*, Twain's *The Adventures of Huckleberry Finn*, and throughout Faulkner's work became representative of the nation's moral burden. Ellison calls the illusion of democratic individuality into question by presenting Black Americans as being caught in an ambiguous sociopolitical predicament that must be simultaneously lived in even as they try to change it.

In "The World and the Jug," Ellison argues, "I think that the writer's obligation in a struggle as broad and abiding as the one we are engaged in, which involves not merely Negroes but all Americans, is best carried out through his role as a writer."[21] But although Ellison vehemently insisted at numerous times during his writing life that he saw his primary role to be an artist and not a political leader, it is impossible to read his work—fiction or nonfiction—completely outside of a political framework. This is precisely the point that Jerry Gafio Watts makes in *Heroism and the Black Intellectual* in his argument that Ellison's way of thinking renders everything in the world overly specialized and, in doing so, unnecessarily relegates politics to politicians and art to artists in ways that firmly separated the function of one from the function of the other.[22] But race and identity remained central to Ralph Ellison's writing and public presence. His art ultimately ends up being a tool that functions politically on behalf of his conception of the implications of racial segregation. It has its origins in Emerson's falsely universalizing conception of self-reliance and "American democratic individualism."[23]

Emerson was a man of his times, and his ideas about race are undeniably regressive. His unwillingness to recognize Black people as independent subjects is particularly difficult to reconcile in the broader recognition of his thoughts on egalitarianism and human possibility. Emerson's thoughts on race are broadly represented throughout his writing. In an 1822 journal entry, Emerson describes the "large lipped, lowbrowed black men who, except in the mere matter of languages, did not exceed the sagacity of the elephant." An 1848 journal entry argues that "It is better to hold the negro race an inch under water than an inch over." In the 1850s, he argues that Black people have a "weakness" and "too much guano in the race" and exist "on a lower plane" than white people and are ultimately destined for extinction and "for museums like the Dodo." His antislavery pronouncements largely focused on the ways the system limited and contaminated white possibilities.[24] While his racism cannot be dismissed, neither can his position as potent cultural critic of America. In *The American Evasion of Philosophy,* Cornel West notes Emerson's cultural influence by saying that Emerson "is a cultural critic who devised and deployed a vast array of rhetorical strategies in order to exert intellectual and moral leadership over a significant segment of the educated classes of his day. The rhetorical strategies, principally aimed at explaining America to itself, weave novel notions of power, provocation, and personality into a potent and emerging American ideology of voluntaristic invulnerability and utopian possibility."[25] In the act of explaining America to itself, Emerson's ideas reveal that race is far more than a tangential component. Race is central to how the nation understood itself. And as such, race is nothing less than an irrefutable fact of the American experiment. That centrality is the area of thought that Ralph Ellison appropriated and transformed.

Henry Louis Gates referred to this process as "signifyin(g)." Ellison generally tends to be more inclined to liken the process to the improvisatory theme-and-variation of jazz. When Ellison "change[s] the joke and slip[s] the yoke," what he is really doing is emphasizing the shortcomings of Emerson's ideas about race to foreground the presence and influence of Blacks in America. Ellison clearly recognized that he was not part of the intended audience for Emerson, Henry David Thoreau, Nathaniel Hawthorne, Herman Melville, Walt Whitman, or any of the canonical writers generally associated with nineteenth-century American Renaissance writing. But he also understood the immense role that Black people played in the psychological world of white Americans and how they saw themselves. The view of Black people presented in nineteenth-century American writing was more than simple racial clichés that these writers inserted into society as a way of maintaining and controlling political and economic power: "Color prejudice springs not from the stereotype alone, but from an internal psychological state; not from misinformation alone, but from an inner need to believe."[26]

In a lecture he gave at West Point, subsequently published as "On Initiation Rites and Power," Ellison recognized that race firmly separated Black Americans from American literature: "I felt that I would have to make some sort of closer identification with the tradition of American literature, if only by way of finding out why I was *not* there—or better, by way of finding how I could use that very powerful literary tradition by way of making literature of my own, and by way of using literature as a means of clarifying the peculiar and particular experience out of which I came [*emphasis in original*]."[27] Ellison also recognized that the nation's greatest power could not be separated from the rhetorical power of the language used to describe the nation itself. If language could be used to define the nation, language could also be used to define and critique the Black presence at the nation's heart.

Emerson's thought particularly gave Ralph Ellison the opportunity to think beyond the conception of America as being composed of a nation of individuals and allowed him to think of the individual as America itself. For Ellison, Emerson's inability to get beyond his racial biases is the very heart of Emerson's thoughts on democracy and his vision of America. And this is where Ellison's intellectual relationship to his namesake becomes uncomfortable. Ellison's recognition of Emerson's intellectual evasion is one of the primary points of *Invisible Man*. Emerson is a nonlinear thinker whose consistency lies in his inconsistency.

Ellison does not explicitly name the racism that defines the vision of Emerson's democratic ideal. Instead, Ellison places it as the element that defines the "usable past" that he wants to draw from the "intellectual evasion" of American Renaissance writers in general and of Emerson in particular. Ellison regarded the Black presence in America as a subject abjectly taboo in the years that led to the Civil War. The dispossession of Black Americans in the wake of Reconstruction (just as the couple is dispossessed during the Harlem eviction scene in *Invisible Man*)—and the collapse of the ideals in whose name the Civil War was fought in the first place—were reflected in the cultural and legal segregation of Black people from truly meaningful humanistic democratic values. This pushed Black people underground in the American consciousness: "Instead of the single democratic ethic for every man, there now existed two: one, the idealized ethic of the Constitution and the Declaration of Independence, reserved for white men, and the other, the pragmatic ethic designed for Negroes and other minorities, which took the form of discrimination."[28]

READING EMERSON, WRITING DIFFERENCE

Original power is usually accompanied with assimilating power.
  RALPH WALDO EMERSON, "Quotation and Originality"

Ellison foregrounds the insidious presence of white supremacy at a time when the nation so persistently built a mythology that functioned on a democratic vision of itself as a melting pot offering equal possibilities to all. There was both a diagnostic process and a revisionary process at work. As reflected in Ellison's antipathy to sociological theory that equated Black life and cultural production solely with oppression, the nation could not fully eliminate the Black presence from its character. The Black presence was not superfluous. It was essential, particularly in its centrality to the nation's moral center.

Emerson's presence exerts itself several times in *Invisible Man,* particularly before Ellison turns his attention to a critique of leftist ideology in the Brotherhood section of the novel. Beginning in the prologue, the narrator very self-consciously invokes Emerson in the examination of his past as the origin story for his subsequent (and elusive) quest for identity. The narrator, in his theft of power and his obsession with light, becomes reflective of Emerson's conception of the poet. But Ellison's presentation of his namesake is rarely positive. Emerson's ideas are subsequently reflected in the novel by characters like Mr. Norton, a white benefactor of the college who is described as a "smoker of cigars [and] teller of polite Negro stories." Mr. Norton is, at best, representative of racists who hide their true attitudes behind a patina of philanthropy and meaningless words. At worst, Nr. Norton's attitudes are nothing less than dangerously self-inflating.

Mr. Norton's arrival in the novel, with his vague references to self-reliance and fate, is the beginning of the narrator's descent underground. Mr. Norton tells the narrator that "as you develop you must remember that I am dependent upon you to learn my fate. Through you and your fellow [Black] students, I become, let us say, three hundred teachers, seven hundred trained mechanics, eight hundred skilled farmers, and so on. That way I can observe in terms of living personalities to what extent my money, my time and my hopes have been fruitfully invested." As Mr. Norton says that, the narrator wonders how any of this could apply to him: "But you don't even know my name, I thought, wondering what it was all about."[29]

Similarly, Dr. A. Hebert Bledsoe, the Black president of the college charged with carrying out the vision of the Founder, is known for his empty recitations of the Founder's "Cast Down Your Bucket" speech emphasizing Emersonian values of self-reliance, service, and humility above all else. Dr. Bledsoe has no true power, and the college has no true educational value beyond the illusion it presents as a place in which its students can uplift their social position through diligent hard work.

The true corruption of the college is that it is a representation of race that is fundamentally unwilling to change the representational limitations of race. For white benefactors of the college, Dr. Bledsoe's work overseeing the vision of the Founder is a fairly viable illusion of racialized progress and social propriety. Instead, the narrator belatedly realizes that Dr. Bledsoe is only interested in protecting his own self-interest: "I didn't make it [the system], and I know that I can't change it. But I've made my place in it and I'll have every Negro in the country hanging on tree limbs by morning if it means staying where I am."[30] Dr. Bledsoe undermines the narrator's dream to be a leader of his people and instead oversees the narrator's expulsion on the grounds that the narrator has overstepped his role as a Black man.

Dr. Bledsoe realizes that he can profit—and is implicitly encouraged to do so—from white trustees eager to donate money to southern schools to appease the guilt of their own exploitation. These schools work to entrench

Lifting the Veil of Ignorance. Statue by Charles Keck, located at Tuskegee University in Tuskegee, Alabama. The standing figure is Booker T. Washington. George F. Landegger Collection of Alabama Photographs in Carol M. Highsmith's America Project in the Carol M. Highsmith Archive, Library of Congress, Prints and Photographs Division, LC-DIG-highsm-05949.

segregation, which in turn enriches people like Dr. Bledsoe. Dr. Bledsoe is not the president of the college because he is invisible. He is the president of the college because he is hyper-visibly Black in a world defined by race. He thrives in the benevolent collegiate environment that uses education as a strategy for the kind of racial progress espoused by Booker T. Washington because of his awareness of that hyper-visibility.

The narrator is instructed by Dr. Bledsoe to deliver a series of unopened introductory letters of recommendation to influential men in New York. Rather than serving as letters of recommendation, the letters push the narrator's vision of being a Black leader further away from him. The last person to whom he is instructed to deliver a letter is named Emerson. But the narrator never actually meets Mr. Emerson. Instead, he meets Mr. Emerson Jr., the self-indulgent son of a college trustee in New York who is described as "a trustee of consciousness." Mr. Emerson Jr. apparently empathizes with the narrator (perhaps because of their shared alienation), shows the narrator the contents of the letter, and begins the narrator on a course that leads him to a union-busting job at the Liberty Paint Factory.

The narrator, who asserts in the prologue that he is part of a long line of American thinker-tinkers, similarly tinkers with Emerson's ideas. Those revisions make those ideas relevant for Black people living in a country unable to see the racialized social realities of historical context. The nation's failure is a failure of vision. Ellison recognizes in his praise of Emerson, Thoreau, Whitman, Melville, and perhaps even Twain that they are unable to confront the pompous, overblown rhetoric of Emersonian human potential. Because of that, they fail to recognize that the realities of that idealism are far from ideal, particularly for Black people living in America.

Ellison knowingly distorts what Mr. Norton espouses to the narrator about Emerson as a way of revealing the limitations contained in Emerson's beliefs. The American Romantic "was in revolt against the old moral authority, and if he suffered a sense of guilt, his passion for personal freedom was such that he was willing to accept evil (a tragic attitude), even to identifying himself with the 'noble slave'—who symbolized the darker, unknown potential side of his personality, that underground side, turgid with possibility, which might, if given a chance, toss a fistful of mud into the sky and create a 'shining star.'"[31] The narrator leaves behind one version of Emerson when he leaves behind Mr. Norton's muddled, self-important portrait of Emersonian transcendence. He replaces him with the kind of pragmatism contained in Mr. Emerson Jr.'s insistence that the narrator read the final letter of recommendation that Dr. Bledsoe has given him and recognize that the college and its trustees are not truly interested in his education. They are only concerned with maintaining their own social positions. They do that by recognizing the threat of people like the narrator and conspiring to "hope him to death and keep him running."[32]

Ellison's first, and most direct, critique of Emerson is introduced by Mr. Norton to the narrator and the novel's reader. Ellison's critique, which first occurs during the narrator's college years, is a repudiation of the conventional narrative commonly associated with the American experience. The narrator is not yet disillusioned by the racist vision that others map onto him throughout the novel. Any sense of consciousness that he has acquired is artificially bolstered by his lack of awareness that true self-reliance is largely unattainable for him. The truth contained in the present that ultimately gives the present the context for its meaning is ultimately buried in a long-forgotten past. Ellison sprinkles references to Emerson and his ideas of self-reliance and democratic individualism throughout the novel. It becomes increasingly unclear what values those references mean for a narrator in the segregated period between the failure of Reconstruction and World War II.

The narrator's identity and, by extension, the identity of Black people like him, is inordinately distorted by the perceptions of white Americans. There can be no tangible aspiration to freedom in a nation unable to confront the racist legacies that define the American character. This is a facet of modernity that affects all Americans. But it disproportionally affects Black Americans. Ellison invokes Emerson's ideas about self-reliance and representative men to produce difference rather than unseeing repetition. His effort is to demonstrate that Emerson's ideas are fundamentally incompatible with the lived experiences of Black people in the United States.

In *Invisible Man,* Mr. Norton is proudly and self-consciously "forty years a bearer of the white man's burden, and for sixty a symbol of the Great Traditions." He is also "a New Englander, like Emerson."[33] Like the historical figure of Ralph Waldo Emerson, with whom Nr. Norton aligns himself and his philanthropic activities, Mr. Norton professes a sense of destiny linking him with the lives of Black people whom he does not know and who are ultimately invisible to him as anything more than representatives of a cause. This facade conceals and disguises the hierarchy and paternalism of racism: "You must learn about him [Ralph Waldo Emerson], for he was important to your people. He had a hand in your destiny. Yes, perhaps that is what I mean. I had a feeling that your people were somehow connected with my destiny. That what happened to you was connected with what would happen to me. . . ."[34]

Mr. Norton is presented as a trustee of the college. He is also the trustee of Emersonian ideology that was built on racialized authority and that ultimately deprives Black people of the opportunity for upward mobility and cultural advancement. The college to which he contributes reinforces racial barriers rather than eliminating them. The college is not interested in helping students realize the vision of self-reliance and democratic individualism. The school's deepest investment is in teaching Black people their place in society rather than how to rise above those limitations. Mr. Norton, who has earlier urged the narrator to read Emerson, is a man representing all the other "Representative Men" who are deceived by their own ideological fantasies. From this perspective, Black people are the cultural trustees of the true possibilities of liberal democracy.

Mr. Norton is little more than a man representative of all the Emersonian "Representative Men" who espouse but fundamentally misunderstand the true essence of self-reliance. Mr. Norton espouses an Emersonian focus on self-reliance. But understanding Mr. Norton in that way is a misreading of Emerson's essay "Self-Reliance" relative to the kind of demeaning philanthropy that Mr. Norton undertakes in his mission at the narrator's Black college. It is also a misreading of Ellison's critique of Emerson. If anything, Ellison parodies the idealized construction of this part of nineteenth-century history and the literature it produced. Mr. Norton's vision of fate and its consequences is naive and short-sighted. Alan Nadel, writing in *Invisible Criticism,* sees Norton as a parody of Emerson's thoughts about democratic idealism. James Albrecht, in "Saying Yes and Saying No," goes so far as arguing for a view that sees the novel as calling into question the ways how readers should even understand Mr. Norton's presence in the novel at all. For Albrecht, Mr. Norton illustrates the kind individual that "Self-Reliance" denounces.[35]

Mr. Norton cannot come to terms with the fundamental nature of self-reliance, particularly as that idea relates to Black people. The narrator can never truly reconcile the implications of his race, particularly as race is understood and lived in a segregated society. But Ellison's deeper point is that racial category is ultimately meaningless. Race, particularly as it is presented in the early portions of the novel, is prevented from extending beyond culturally recognized racial categories. Since power is unevenly distributed, those on the margins or those individuals or communities who remain systematically disenfranchised from the ability to define their own identity suffer. Invisibility is reflected in the ambiguities of race. Those ambiguities are for Ellison a function of the perceptions of those, like Mr. Norton or Dr. Bledsoe, who are most deeply invested in maintaining the illusion of social boundaries imposed by racial distinction.

This is the area in which Ellison's revisioning of Emersonian democracy rewrites racial metaphor to recognize a broader sense of hybrid cultural possibility. This rethinking of how Black subjectivity can and should be culturally understood raises the question of whether the idea of whiteness can ever be understood beyond its cultural position of superiority. This has both individual and cultural consequences. Without an awareness of the hybridity of race in America, identity becomes elusive. The history of race, buried as deep it is in the nation's past yet simultaneously existing on its surface, becomes an uncomfortable reminder of the positive and negative complexities of cultural hybridity.

This is the only way that America can truly fulfill its democratic ideal. The nation must recognize, acknowledge, and reconcile its racial past and, by doing so, understand that a truly pluralistic, hybrid nation is composed of individuals. There is a great deal that separates Ellison from Emerson, particularly as that separation relates to race and Ellison's understanding that neither he nor the aspirations of Black people are truly represented in Emerson's thought. If Ellison suffers from an anxiety of Emersonian influence, that anxiety is perhaps most clearly demonstrated in Ellison's attempts to reconcile the consequences of the democratic and individualist ideals he shares with Emerson.

Ellison's recognition is that Emerson's inability fully to reconcile his outlook on race and American identity ultimately undermines his broader democratic aspirations. In "A Very Stern Discipline," drawn from an interview Ellison gave in 1965 and subsequently revised for publication in *Harper's Magazine* in 1967, he argues that identifying with a particular writer does not necessarily interfere with the rejection of that same writer's fundamental assumptions: "When it comes to those writers who have shaped American literature—the framers of the Declaration, the Constitution and Lincoln excepted—we tend to project racial categories into the areas of artistic technique, form and insight, areas where race has no proper place. We seem to forget that one can identify with what a writer has written, with its form, manner and techniques, while rejecting the writer's beliefs, prejudices, philosophy and values."[36] This is precisely what Ellison has done with Emerson, and he does it by enlarging Emerson's core beliefs even as he chips away at their most negative implications.

There is both a diagnostic process and a revisionary impulse at work. Both Emerson's ideology and the perversion of that ideology that is presented in the character of Mr. Norton fail to support the presence of actual Black people rather than the two-dimensional view of Blacks that Emerson employs to support his idealized vision of spiritual transcendence. The philanthropic reduction of Black people that uses education at a college for Negroes obscures true opportunities for upward mobility and instead teaches Black people their true place in society. Mr. Norton employs this tactic to mask his incestuous desire for his deceased daughter and, by extension, his impulse to maintain the purity of the bloodline. That is why the seamless transitions between the narrator's introduction to Mr. Norton, the episode involving Jim Trueblood's story of his incestuous relationship with his own daughter that has made him an outcast in the Black community, and the culminating episode at the Golden Day are so relevant to Ellison's diagnosis of the weaknesses inherent in American thought and to his attempt to resituate his thoughts about the limitations of Emersonian thought in the broader context of Black experience in America.

Although Mr. Norton invokes Emerson to the narrator, Mr. Norton does not embody Emerson's ideology in any meaningful way. Mr. Norton is undeniably racist. His relationship to the narrator in general and the college itself is paternalistic and built on an agenda that is not revealed until he encounters Jim Trueblood and the chaos of the Golden Day. Jim Trueblood, the sharecropper, is shunned by the college as much for his actions as for what he represents to the process of Black cultural aspiration in America. He is "primitive" in all respects. But he is also a performer who is as much an exploiter of the sympathies and anxieties of his white audience as he is exploited by their paternalistic attitudes toward him. Black people in the community want nothing to do with him. Although they have been unable to get him to resettle in another county, they have marginalized him as completely as possible.

Like the college itself, Jim Trueblood is supported by a paternalistic white community that provides him with social status and work. Trueblood's is a story about impregnating his wife Kate and his daughter Matty Lou, perhaps the most aggressively sustained sexual episode in all of Ralph Ellison's writings. Though illiterate, Jim Trueblood reveals to Mr. Norton the possibility of living the very experience that Mr. Norton has, until then, imagined. It is unclear whether Mr. Norton acted on his incestuous impulses. Perhaps he reacts with such distress to Jim Trueblood's story because Trueblood has "looked upon" the chaos of his desire and, not only has he not been punished for those desires, he has also profited from its pubic revelation.

If thinking is the quality that makes, for Emerson, someone a poet, then it is a mistake to identify Jim Trueblood as a kind of Emersonian poet for Ellison to critique. Jim Trueblood's story to Mr. Norton about how he came to impregnate both his wife and his daughter, as well as the dream sequence of going to the home of Mr. Broadnax for some "fat meat" is little more than impulse rather than thought. Jim Trueblood is not fully able to understand the meaning of his experiences. He is only able to perform that experience for the entertainment of people like Mr. Norton.

In the context of Ellison's examination of Emersonian thought, Jim Trueblood is fundamentally unable, by virtue of race and social standing, to universalize his experience. Mr. Norton is clearly drawn to the similarity of their shared desires, but there is no indication that Jim Trueblood is anything more than an emblem of Mr. Norton's repressed desire. In telling his story, Jim Trueblood cannot find a way to be reborn into a new universalizing identity even as he tells and retells a story that becomes as much communal as it is personal. In a profoundly disturbing way, Jim Trueblood's experiences describe a man who has become remarkably self-reliant without ever being able to render that self-reliance in a way that reflects either the consequences of being Black and poor or the unseen, invisible historical realities of what it means to be Black and American.

The historical consequences of Jim Trueblood's status as a poor sharecropper reduce him to a place of social helplessness. Jim Trueblood has not and cannot access some broadly defined Emersonian Oversoul because he cannot unify personal experience with political relevance. Jim Trueblood's experience is meant to be undeniably American, as seen in the fact that it resonates as completely with a representative of northern philanthropy like

Mr. Norton as it does with the southern white community in the area that supports and sustains Jim Trueblood. Even the representation of Jim Trueblood's experiences are saturated in the blues idiom. Trueblood is a reprehensible character whose appearance in the novel forces his readers (the reading audience for the novel, as well as Mr. Norton, the Black and white communities in the area, and the invisible narrator himself) to reassess the ways mainstream American culture represents the full range of the chaotic, complex realities of American experience.

Jim Trueblood exemplifies Ellison's belief that his notion of invisibility is actually grounded in "the racial conditioning which often makes the white American interpret cultural, physical, or psychological differences as signs of racial inferiority; and on the other hand, it springs from a great formlessness of Negro life wherein all values are in flux, and where those institutions and patterns of life which mold the white American's personality are missing or not so immediate in their effect."[37] But Trueblood is a minstrel figure, a parody, and a stereotype who has somehow avoided the fate of white retribution that so many Black people encounter by using his story to manipulate white people like Mr. Norton. Jim Trueblood parodies those people who fundamentally misread Emerson. In a letter to Alan Nadel, Ralph Ellison is careful to clarify that his critique of Emerson should not be read more broadly as being a critique of Emerson himself. Ralph-the-Exhorter, as Ellison referred to Emerson in the letter, was an important part of his worldview. Ellison clarifies by saying that his was an attack on the "bombast" that others had subsequently made of Emerson's ideas. Ellison also acknowledged that Emerson's meaning was often as difficult to determine with any certainty as the meaning contained in the dying words of the invisible narrator's grandfather.

The episode at the Golden Day that follows Mr. Norton's experience with Jim Trueblood is perhaps the logical consequence of an absurd situation. The narrator takes Mr. Norton, who is near the point of collapse after hearing Trueblood tell the unrepressed story of desire that Mr. Norton represses, to a saloon and bordello frequented by disfranchised Black soldiers. The saloon bears the name of the period that Lewis Mumford conceived as being the height of American Romantic accomplishment exemplified by Emerson, Thoreau, and Hawthorne. The Golden Day that Mumford's study envisioned was the period in American history that had moved beyond the cultural expansion of the American pioneer and before the country had begun its transformation away from agriculturalism and toward the industrialism that steadily continued during the second half of the nineteenth century.

Ellison is happy to praise writers like Emerson, Thoreau, and Hawthorne, as he does in his essay "Twentieth-Century Fiction and the Black Mask of Humanity," for their encounters with the repressed humanity of race. Ellison is far less willing to accept Lewis Mumford's simplified account of literary history. He saw in it a failure to distinguish between Emerson's ideas and what Ellison sees as Mr. Norton's reductive misapplication of Emerson's ideas. The Golden Day at which the narrator arrives at the request of Mr. Norton reflects Lewis Mumford's Golden Day in the sense that both blur the realities of their existence. In *The Golden Day* (1926), his cultural and literary study of the American Renaissance, Lewis Mumford argued that the thirty-year period preceding the start of the Civil War was perhaps the only period in the nation's history in which individuals had the brief opportunity to rediscover the American past and envision the possibilities contained in its future. He saw that sense of possibility as being supplanted by the Civil War and, subsequently, by industrialism and the Gilded Age's industrialized greed.

Mumford argues that "An imaginative New World came to birth during this period, a new hemisphere in the geography of the mind. That world was the climax of American experience. What preceded led up to it: what followed, dwindled away from it; and we who think and write to-day are either continuing the first exploration, or we are disheartened, and relapse into some stale formula, or console ourselves with empty gestures of frivolity."[38] Ellison admired Mumford. He had certainly considered his work very carefully. But Mumford's implication was that slavery was of no particular significance in his understanding of the Civil War and its cultural implications. The Civil War was a shared historical experience that was the site of the nation's deepest tragedy. Ellison argues, in the letter he wrote to Alan Nadel dated January 27, 1984, that Mumford had eviscerated its meaning. He had transformed the tragedy into farce by denying Black people "the sacrificial role that they had played in the drama."[39]

Alan Nadel in *Invisible Criticism* and James Albrecht in "Saying Yes and Saying No" each persuasively argue that, for Mumford, the Golden Day—and the literature it produced—is inexorably linked to all that preceded and all that followed in the nation's history.[40] But the Golden Day also represents an illusion. Pre–Civil War America was preferable for Mumford despite the stain of slavery that eventually polarized the nation and led to the Civil War. Ellison's revised Golden Day reflects the unacknowledged tragedy at the heart of the nation's whitewashed aspirations. The students from the narrator's college are prohibited from going there. Those men who frequent the Golden Day are disfranchised professionals largely alienated by the American mainstream: "Many of the men had been doctors, lawyers, teachers, Civil Service workers; there were several cooks, a preacher, a politician and an artist. One very nutty one had been a psychiatrist."[41] While these men are destroyed because of their participation in the nation's aspirations, Mr. Norton can return home largely untouched by the moral issues that Ellison links to democracy, race, and slavery in his re-creation of the Golden Day. To enter the Golden Day—both through Mumford's conceit of it as a kind of golden era in American culture and Ellison's conceit of it as an asylum caused by the traumatic illness of American culture—is to enter a prohibited space that segregates Black people in America from fully participating in the democratic and individualist ideals that Ellison shares with Emerson.

BLACK CODES FROM THE DEMOCRACY

[White Americans] take what they need [from Black people] and then git. Then they start doing all right for themselves and pride tells them to deny they ever knew us.

THE REVEREND ALONZO HICKMAN in the excerpt "And Hickman Arrives" (1960), *Three Days before the Shooting . . .*

Ellison's pluralistic view of race and American culture emerged from his thoughts about democracy. He began to map the indeterminacy of race as a living metaphor for the indeterminacy of the nation itself. But what is the importance of Ellison's thoughts on the matter? His formulation of a sustained critique of white privilege and whiteness itself is the embodiment of American identity that is a prescient anticipation of contemporary thoughts about the ways race is conceived and deployed across American culture. The profound singularity of Ellison's position among others who contemplated the relationship between race and nation is his belief that the elimination of race from American culture by white supremacists and Black nationalists alike ultimately both scapegoat Black Americans. This achieves a dubious cultural catharsis that ignores the fact that American democracy is inescapably characterized by the presence of race. The complex question that Ellison's work continually envisions is: What are the ongoing implications for the formation of national culture?

For a writer whose work, fiction and nonfiction, is so bound up with ideas shaped by the consequences of race on American culture, it is only natural that Ralph Ellison is so often read and considered for the ways he conceptualizes race. Ellison has been seen as the quintessential "race man," intent on foregrounding Black humanity and its centrality as the nation's moral center. Leon Forrest, a novelist praised by Ellison, noted in 1994 that

> Ralph goes back to a fundamental tradition in African-American life. He's what we used to call a race man. Areas that seem conservative, supporting businesses in the community, respecting the workingman, the family—that's part of it. A race man means you're in a barbershop conversation, and there might be a nationalist, an N.A.A.C.P. man, whatever, but they're all concerned with getting African-Americans ahead in the community. I know Ralph had a lot of respect for many of the things Adam Clayton Powell stood for at first, the way Powell broke the back of Tammany Hall, though not the shrill things he said at the end of his life. Ralph is for a robust onslaught against racism but, at the same time, a building within the race. What's happened is that there hasn't been enough building with the race: our families, our businesses, the inner strength of the people. What disappoints him today is that not enough black Americans are learning from the possibilities of the book. We don't read enough. His own literature is informed by a vast library, and yet we are cutting ourselves off from that. You've got a problem in Afro-American society these days: if a woman has a niece and a nephew, she'll give the niece a copy of a Toni Morrison book and take the nephew to the Bulls game. We don't do nearly enough to enrich our kids in the middle class in our body of literature—the body that fashioned Ralph Ellison's imagination and scholarship.[42]

He has also been seen as little more than someone who has been disloyal to the race and who has pandered to white expectations of the Black subject. In *So Black and Blue,* Kenneth Warren refers to Ellison as "a transracial messiah heralding the return of humanism and reason to redeem an American society threatened by racial medievalism."[43] It is certainly true that Ellison sees race, both before and during Jim Crow and following desegregation, as a hybrid construction that looks forward to the ways Blackness as identity has come to be treated in the work of Black writers like Colson Whitehead and Paul Beatty, whose work began to appear at the end of the twentieth century and during the early decades of the twenty-first century. Ellison's pluralistic, integrationist, multicultural outlook on race functions around his cultural view of race that replaces the separate cultures that comprise the nation with a more expansive vision of American culture dependent on cultural exchange. American culture, and race itself, are, for Ellison, engaged in a constant process of identification, appropriation, and transformation. American hybridity is a fact, not an aspiration.

On an occasion in celebration of his eightieth birthday, Ellison noted that "It behooves us to keep a close eye on this process of Americanness. My grandparents were slaves. See how short a time it's been? I grew up reading Twain and then, after all those Aunt Jemima roles, those Stepin Fetchit roles, roles with their own subtleties, here comes this voice from Mississippi, William Faulkner. It just goes to show that you can't be Southern without being black, and you can't be a black Southerner without being white. Think of L.B.J. Think of Hugo Black. There are a lot of subtleties based on race that we *will* ourselves not to perceive, but at our peril. The truth is that the quality of Americanness, that thing the kids invariably give voice to, will always come out [*emphasis in original*]."[44] Ellison's conception of race, even forty years after he had begun writing his second novel, remained unwaveringly resistant to prescriptive ideas of race and culture. Race, as important as it is to Ellison and his work, is for him a metaphor for something even larger, if that's possible. Ellison often writes of what he referred to as chaos and complexity. In the context of race and culture, the chaos that he described is the confrontation of possibility and ambiguity.

Like Ralph Waldo Emerson, Ellison uses the idea of America as precisely that: A concept that is broadly inscribed with possibility and ambiguity, chaos and uncertainty. Ellison's hybrid vision of a multicultural nation is surprisingly uncategorized and egalitarian in the democratic sense of the word. Race as a lived experience is real for Ellison. But race also serves as a metaphor for indeterminacy. The boundaries of race are, by their very definition, imprecise. By extension, America itself is similarly unsettled relative to preconceived notions of what America is and what it can be. For Ellison, the ever-shifting concept of America was inseparable from the indeterminacy of race. This is a primary theme explored in both of his novels. Racial categorization should not be conflated with the individual cultures that comprise the nation.

Black people had certainly been politically marginalized since long before the formation of the nation itself. But culturally, Black people are essential to the conception and moral responsibilities and aspirations of the democratic republic. Ellison makes the tension between these two ideas most evident in an essay entitled "What America Would be Like Without Blacks" that appeared in *Time* on April 6, 1970. In it, he addresses a mainstream audience with what may be his clearest dismantling of the "concept of race." He situates his remarks in the broader conceit of ridding the nation of Black people. In doing so, he emphasizes his belief that fixed cultural categories that are defined by Black and white are unsophisticated and naive at best and downright dangerous to the difficult work of realizing the nation's aspiration of democratic equality. Although Ellison seems to be conceptualizing his audience as white, he is writing from a position of considered discretion that understands the pressures exerted by both white people and Black people on the indeterminate "concept of race." The battle that Ellison is fighting is to get his reader to recognize that race is stitched—often visibly, sometimes not—into the very fabric of the American experiment while simultaneously presenting a vision of the American experiment that is culturally egalitarian precisely because of the presence of race.

The binary view that reduces race to white and nonwhite also reduces people who are Black to a racially imposed status that ignores the broader cultural realities of the nation. Whatever modifiers people chose when they characterize themselves as American—Native, European, African, Asian—do little more than emphasize Ellison's point about the hybrid nature of being American. Mainstream American culture often relegated Black people to the status of other, outsider, or scapegoat and relied on phenotypic difference as a way of providing a marker delineating insider from outsider.

By examining assumptions about Blackness, Ellison is interrogating the assumption that whiteness equates with being American. But the insistence on whiteness as a qualification for being American has as much to do with racism as it does with a larger question about a more fundamental set of values: "Despite his racial difference and social status, something indisputably American about Negroes not only raised doubts about the white man's value system but aroused the troubling suspicion that whatever else the true American is, he is also somehow black."[45] As white Americans reached for something fixed and unchanging as the foundation of their American status, the hybrid sensibility that Ellison argued for was nothing less than an assault on the systemic privileges casually associated with whiteness. Whiteness can only be held up as the embodiment of the central American identity if Blackness is understood to be its opposite. All of this speaks to Ellison's criticism of white anxieties over its own privilege.

Ralph Ellison was certainly no proponent of post-racialism since that term is a response to some undefinable concept of "authentic" racial expression. Far from it. If America is seen, beginning with the nation's founders, as an entity in which many become one, Ellison's view is that the only way truly to see the nation is through a lens that acknowledges the influence of cultural pluralism. In Ellison's assessment, "most American whites are culturally part Negro American without even realizing it."[46]

This is precisely the place in which Ellison's critique of whiteness and the privileges of whiteness begin to overlap with the broader possibilities of the democratic process. The objective of the democratic process is cultural inclusivity rather than racial assimilation. This is an important distinction to make. Ellison has been criticized as being simultaneously trapped in a sentimental recollection of an Oklahoma childhood that no longer exists and an idealized conception of a future. That idealized vision looks beyond the realities of the troubled racialized present in which he was writing by focusing instead on an idealized future that acknowledges the need to recognize and include cultural difference. Ellison certainly recognizes that individuals of all races need to work to find ways to *be* individual. This is a prescient way of describing contemporary attitudes about race. There can certainly be no singular, culturally agreed-upon way to express some "authentic" experience of race and ethnicity. Ellison's is not a recommendation to reject race entirely in favor of a color-blind nation. His recommendation is that the nation leave behind conceptions of race that ultimately render it narrowly expressed and naively finite.

The options available for the expression of racial and ethnic identity are limitless. But the democratic principle upon which the founders of the nation based the American experiment was the possibility of disparate individuals being able to put their individualism aside in favor an aspiration to form a more perfect union: "[T]he true subject of democracy is not simply material well-being, but the extension of the democratic process in the direction of perfecting itself."[47] Though his thinking gestures toward contemporary attitudes about race and ethnicity, his thoughts substantially revise those assumptions.

> During the nineteenth century an attempt was made to impose a loose conceptual order upon the chaos of American society by viewing it as a melting pot. Today that metaphor is noisily rejected, vehemently disavowed. In fact, it has come under attack in the name of the newly fashionable code word "ethnicity," reminding us that in this country code words are linguistic agencies for the designation of sacrificial victims, and are circulated to sanction the abandonment of policies and the degrading of ideas. So today, before the glaring inequities, unfulfilled promises and rich possibilities of democracy, we hear heady evocations of European, African and Asian backgrounds accompanied by chants proclaiming the inviolability of ancestral blood. Today blood magic and blood thinking, never really dormant in American society, are rampant among us, often leading to brutal racial assaults in areas where these seldom occurred before. And while this goes on, the challenge of arriving at an adequate definition of American cultural identity goes unanswered.[48]

The basis of Ellison's critique is perhaps the sense of ownership contained in so many of the claims made on behalf of culture. The very definition of plurality makes membership in any group, racial or ethnic, subjectively arbitrary, at best.

Plurality exists between groups, between individuals, and within individuals, particularly as the inward formation of identity separates itself from the cultural elements grounding that identity. There is an infinite number of ways to perform identity, particularly as that identity is thought of as specific cultural components. While individuals cannot choose the cultural elements that contribute to their sense of their performance, they can make conscious and unconscious decisions about their relation to cultural tradition. As Ellison makes the point in "What America Would Be Like Without Blacks," "Since the beginning of the nation, white Americans have suffered from a deep inner uncertainty as to who they really are."[49] Perhaps the basis of this uncertainly has to do with the easy relationship white Americans have long had with a cultural entity outside of the United States. Democracy does not eliminate that relationship. Instead, democracy serves as a conduit through which the fragmentation of individual experience could be made whole by incorporating it into the broader project of American pluralism.

What complicates the deployment of democracy is, for Ellison, nothing less than historical denial. Blackness does not need to be assimilated into the nation's cultural fabric because it is already there. It was there from the very beginning. Ellison recognized that when he noted Thomas Jefferson's 1777 proposal for gradual emancipation of enslaved Black people and their return to Africa when Jefferson served in the Virginia legislature. Subsequent fantasies of eliminating America's race problem led to various back-to-Africa movements aimed at ridding the country of Blackness and, more specifically, of Black resistance to slavery. Eliminating race from the fabric of American culture was nothing more than a fantasy that Ellison saw appealing to white racists and Black nationalists alike: "Both fantasies [colonization and secession] become operative whenever the nation grows weary of the struggle toward the ideal of American democratic equality. Both would use the black man as a scapegoat to achieve a national catharsis, and both would, by way of curing the patient, destroy him."[50]

Ellison understood the nation as being a series of identities that were simultaneously individual and codependent. At best, democracies demand social equality for all members. At the very least, they require recognition of difference (social, cultural, historical, economic, and so forth). The social movements that shaped Ellison's thinking about race and nation were criticized for what some saw as being overly invested in a version of identity politics that did little more than segment the nation into a mosaic of individual groups. All advocated for recognition and acknowledgment in the face of their cultural invisibility. What makes Ellison's thinking so important in this context is his recognition that much of what came to be labeled identity politics is little more than an extension of what had been part of the nation—and hidden in plain sight—since its founding.

The hard truth is that this part of the nation's past had most often been rendered as either a movement toward assimilation or exceptionalism. People could either seek to be recognized as a nation of equals or as a nation of equals composed of individuals who are recognized for their difference. Early in Ellison's life, the Left gave him an ideological stance predicated on the importance of the working class. The movement for civil rights, particularly its early years, fought for an end to legal apartheid in the nation. The Nation of Islam and the Black Left argued for a separate Black consciousness that saw itself outside of the assumptions of the white mainstream. More specifically, Black consciousness became something that was not simply the byproduct of being Black but unambiguously a product of being Black in a society hostile to Black presence and agency in the nation. All of this presupposes that there is an intrinsic gulf between the ways living in America has been understood by Black and white people. Contemporary experiences of race are little more than an extension of a long national history of racial experiences.

Because he lived until the very dawn of the internet age, Ellison's recognition of lived experiences was largely relegated to geographic region: The South, the former Oklahoma territories, and Harlem among them. Ellison was concerned with the presence and experiences of individuals living in group boundaries. But he was also profoundly aware that modern culture was simply too complex to minimize the pluralism of which it is composed. By its very nature, the nation is diverse and pluralistic. The idea toward which Ellison reached, and for which he received criticism from Black and white people to the right and to the left, is that the various cultural spheres that comprise the United States experience life differently. Because of the nation's complex relationship with race, all of those lived experiences, particularly those experiences that had been made culturally invisible, should be recognized with a similar level of acknowledgment.

In "What America Would Be Like Without Blacks," Ellison seems to be addressing a latent attitude of resentment held by some in his white reading audience who believe that Black people have somehow historically failed to live up to the values of work and cultural contribution they associate with the responsibility of being American. The resentment he addresses reflects broader cultural anxiety about privilege and cultural advantage. The vision of liberal democracy that Ellison envisioned reflected meaningfully robust individual autonomy even as American democracy systemically diminished the freedom and self-determination of some of its citizens. In this respect, Ellison's thinking anticipated the ideas about multiculturalism that arose at the end of the twentieth century and the social movements in the twenty-first century that have addressed various forms of social justice.

Perhaps the basis of some of the criticism that Ellison experienced had to do with the ways group identity disintegrated beyond racial and geographic boundaries. These rubrics have been replaced with an awareness, as Kimberlé Crenshaw pointed out in "Mapping the Margins," that defining group experience without acknowledging intersectional influences is ultimately confining and perhaps self-defeating. This is entirely consistent with Francis Fukuyama's thoughts in *Identity* about the roles that individual and group identities play in the formation of national identity and the threats to democracy posed by cultural fragmentation.[51] The basis of this critique ultimately points toward the question of whether racial solidarity alone is robust enough to serve as the foundation for meaningfully sustainable responses to social and cultural injustice. Ellison was well acquainted with the argument that class-based solidarity should be favored over race-based solidarity. This idea was certainly nothing new for him. He encountered these same arguments earlier in his writing career when his thinking was more closely aligned with Marxist ideology.

But Ellison's primary belief, reflected throughout his work, is that American democracy is inexorably connected to a meaningful engagement with race. Ellison's preoccupation with American democratic individuality functions on the presence of Black and white experience precisely because Black experience is essential to the nation's moral center. Perhaps what Ellison's thinking illustrates most effectively is an explication of the ways the legacies of slavery and the failures of Reconstruction as well as Jim Crow contribute to a vision of transracial democracy. That vision explains the ways white privilege distorts the basic, fundamental tenets of American character.

His thoughts about democracy reveal an attempt to illuminate the complexity of cultural hybridity to redefine the cultural significances of racial identity. That illumination relies on perspective. One of the things that comes with racial privilege is the privilege of avoiding uncomfortable historical realities by relying on viewpoints that minimize or even erase entirely the experiences of those who cannot participate in that cultural privilege. Even in the founding years of the American republic, white privilege and supremacy coexisted uncomfortably with Black enslavement while the new nation ostensibly sought to form a more perfect union dependent on natural equality.

This was the fundamental, tragic drama of American democracy that all of Ellison's work after *Invisible Man* addresses: "[Race] made for a split in America's moral identity that would infuse all of its acts and institutions with a quality of hypocrisy. Worse, it would fog the American's perception of himself, distort his national image, and blind him to the true nature of his cultural complexity." As Jack Turner emphasizes in "Awakening to Race," "Ellison detects in the white supremacist deep ambivalence about freedom" even as he attempts to encourage his white readers to confront the realities of race in America.[52] While Ellison's rejection of anything suggesting racial essentialism was complete and uncompromising, his conception of American cultural pluralism was far more complex than that.

The individual, diverse characteristics of American culture are perhaps easier to recognize than the hybrid characteristics of democratic unity. Put differently, Ellison's vision of the democratic whole is greater than the sum of its individual elements. As he noted in 1978, "This difference, that new and problematic quality—call it our 'Americanness'—creates out of its incongruity an uneasiness within us, because it is a constant reminder that American democracy is not only a political collectivity of individuals, but culturally a collectivity of styles, tastes and traditions."[53]

5

NEGRO-AMERICANIZING THE NOVEL

Finally: It was stated at the outset, that this system would not be here, and at once, perfected. You cannot but plainly see that I have kept my word. But I now leave my cetological System standing thus unfinished, even as the great Cathedral of Cologne was left, with the crane still standing upon the top of the uncompleted tower. For small erections may be finished by their first architects; grand ones, true ones, ever leave the copestone to posterity. God keep me from ever completing anything. This whole book is but a draught—nay, but the draught of a draught. Oh, Time, Strength, Cash, and Patience!

HERMAN MELVILLE, *Moby-Dick; or, The Whale*

ELLISON'S COPESTONE TO POSTERITY

The problem with *Juneteenth* is that it does not show the scope or the ambition of what Ralph was doing. The man was trying to write something as big as Moby--Dick!

ALBERT MURRAY, "Ralph Ellison Remembered"

The tension between Ellison's attraction to the possibilities contained in the closed-end focus of the essay form and the expansive possibilities of space contained in the novel form is nowhere more apparent than in his composition of *Three Days before the Shooting....* There were risks involved in Ellison's reliance on an episodic writing style, particularly when it came to resolution and closure. Adam Bradly's account of Ellison's composition of the second novel in *Ralph Ellison in Progress* certainly chronicles Ellison's production of episode and revision in both novels.[1] Ellison's attempt to write an epic novel of Americana was, by its very design, an unfinishable process. There could be no closure because American culture was, and continues to be, an unfinishable process of statement and revision.

Ellison provided ongoing commentary about how to read *Invisible Man* in the decades following its publication, even as he said that his role as a novelist was to present rather than to interpret. If readers can, even temporarily, give up the impulse to confine *Three Days before the Shooting…* to a particular form, it becomes clear that *Invisible Man* has the beginning, middle, and end that the second novel lacks. But the second novel contains the scenes, many of which Ellison published as standalone stories in anticipation of the complete novel, that resonate as powerfully as the most memorable scenes from *Invisible Man*. The second novel contains the gravitas of race and democracy in the formation of national culture that Ellison never abandoned, even if he could not entirely contain it and wrestle it to closure. More specifically, Ellison was attempting to integrate Black identity into the nation's identity at a time when Black identity as a collective endeavor had become culturally diminished.

The reasons for Ralph Ellison's prolonged period of composition for his second novel are as perplexing as they are mysterious. But the question of "why not?" is also largely irrelevant. The reasons the novel remained incomplete at the time of Ellison's death are elusive, at best. What is less ambiguous is that Ellison was trying to address the question of what the Black presence in America would mean as the nation quickly changed in all aspects of public and private life. Culture and politics were inseparable in the nation's fabric. His second novel integrated politics, illustrated by the senator, the action that takes place in the nation's capital, and the presence of Lincoln, with the religious and cultural traditions that are so much a part of Black America.

These are unique histories with their own ways of being in the world. And they are components essential to what the nation has been and what it aspires to become. It is virtually impossible not to read *Three Days before the Shooting … outside of the long shadow that *Invisible Man* continues to produce. At the time *Invisible Man* was published, Ellison was understandably apprehensive about its potential reception. In a letter to his friend Albert Murray that was dated June 6, 1951, Ellison mentioned his intention to begin work on a new novel.[2] His thoughts necessarily revolved around his desire to immerse himself in work on his second novel as a way of diverting his attention from responses to the first. This is one of the first references that Ellison made to his thoughts about the novel that he intended to write following the publication of *Invisible Man*. As he suggested to Murray, Ellison slowly began work on the

House in Washington, DC, where Lincoln died. Library of Congress, Prints and Photographs Division, LC-DIG-fsa-8a02991.

novel that consumed the next forty years of his life and remained unfinished at the time of his death in 1994.

John Callahan's "General Introduction to *Three Days before the Shooting...*" offers perhaps the clearest insight into the challenges involved in evaluating Ellison's work in the second novel. As Callahan notes, Ellison did not leave behind a coherent, definitive manuscript. Instead, what Ellison produced is "a series of related narrative fragments, several of which extend to over three hundred manuscript pages in length, that appear to cohere without truly completing one another. In fact, the thousands of handwritten notes, typewritten drafts, mimeographed pages and holographs, dot-matrix and laser printouts, testify to the massive and sustained effort Ellison exerted upon his fiction, but also to his ultimate failure to complete his manuscript so long in progress."[3] This novel, which Ellison began writing during a time when America was legally segregated and "separate but equal," through *Brown v. the Board of Education of Topeka, Kansas,* and the opening years of the civil rights movement, was subsequently influenced by the social events surrounding

America's increasing involvement in the conflict in Southeast Asia, the Black Power movement, and the identity anxieties that characterized America in the 1980s.

The novel's latest revisions suggest a broad transformation away from its earliest themes of race and individuality toward contemporary issues of racial identity, national identity, and the uneasy coexistence between the two. Unlike many writers, Ellison saw his intellectual and writing lives as being inextricably tied to the sweep of the historical moment. The themes that Ellison confronted in his writing after 1970 reflect his awareness of what he called "the complexity of freedom"—that is, the anxieties contained in the post-segregation era—and the ways those complexities influenced his conception of post–civil rights politics. *Invisible Man* largely focused on the alienation and anger that was contained in America in the years preceding *Brown v. the Board of Education of Topeka, Kansas*. Ellison's writing in the second novel suggests his ongoing re-visioning of America in the post–civil rights years and his attempts to address the legacies of Black cultural nationalism and identity politics.

There are far more questions raised about the second novel than there are answers: Why did Ellison have such difficulty bringing his novel to a close? Was it simply that the novel, which he held up as a kind of mirror to American society, could not keep up with actual events at a time when the country was embroiled in foreign war, domestic unrest, and rapid social changes? Perhaps, as John Callahan puts it in his introduction, instead of asking why Ellison invested so many years working on a novel that he was ultimately unable to bring to resolution, the question that should instead be posed (particularly in light of the volume of manuscript material related to the novel that is contained in Ellison's papers at the Library of Congress) is "What is it about this material—either in focus, form, or theme—that kept Ellison writing so much for so long?"[4]

Ellison's first novel took invisibility and its implications as its main subject. *Three Days before the Shooting* . . . does the same. The visibility of race is manifested most obviously in skin color. It is, in Ellison's work, the most apparent place of connection between the racial history of life in America, the ways race is remembered and memorialized, and the implications America's racial history has for its present and future. Part of Ellison's success in crafting *Invisible Man* is that he was able successfully to distill the lived experience of race in America into an ambitious novelistic amalgamation—Ellison would have most likely thought of that mixture as a kind of "integration"—that reflected the highest aspirations of American democracy. But integration brings with it a conscious need to revisit the past.

In his introduction to *Shadow and Act,* Ellison spoke very directly to the influence of memory and the past: "The act of writing requires a constant plunging back into the shadow of the past where time hovers ghostlike. When I began writing in earnest I was forced to relate myself consciously and imaginatively to my mixed background as American, as Negro America, and as a Negro from what in its own belated way was a pioneer background."[5] For Ellison, what members of the American democracy choose to remember is as crucial to his understanding of race as the future to which Americans aspire. "Consciousness and conscience are burdens imposed upon us by the American experiment. They are the American's agony, but when he tries to live up to their stern demands they become his justification."[6] Ellison fully recognized that, for America to move toward a future that is somehow less consumed with race, America must somehow forget the very past that enabled the present and anticipated the future.[7]

Ellison's second novel was a maze that has mystified readers, perhaps in some of the same ways that the project mystified Ellison himself. He wanted to write a novel epic in its examination of implications of race, democracy, religion, and identity in the United States. The novel stretches from Washington, DC, to Georgia and Oklahoma. Temporally, it was set in the 1950s, when Ellison began work on it, but even its temporal scope reaches back to the 1920s and to the years when the Oklahoma Territory was being transformed into statehood. But while his objective was to write a novel epic in dimension, what Ellison left after his death is something far less cohesive. In the thousands of manuscript pages, notes, outlines, and revisions that he produced, there is no sense of unity—conceptual or physical—available to unite his ideas into the cohesive vision that his work stretching from the 1950s into the 1990s seemed to seek.

Although the last of the eight excerpts of the novel in progress that Ellison published during his lifetime in a span of seventeen years between 1960 and 1977 was a section that he entitled "Backwacking: A Plea to the Senator" in 1977, the writing that Ellison left behind suggests the same attention to episodic writing and revision that his work on *Invisible Man* reveals. John

Callahan, Ellison's literary executor, notes, for example, Ellison's inclination for revision in *Invisible Man* when Ellison pruned the penultimate version of the manuscript from 781 pages down to the 612 pages that comprise the final manuscript. In the final revision, he added a prologue and epilogue. His commitment to revision in the work in progress was, even for Ellison, relentless. According to Callahan, as Ellison was completing work on *Invisible Man* in April of 1951, Ellison had begun to think about working on his second novel. In a letter sent to Albert Murray on June 6, 1951, Ellison notes his desire "to get going on my next book before this one [*Invisible Man*] is finished. . . ." He had previously made a reference to his thoughts about the second novel several weeks earlier in a brief letter to Albert Murray from May 14, 1951, which he concluded by saying that "Fanny [Ellison's wife] is well and glad it's finished [the composition and revision of the manuscript for *Invisible Man*], I'm back at 608 Fifth trying to get started on my next novel (I probably have enough stuff left from the other if I can find the form."[8] Callahan notes that Ellison may not have actually begun writing until 1954. His uncertainty about form certainly haunted his work on the second novel.

In *Ralph Ellison in Progress,* Adam Bradley makes a similar comment about Ellison's work in progress. He notes that the process that Ellison used from the mid-1950s, when he first conceived the novel's plot, until the early 1980s remained largely unchanged. Ellison often sketched ideas and notes for the novel that he then expanded, revised (sometimes as many as a dozen times), and eventually assembled into a cohesive manuscript that he would then submit to additional revision. For Bradley, the greatest change in Ellison's writing style occurred when he switched from initially handwriting his ideas to composing on the computer in 1982. More significantly, Ellison seemed to stop the work in books I and II on which he had focused throughout the 1970s in favor of reconsidering older typewritten fragments, some dating back as far as the mid-1950s.[9]

To some extent, it is fitting that Ellison returned near the end of his life to reconsider the episodes he had written at the inception of the project in the mid-1950s. On May 17, 1954, the Supreme Court's unanimous decision in favor of *Brown v. the Board of Education of Topeka, Kansas,* successfully overturned the system of separate-but-equal, at least in the sphere of public education, that had been in place since the court's decision on *Plessy v. Ferguson* in the concluding years of the nineteenth century. The configuration of American society in which Ellison had lived his entire life had been overturned by the court's ruling that segregation violated the Fourteenth Amendment. The enormity of the decision is that it sought to remedy fundamental cultural attitudes of racial injustice. Segregation clearly had nothing to do with distributing benefits equally to Black people and white people. It had everything to do with systematically creating and maintaining a cultural position for Black people living in America to occupy that was fundamentally inferior to the cultural position occupied by white Americans. The court's corrective initiated one of the most aggressively combative periods of American history since the Civil War and Reconstruction.

When the Supreme Court ruled that *de jure* racial segregation was a violation of the Equal Protection Clause of the Fourteenth Amendment of the US Constitution, Ellison, among others, recognized that all aspects of the composition of American public life—its politics, its social interactions, its understanding of national history, its sense of racial identity and the literary representations of race, among others—were about to change in ways unimaginable during the first half of his life. If the assumption is correct that Ellison began the work of writing his second novel in earnest in 1954, the novel represents an important revision of cultural attitudes toward democracy, Black American racial identity and social continuity, and literary representation. Like the nation itself, the second novel, even from its very beginning, embodies a literary representation of an unfinished—and unfinishable—process.

Adam Bradley supplies several important observations about Ellison's process, particularly as it relates to Ellison's intentional isolation from Black nationalist and separatist movements. Bradley comes to see Ellison as being "conscious of racism, but mindful of possibility; cognizant of difference, but alive to interplay of racial categories." Part of the process in which Ellison found himself immersed was an attempt to find a novelistic solution to the intersection of race and culture contained in his unwavering devotion to a pluralistic vision of nation. While Bradley sees the links between *Invisible Man* and the unresolved revisions of the second novel as challenging critiques of the limitations of Ellison's attitudes about politics and culture, it should also be emphasized that a good measure of the sprawling manuscript of the second novel reflects Ellison's sensibilities dating back to the 1950s and even preceding *Invisible Man.*[10]

Bradley's naming of Ellison's "progress" acknowledges the expanse of

Ellison's writing production mapped out over the sprawling archive of drafts, notes, and correspondence. Bradley's evidence reveals a compositional process devoted to finding a literary form capable of considering race and democracy. By reading backward and by using an archeological, document-based approach like Barbara Foley's in *Wrestling with the Left,* though with a strikingly different series of objectives, Bradley illuminates Ellison's complex relationship to the world his fiction worked so hard to describe. In short, for Bradley, all of this, including Ellison's unresolved process of revision, was congruent with his thoughts about the role of the novelist and what the novel, as both a form and a cultural artifact, should achieve, particularly as that relates to ambiguity and plurality.

In "Ralph Ellison's Novel without Qualities," Timothy Parrish recognizes the significance of Ellison's unfinishable literary endeavor by persuasively arguing that "it [the unfinished second novel] cannot end but through the counterreaction from the reader, who carries the book's story into the future."[11] Much like the effect that *Invisible Man* achieved, he sees the indeterminate future as being as important to the novel as its past and present. Its relationship to the nation is undeniable, particularly as its composition reflects a nation emerging from the second reconstruction signaled by *Brown v. the Board of Education of Topeka, Kansas.* Danielle Allen's intervention in *Talking to Strangers* provides an important lens through which to consider Ellison's contribution to political theory. In her reading of *Invisible Man,* Allen recognizes Ellison's awareness that democracy is not entirely democratic by noting the tension described by acting as an individual within the limitations of a greater sovereign will.

What Allen sees in Ellison is his awareness of the ways the nation's institutions reinforce an unequal distribution of resources. This, after all, is the realization the invisible narrator realizes in his trajectory underground. Put differently, Allen's argument is that citizens look to the Constitution for guidance. When, inevitably, that document cannot fully respond to all the questions asked of it, its citizens look to the world in which they live for clues. When the world changes, as it did after *Brown v. the Board of Education of Topeka, Kansas,* so do the answers. Allen saw this in relation to democracy. It is also true in relation to Ellison's work on the second novel.

Ellison experienced financial difficulties in the winter quarter of 1936 at Tuskegee Institute that made the music school too expensive for him

African American demonstrators outside the White House, with signs demanding the right to vote and signs protesting police brutality against civil rights demonstrators in Selma, Alabama. Library of Congress, Prints and Photographs Division, LC-DIG-ds-05267.

to continue to attend. Although unable to pursue his musical aspirations, Ellison found himself increasingly interested in literature. During that quarter, Ellison enrolled in a course on the English novel taught by Morteza Drexel Sprague. Unlike many other Tuskegee instructors, Sprague emphasized interpretation and analysis over rote plot memorization. Sprague also recognized the need to expand the literary canon to include writers like Sinclair Lewis and Theodore Dreiser, as well as the writing that was appearing in current literary magazines. Ellison thought highly enough of Sprague that he dedicated *Shadow and Act* to him. When asked about Sprague in an interview from 1965, Ellison noted that "As a Tuskegee freshman I took his senior course in the nineteenth century English novel. He was an honest teacher, for when I went to him about Eliot and such people, he told me he hadn't given much attention to them and that they weren't taught at Tuskegee. But he told me what to do about it: the places to find discussions and criticism.... Yes, I consider Sprague a friend and dedicated my essays to him because he was an honest teacher."[12]

When the decision that struck down legal segregation was handed down by the US Supreme Court on May 17, 1954, Ellison wrote to his friend and teacher to convey his happiness and reservations:

> Well so now the Court has found in our favor and recognized our human psychological complexity and citizenship and another battle of the Civil War has been won. The rest is up to us and I am very glad. The decision came while I was reading *A Stillness at Appomattox,* and a study of the Negro Freeman and it made a heightening of emotion and a telescoping of perspective, yes and a sense of the problems that lie ahead that left me wet-eyed. I could see the whole road stretched out and it got all mixed up with the book I'm trying to write and it left me twisted with joy and a sense of inadequacy. Why did I have to be a writer during a time when events sneer openly at your efforts, defying consciousness and form? ... For me there is still the problem of making meaning out of the past and I guess I'm lucky I described Bledsoe before he was checked out. Now I'm writing about the evasion of identity which is another characteristically American problem which must be about to change. I hope so, it's giving me enough trouble. Anyway, here's to integration, the only integration that counts: that of the personality.[13]

There is a great deal in Ellison's brief letter to his friend and teacher marking the end of legal segregation that speaks toward the work he had recently published in *Invisible Man,* the project he was about to undertake, and the insecurities that he reveals. By legally recognizing Black American psychological complexity and citizenship, Ellison rightfully saw an important corrective to the failures of the nation's founding documents, the Civil War, and the failures of Reconstruction. The "telescoping of perspective" that Ellison notes by referencing *A Stillness at Appomattox* and the Freeman study that he was reading when the decision was handed down clearly places the court's decision in the kind of broad perspective to which Ellison had alluded in *Invisible Man.*

He recognized this decision as being a victory—a singular victory, but a victory nonetheless—in the unfinished business of the Civil War. The ruling affirmed that Black American presence in all aspects of the nation's activities would no longer be whitewashed into invisibility. In some ways, Ellison recognized that a character like Dr. Bledsoe had the potential to be ruled out of existence by the Supreme Court. But the decision brought with it a more paralyzing crisis of identity and the past, which Ellison had clearly, even at this nascent stage of conceptualizing his new project, anticipated employing as a central theme of the novel. How was Ellison, especially after the success of *Invisible Man,* to address the relationship between identity and the past, particularly since Black American expressions of identity would undoubtedly be culturally reconsidered with the legal end of Jim Crow? For all that it did, with its insistence on separation in all things social and cultural, legal segregation forced Black people living in America to develop modes of being that were in, though not necessarily of, America.

Ellison's letter seems to acknowledge that desegregation came with costs as well as benefits. Jim Crow mattered but not as completely as the "integration of personality" that he commends at the letter's conclusion. Segregation was repressive and exploitative. But because it imposed boundaries on the participation of Black people in the public sphere, it caused Black Americans to establish systems of social support and organization that uniquely addressed the needs of Black people. Integration was a worthy aspiration. It was also a gamble on whether the assumption that cultural compromise in the form of integration would be uniformly beneficial for Black Americans or simply lead to nonending battles in the Civil War that Ellison references in his letter to Morteza Sprague. Ellison's letter indicates his anxieties about desegregation as well as his realization that Black identity itself was now a quality negotiable in ways that it had not been in the first half of the century.

Ellison had been able in *Invisible Man* to create a cohesive novel whose narrative relevance was grounded in the tension between the limitations of segregated life in the United States and the aspirations of the Founders that called those limitations into question. This, perhaps, is "the evasion of identity" to which Ellison's letter alludes. The circumstances "defying consciousness and form" reflect Ellison's prescient understanding that his epic novel in process, even at this early stage of its conceptualization and composition, was forever transformed by changes in the culture and identity that Ellison envisioned giving the novel its meaning.[14] Ellison saw the novel as a literary form capable of reducing the chaos of lived experience into a coherent pattern. In an interview in 1972, Ellison argues that "Literature is a form of art wherein time can be reduced to manageable proportions; and the diversity of experience can be assembled to show an immediate pattern: to conserve memory, focus energies, ideals and to give us some idea of the cost and glories of those ideals.... Literature is a form through which a group recognizes its values—values from without and values from within."[15] Ellison's desire to devise a prism through which the sweep of history could be distilled into a manageable form is precisely what desegregation denied him as a writer committed to examining particular aspects of race and the human condition.

While this seems to be a psychological rationalization of Ellison's inability to bring his second novel to fruition, it is a compositional assessment. The tension that Ellison struggled with was how his novel could best integrate Black identity with American identity at a time when the identities of Black people living in America were being rapidly redefined. Jim Crow's strange career had been characterized by the restrictions it placed on Black Americans. Jim Crow's demise suggested to Ellison that any sense of collective identity had also met its cultural demise. The archetypal characters like Dr. Bledsoe, Jim Trueblood, and even the narrator himself that Ellison had created in *Invisible Man* may eventually no longer exist and would certainly not culturally function in the ways they had before *Brown v. the Board of Education of Topeka, Kansas.* While the cultural legacy of the court's decision was uncertain, at best, its social implications were borne out in the subsequent emergence of the civil rights movement and the legislation the movement advanced.

Black American identity was never homogenous. The viability of diverse social, political, and cultural movements emerged in the decades following *Brown v. the Board of Education of Topeka, Kansas,* when race came to mean something different for people of color, particularly when the court no longer defaulted to envisioning the American mainstream as exclusively white. At the very least, the court's decision allowed for court-mandated acknowledgment of the infiltration of blackness into the nation's public sphere. For a novelist like Ellison, the importance of American history finds its focus through the prism of race. Danielle Allen's work in *Talking to Strangers* is most compelling and persuasive when it discusses Ellison's relationship to *Brown v. the Board of Education of Topeka, Kansas,* through the lens of political theory and the ways the court's decision "reconstituted" the United States between 1954 and 1965. It is certainly not alone in citing the influence of *Brown v. the Board of Education of Topeka, Kansas,* on Ellison's thought. There is a second reading strategy proposed in Kenneth Warren's *So Black and Blue.* Warren reads Ellison's essays as making historically specific commentary as the events contributing to their composition unfolded and writes that "[W]hat has made possible the contradictory appropriation of Ralph Ellison's work is that his writing so effectively rings the changes on black political and social life during the era of formal and explicit American racial segregation, stretching from the end of the nineteenth century until the mid-1960s."[16] Warren bases this assertion on the thesis that, rather than transcending time, *Invisible Man* remains culturally relevant because the issues it raises relative to Jim Crow America continue unabated.[17] Situating the novel, and Ellison's ongoing commentary about the novel, in this way, the question Warren implies is to what extent would the end of Jim Crow bring cultural and political change to Black Americans? Even as younger generations of Black Americans were consciously beginning to abandon all influences associated with American culture, Ellison specifically chose to use his writing as a way of expanding the world for those for whom ideology primarily defined their identity in terms of group membership.

At the conclusion of an article from July 1969 about Ralph Ellison entitled "Indivisible Man" that was published in *Atlantic Monthly* in December 1970, James Alan McPherson says of the novel in progress that

> I have never read the book, but I remember one night, back in the summer of 1969, when he read a section of it to me. The prose was unlike anything I had ever heard before, a combination of Count Basie's sense of time and early American minstrelsy and Negro Baptist preaching. And the narrator was riffing everything, from coffins to the Book of Numbers. I have been thinking about those five or ten minutes for many years now, and what I think is that, in his novel, Ellison was trying to solve the central problem of American literature. He was trying to find forms invested with enough familiarity to reinvent a much broader and much more diverse world for those who take their provisional identities from groups. I think he was trying to *Negro-Americanize* the novel form, at the same time he was attempting to move beyond it [*emphasis in original*].[18]

On the afternoon of November 29, 1967, the country house in Plainfield, Massachusetts, where Ellison had been working during the summer, burned in a fire that consumed the work that Ellison had completed since his arrival. Although the decades after the end of Jim Crow brought with them the instability that Ellison had been concerned about, this period also seems to have focused Ellison's work on the first two books of the novel. In addition to the fire that destroyed a portion of his work, the concluding years of the 1960s brought with it the prominent assassinations of the Reverend Dr. Martin Luther King Jr. and Robert Kennedy. This was coupled with the transition from nonviolent to violent confrontation that focused less on integration and more directly on political encounters characterized by the Black Power movement, the Black Panthers, and other radical responses to the nation's pervasive social conditions. The objectives of the civil rights movement shifted from the South to urban agendas. The war in Southeast Asia was escalating, and college campuses across the nation were responding with confrontations that often turned violent. Lyndon B. Johnson had decided not to run for presidential reelection, and Richard M. Nixon took office in what some cite as a symbolic conclusion of the movement for civil rights. Urban unrest engulfed cities across the country. Even the hostile receptions that Ellison himself received on college campuses across the country from protesters and activists reflected a nation in turmoil. But out of all of this, Ellison seems to have been able to find a kind of unity connecting the episodes that he had composed for the novel's first two sections.

In Adam Bradley's reading of the matter, the issue of cultural change is notably absent in the second novel. As Bradley observes, "At this moment of national foment in politics and in culture, Ellison renders a world surprisingly untroubled by the growing tensions forced on the American consciousness by segregation." Rather than seeing the nation in a moment of "reconstitution," Bradley sees in Ellison's writing "a world surprisingly untroubled by the growing tensions forced on the American consciousness by segregation."[19] This had very much been Ellison's preferred working strategy, as Arnold Rampersad notes in his observation of *Invisible Man* that "Ralph did not seek to align his plot according to the facts of history.... Major events and eras are ignored in *Invisible Man*. The Depression is not identified. Allusions are made to World War I, but not to World War II. These omissions deliberately boost the allegorical element so important to Ralph's aims."[20] Similarly, from the second novel's inception, Ellison had very consciously been trying to see beyond the moment to something more expansively assimilating. It was a political novel that refused to be political in its orientation. Or perhaps, as Bradley clarifies, it was a civil rights novel that functioned around aesthetics rather than politics.[21]

Culturally, emerging from Jim Crow required leaving behind the limitations of an engrained way of life. Some parts of that life needed to be discarded. Other parts needed to be treated as values that made Black American life whole by connecting it to its historical past. Ellison made this point in an interview as early as 1960: "What part of Negro life has been foisted on us by Jim Crow and must be gotten rid of; what part of Negro life, expression, culture do we want to keep? We will need more true self-consciousness. I don't know what values, what new tragic sense must emerge. What happens to the values of folk life, of church life? Up to now it has been a matter of throwing things off. But now we have to get conscious of what we do not want to throw off."[22] To some extent, between the publication of "Night-Talk" in *Quarterly Review of Literature* (1962) and "A Song of Innocence" in *Iowa Review* (1970), Ellison may have arrived at a point where he was as satisfied as he had been with his composition of an epic novel in which the central action was capable of addressing the shared experiences, realities, and emerging possibilities of both Black Americans and the nation. His work emphasized the importance of race, in all the ways that racial identity was being revised and redeployed. Race, for Ellison, continued to be the single greatest metaphor of national aspiration because of the ways it simultaneously defined and challenged collective identity and the limits of American democracy.

THE DARK, MYSTERIOUS YEARNINGS OF THE NATION

And isn't a nation a larger, more intricate form of the family and thus, like most families, thronged with dark, mysterious yearnings?

    WELBORN MCINTYRE, in *Three Days before the Shooting . . .*

In an interview from 1965, Ellison was asked about the progress of his second novel and the reason for its delay, particularly since portions of it had already appeared in print. His response candidly speaks toward the expanse of his project and his uneasiness about the direction of his progress: "Well, it takes me a long time because I have a deep uncertainty about what I am doing. I try to deal with large bodies of experience which I see as quite complex. There is such a tendency to reduce the American experience, especially when it centers around the Negro experience. I'm constantly writing—I write a lot—but I have to put it aside. It has to gel, then I come back. If I still react positively to it, if I can still see possibilities of development, then I keep it."[23] As Ellison's comments here suggest, and they are subsequently borne out in its composition, the second novel functions around an unshakable belief in a complex, chaotic present that embodies the past and anticipates the change contained in the future.

Timothy Parrish argues in his essay "Ralph Ellison's *Three Days*" that the second novel asks readers "to reorient our understanding of what the Ellisonian novel is and what it tries to do."[24] Parrish asks readers to recognize that the second novel is more than a disorienting, unfinished novel. It is the coalescence of Ellison's thoughts about the novelistic form with his well-documented conception of the nation's past as an active, ongoing influence (a boomerang, as he described the process in *Invisible Man*) on the present. As for the form of the novel itself, "other writers gave him a form to tell a story that was not his alone but that of a people into which he was born."[25] This is an expansive claim, but Parrish clearly means to emphasize the role Ellison saw himself occupying rather than emphasizing a critique of the novelistic product that Ellison produced. For a novel describing a world "that is in the process of being made, or remade, in every moment," there can, for Parrish, be no traditional end, particularly since the process of making and remaking is so intimately tied to the reader's sense of that process.[26] Parrish is certainly right to observe that the indeterminacy of the novel's form, structure, and even its central conceit about a novel in which race is central, yet unrelentingly indeterminate. What he says implies the novel's attempts to resist the restriction that so often accompanies categorization.

The novel, begun with the urgencies of mid-twentieth-century America in mind, stretches in its incomplete fullness into the twenty-first century, where it exists among Ellison's papers in the archives of the Library of Congress. Engaging its meaning requires its reader to engage the sprawling mass of notes, drafts, and revisions to discern an authorial intent that eluded the author himself. Without a clear roadmap for even deciding what is contained in the novel, the reader is made complicit in the novel's composition as well as its potential meanings.

The expanse of Ellison's conception of the project is undeniable. *Invisible Man* was the work that established and defined Ellison's intellectual and creative life. *Three Days before the Shooting...* was the work to which he dedicated the greatest portion of his intellectual and creative energies. When Ellison was asked at the conclusion of the interview about the role of the novelist and whether the novelist could have meaningful power to create change or to speak for a particular point of view, Ellison's response illustrates both his thoughts about the role of the novelist and of his novel in progress:

> I think that the good novelist tries to provide his reader with vivid depictions of certain crucial and abiding patterns of human existence. This he attempts to do by reducing the chaos of human experience to artistic form. And when successful he provides the reader with a fresh vision of reality. For then through the symbolic action of his characters and plot he enables the reader to share forms of experience not immediately his own. And thus the reader is able to recognize the meaning and value of the presented experience and the essential unity of human experience as a whole.[27]

The novel is as incomplete, indeterminate, and as imperfect as the American experiment itself. To echo Parrish's point in "Ralph Ellison's *Three Days*," it is the story of a nation with no real beginning and no discernable end. It compresses and expands the broad period in American history circumscribed by the Civil War and the civil rights movement. It is also painfully difficult to summarize and encapsulate in a traditional arc of narrative exposition, development, climax, and conclusion. Broadly speaking, Ellison seemed to conceptualize the novel in three sections that were to be connected by an assassination attempt in the chamber of the US Senate on the life of a racist senator from New England named Adam Sunraider. The reader later learns that the assassin is the biracial son whom the senator had abandoned. A Black minister named Alonzo Hickman tries to save the senator's life. Beyond that, there is really no plot. In its place, there is perspective. The novel's two primary characters are a Black minister named Alonzo Hickman and the boy of uncertain racial background named Bliss that Hickman and his church community have raised. Bliss eventually runs away and is reborn as Senator Adam Sunraider, who is described as having the gift of language that he learned from Hickman in the Black church. The action that animates the story is that the senator's son Severin, whom the senator long ago abandoned, arrives in Washington and shoots the senator.

Book I includes the activities of Reverend Alonzo Hickman and the members of his congregation who want to meet with the senator to warn him of the possibility of an assassination attempt. Ellison's working notes suggest that, in their attempt to warn the senator of the impending danger to his life, they lead his assassin to him. But the novel's tragic mistake belongs to the senator, who refuses to see Hickman and his associates.[28] They are unable to arrange that meeting and instead bear witness to the shooting from their seats in the spectator's gallery of the Senate.

Boys in front of the Lincoln Memorial, Washington, DC. US Farm Security Administration / Office of War Information Collection, Library of Congress, Prints and Photographs Division, LC-DIG-fsa-8d20423.

The present time of the novel takes place "roughly from 1954 to 1956 or 1957" and bookends *Brown v. the Board of Education of Topeka, Kansas*, Emmett Till's lynching, the arrival of the Reverend Dr. Martin Luther King Jr. into a leadership position in the Montgomery Improvement Association and his guidance in organizing the Montgomery bus boycott. The boycott brought national attention to the repressive segregation that was so much a part of the fabric of the South. In an undated working note, Ellison stipulates that, although the action of the novel takes place in this very specific point in American history, its implications are intended to be far-reaching: "Action takes place on the eve of the Rights movement but it forecasts the chaos which would come later. This is a reversal of expectations to consider inasmuch as it reaches beyond the frame of the fiction. This looks forward to the reassertion of the Klan and the terrible, adolescent me-ism of the '70's."[29]

The senator (who is known as Bliss in his childhood) is little more than a con man, initially modeled on the character Rinehart in *Invisible Man*, who takes numerous forms in the novel and for whom the invisible narrator is mistaken. In an undated working note, Ellison comments that "Bliss rejects Christianity as sapping of energies, Hickman sees it as a director of energies. In this he [the Reverend Alonzo Hickman] foreshadows Martin Luther King, while Sunraider repeats the betrayals of the past."[30] It is not clear what the betrayals are to which Ellison refers in this note. But part of the senator's ability to betray is his ability to assume multiple disguises. He is first introduced in the novel as a baby who has been born to a white mother. His mother had been raped. His paternity is unclear. The Black man accused of the rape and subsequently lynched was Alonzo Hickman's brother. Although it is unclear, in a layer of ambiguity reflecting William Faulkner in *Absalom, Absalom!* and *Light in August,* whether Hickman's brother is the father of the child, Hickman, a former jazz trombonist who has joined the ministry, agrees to raise the child, whom he names Bliss.

Hickman envisioned Bliss as a kind of sacred and secular salvation figure. He hopes to lead Bliss into the ministry and then into public service so that *"by embracing that child as the unique symbol of unity to come we hoped that the combined promises of Scripture and this land's Constitution would be at last fulfilled and made manifest [emphasis in original]."*[31] Reverend Hickman does indeed turn Bliss into a child preacher. It is not entirely clear if Bliss is to be understood as a representative of sincere faith or what Ellison referred to as a "circus-sideshow," which is represented in the novel by Bliss being taught to rise from a small coffin on cue during services to recite the line "Lord, why hast Thou forsaken me?" What is clear is that Ellison envisioned this child of mixed race as being "tied up in some way with the significance of being a Negro in America, and at the same time with the problem of our democratic faith as a whole."[32]

Bliss eventually escapes his role and runs away to Oklahoma. He becomes the father of a son somewhere around 1930 when he enters a sexual relationship with a woman of Black, white, and Native American ancestry named Lavatrice. Bliss abandons Lavatrice during her pregnancy. The child, who is named Severen when he is born, has no relationship with his father and eventually tries to assassinate him on the floor of the US Senate when Bliss resurfaces as Senator Adam Sunraider. The racist senator is a prodigal son who has returned to the arms of Reverend Hickman and the race he had long abandoned. This is the backstory that precedes the arrival of Reverend Hickman and several members of his congregation in Washington, DC, where they have gone to warn the senator of the danger to his life.

A portion of book I is told from the perspective of a white newspaperman named Welborn McIntyre who reports on Washington politics and who has been given the assignment of investigating the shooting. But even as McIntyre searches for the betrayal at the heart of the nation's politics that has led to the assassination attempt on the life of the senator, Ellison reveals that McIntyre has himself betrayed the trust of a Black woman whom he has gotten pregnant and subsequently abandoned. As with other parts of the novel, this area toggles between McIntyre's present and past actions. He is a hypocrite who ultimately feels relief at the prospect of not carrying out his paternal responsibilities. His personal shortcomings reflect a more deceptive strand of racism; he is a white liberal who can only see the world in terms of racial difference.

Before being shot, the senator had given a mean-spirited speech about Black people and their cars. In response, LeeWillie Minifrees decides to burn his own car on the senator's lawn. This is an episode of the novel that Ellison published in 1973 as "Cadillac Flambé." When McIntyre gathers with other reporters to discuss the event, the conversation inevitably turns to the political subtext contained in the act and the incorrect assertion that all Black action is ultimately political. Ellison refutes this opinion when it is revealed that the senator's assassin is his son Severin, who shoots his father and subsequently kills himself. After witnessing the senator's shooting on the floor of the Senate, McIntyre conflates political violence with patricide. But only Reverend Alonzo Hickman, who is the adopted father of the senator and the grandfather of the assassin, knows the depth (if not the entire truth) of their racial bloodlines.

As he lies dying, Senator Sunraider requests that Reverend Hickman remain with him. Reverend Hickman offers comfort to the dying senator by recalling their shared past. These reflections comprise book II. McIntyre's white, liberal perspective disappears and is replaced by the interactions between Hickman and the senator. Book II is largely the part of the manuscript that was published as *Juneteenth*. It is a standalone area that encapsulates that depth and meaning of the relationship between Reverend Hickman and the senator. The Black minister is the only person to whom the dying senator can turn to try to reconcile the details of a background that remained invisible even to him throughout his life. While the senator was certainly switched at birth, it is not clear that his biological parents were anything but white. But since he grew up in Reverend Hickman's care and was collectively mothered by the women in the Black church, his true family are the Black people on whom he has turned his back. This is certainly consistent with Ellison's assertion that race is as much cultural as it is biological. The senator is ambiguously raced just as Ellison believes most Americans to be. But in the shadow of segregation, ambiguity was impossible to live. The senator, as reflected in his political stances, resents Black Americans. But he loves Reverend Hickman and perhaps resents Reverend Hickman for the conflict he feels.

Book III is the least cohesively developed. Perhaps Ellison intended to provide additional background to the senator's story but remained undecided about who would be best suited to provide that background. This section is largely composed of episodes that Ellison had difficulty connecting into a coherent narrative form. Even Ellison's literary executor had difficulty discerning the sequence of these episodes and necessarily made editorial decisions about what to include in *Three Days before the Shooting…* and what to leave out.

The difficulties of reducing the chaos of human experience to artistic form that Ellison cites as the difficulty of bringing the novel to completion is ultimately a comment about the novel itself. The United States is composed of multiple narratives, each of which contributes in some way to a broader conception of democracy and what it means to be American. Simply put, the form of the novel reflects a place of cultural and aesthetic integration that defines a national type even as it calls that type into question. If the nation's democracy is one of contradiction, the form of the novel unsettles the artificial sense of cohesion reflected in the national narrative. The nation, particularly in the context of race, is most often read in the context of external cultural events like the Civil War, Reconstruction, Jim Crow, *Brown v. the Board of Education of Topeka, Kansas,* the civil rights movement, and post–civil rights influences on identity.

But external events can never be brought to integration. External events, with the help of the novelist and the form of the novel itself, can only reflect the confusion that defines democracy and gesture toward the necessity of individuals working to reconcile the meaning of their experiences. As Ellison's invisible narrator suggested, the incomprehensible can only be made intelligible at the individual level and certainly not by way of the external application of cultural, familial, or ideological expectations. Coming to this realization drives the narrator underground at the conclusion of *Invisible Man* to consider and reconcile what he has come to recognize as his own invisibility. Unfortunately, the more the individual searches for some sense of individual completion, the further that completion recedes on the horizon. Individual meaning can only be approximated in relation to the unwavering democratic ideal that is America itself.

McIntyre references this search when, in book I of *Three Days before the Shooting...*, he reflects on an experience he had in World War II in which he felt a sense of pride that reflected "that helpless, American, most democratic yearning which seeks ever to effect some sense of personal connection between the self and historical events" that "arises, perhaps, out of the fluid, shifting center of power and the absence of ancient hierarchical structure which is native to our form of government."[33] McIntyre is directly confronted with the collision of self and history when hearing the name "McMillan" causes him to return to an experience in which he accompanies the police to the home of a ninety-five-year-old Black man named Jessie Rockmore. McIntyre and the police arrive to find Rockmore sitting dead in a coffin that had become infested with termites. He had bought the coffin before becoming disillusioned at having outlived the usefulness of a coffin in which he had long intended to be buried. Even with the help of Aubrey McMillan, the handyman and custodian who works in the house and is questioned by the police, McIntyre cannot decipher the truth or even construct a coherent narrative that could explain a series of circumstances that are at once surreal and undecipherable. This is, somehow, an episode that is at once racial and historical while simultaneously standing outside of each of those ways of understanding individual and historical experience. Welborn McIntyre inherits the dilemma, but it is a problem that he cannot understand and certainly cannot reconcile.

Jessie Rockmore's house is some combination of home and museum. It was chaotic, though McIntyre sensed the possibility of unity connecting the fragmentation. The contents of Rockmore's house—which seems to be a random collection of clutter that includes books, lamps, vases, musical instruments, art, and furniture of various styles and periods—is disturbing to McIntyre. What disturbs him the most is that the invisibility of this ongoing history has been compiled in the shadow of a historical narrative that McIntyre recognizes and understands: "*Perhaps, I thought, it's simply the fact of finding such a place so close to the Capital, so near the center of our national source of order. There are slums nearby, of course, but slums are different. They emerged from history and are unhappy marks on the road of progress. What's more, we were doing something about the slums. But this place—my God, the fact that it exists means that something has been going on that has completely escaped me and everyone else.... [emphasis in original].*"[34] Jessie Rockmore's house stands as a physical manifestation of a historical counternarrative that had for so long been hiding in plain sight.

In this context, McIntyre has no frame of reference for judging what is meaningful and what is not. Jessie Rockmore is dead. Adam Sunraider is dying. And Welborn McIntyre cannot solve the mystery of death that, incongruously enough, connects each of these stories to an unseen, repressed, complex past. Even as Aubrey McMillan, the handyman and custodian at Rockmore's house, tries to provide a coherent narrative to McIntyre and the police explaining the unexplainable, McIntyre is overwhelmed by a wave of humiliation at his inability to make sense of the chaos around him. To some extent, the contents of Rockmore's house is an expansion of the objects that the narrator of *Invisible Man* collects and carries in his briefcase throughout the novel and cannot discard. It reveals an alternative understanding of the ways the nation's history has disproportionate effects on Black and white citizens. In Jessie Rockmore's house, time disintegrates and is unappreciated even as it is reconstructed into a new image of unacknowledged experience. After all, what Jessie Rockmore has assembled during his ninety-five years of life ultimately led to disillusionment and death rather than to individual or cultural transcendence.

Jessie Rockmore's story is a tragedy, right down to his attempts to integrate the fragmented worldview reflected in his house. If there is an argument to be made for catharsis, it is his recognition of the nation's moral evasion of its own democratic ideals. This episode, writ small, depicts the sense of tragedy that the novel represents in the assassination of Adam Sunraider. McIntyre, in his attempt to integrate the meanings of the assassination of Sunraider, the car burning of LeeWillie Minifrees, his own complicated relationship to his former girlfriend Laura, and the drunken narration about Rockmore passed along to him by Aubrey McMillen, is the conduit through which the reader grapples with America in book I. McIntyre's recognition is that his liberal attitude is a tool inadequate for reconciling the complexity of racial history in America with its chaotic present. Perhaps the deepest disillusionment that Jessie Rockmore experiences is the realization that perhaps the United States can never fully move beyond the legacy of slavery, the failures of Reconstruction, and the ongoing present contained in the civil rights years.

While Ellison regularly referenced the work of William Faulkner, often to point toward its paternalistic shortcomings regarding race, his second novel revises Faulkner's sense of the influences of the past by emphasizing, particularly in the Jessie Rockmore episode, Faulkner's point in *Requiem for a Nun:* "The past is never dead. It's not even past." Jessie Rockmore's past is relived in the flashback in which he tells it to Aubrey McMillen. But the past contained in Rockmore's house is alive and well as it revises the lens through which McIntyre (and, by extension, the reader) sees the past. The connection to Faulkner is pertinent, if not entirely accurate. *Go Down, Moses* (1942) is perhaps a more fitting example of Faulkner's desire to examine the ways in which individuals struggle to overcome the past. That effort takes on moral implications since individuals must either remain in servitude to the past or find ways to move beyond its limitations.

This is certainly consistent with the experiences the invisible narrator faces in *Invisible Man* when he is forced to confront the meaning of his grandfather's deathbed confession, Dr. Bledsoe's expulsion of him from college, and the ways he is subsequently manipulated by Lucius Brockway, leftist ideology, and Black nationalism. The conclusion of *Invisible Man* ambiguously sends the narrator underground while implying a possible end to his hibernation. Welborne McIntyre leaves the Jessie Rockmore episode unable to reconcile history with the present. Perhaps it is self-defeating for individuals to even attempt to reconcile the past with the present. This may be supported by the fact that Ellison uses a different strategy for reconciliation in book II when he reunites the Reverend Alonzo Hickman with Senator Adam Sunraider in a collaborative process of reconciliation. Their conversation integrates the communal call-and-response characteristics of folklore, religion, and tragedy with an acceptance of America as an allegory connecting the plurality of race and culture.

The story that Welborne McIntyre learns about Jessie Rockmore is certainly no requiem for an idealized past that needs to be reclaimed. As a matter of fact, Jessie Rockmore becomes disillusioned by a more fundamental betrayal of all that he has experienced in life. In a character like Rockmore, Ellison belies Faulkner's pattern of repetition in favor of something that transforms past inequalities into an ambiguous present. People are shaped by their past but recognized as individuals dedicated to reconciling the past and pursuing an equal present.

The Jessie Rockmore episode, which arrives as a flashback to McIntyre as he waits in the hospital, trying to make sense of LeeWillie Minifree's Cadillac-burning, the senator's shooting, and the presence of the Reverend Alonzo Hickman, never achieves the kind of integration to which Ellison aspired in his letter to Morteza Sprague back when he first began thinking about the novel. But it is an aesthetic process to which he is committed because, as he says in his "Haverford Statement" from May 1969, "As a writer who tries to reduce the flux and flow of life to meaningful artistic forms, I am stuck with integration, because the very process of the imagination as it goes about bringing together a multiplicity of scenes, images, characters, and emotions and reducing them to significance is nothing if not integrative. Further, the object of my fictional imagination is American society and the American experience as experienced fundamentally by Negroes, and I find it impossible to deal with either in isolation, for they are intricately united in their diversity."[35] But it is an ambitious assessment of history that supports Ellison's assertions that the United States cannot function as a nation without acknowledging the national betrayals of race and slavery that inform the ways the present unfolds. McIntyre and Rockmore are separated by race and history, and there is no true resolution to the scene. Welborne McIntyre simply leaves, relieved to be out of the chaos of the house and thankful that he "had been born to a stable level of society in which such chaos had been eliminated, tamed, filtered out. It had difficulties, true, but at least there was ORDER [*emphasis in original*]."[36] McIntyre has to resolve the contradictions of history, the past, and democratic belonging that he has witnessed. And, like Ellison's invisible narrator, he ultimately has a generative responsibility to reconcile the implications of American experience for himself.

WHAT A CONFUSION HAS BEEN RELEASED

Find the myth in which the hero descends into hell by following cord and is thus able to escape. This seems like a basic form to give this thing organization. Because, god knows, it seems to run all over the world.

RALPH WALDO ELLISON PAPERS, Library of Congress

After Ellison's death, when Fannie Ellison gave John Callahan, Ellison's literary executor, access to Ellison's papers, she asked if the second novel had a beginning, middle, and end. It did not. The second novel has none of those characteristics because it is perpetually in the middle of a form. Cheryl Alison makes the point in "Writing Underground" that, in *Invisible Man,* "The narrator moves from passage to passage in the course of his tale, and we feel these series of enclosures for the strange inelegance of the byways through which we are made to burrow, traversing as it were the ellipses in ... and ... and ... and...."[37] That is a very fair and accurate assessment of *Invisible Man,* but in *Three Days before the Shooting...,* the reader has neither the benefit of a single narrative presence nor any compelling sense of narrative pattern or trajectory whatsoever. The fact that the novel is untitled suggests its compositional status. It is all middle and episodically spins out, forward and backward, with no beginning and no end, from its center.[38] The compositional aspirations of the second novel and the difficulties that Ellison faced in realizing those aspiration were intrinsically tied to the presence of Black culture in the foundation nation's democratic experiment.

The form of the novel, like jazz itself, was for Ellison democratic by its very definition. It could provide order to the past and offer coherence to a chaotic present. In book I, as Welborn McIntyre waits at the hospital for news about the senator's condition after the shooting and tries to formulate some understanding of what has occurred—"Politics and blood, blood and religion, I thought, what a confusion has been released"[39]—Ellison includes a curious flashback to an episode in McIntyre's life in which he has a brief relationship in Harlem with an Black woman named Laura. The sense of conflict that McIntyre feels in Jessie Rockmore's house is echoed in the contradictions included in this brief flashback. The thrill he felt as a young, white man in a relationship with a Black woman in the midst of the New Deal challenges the assumptions and hostility of those who witness their youthful infatuation: [B]asically we were in love, and in our circles it was agreed that Laura and I represented, if not the future, at least a good *earnest* of that time when the old conflicts left unresolved by the great war between the states (and we were nothing if not historical-minded) and the wounds, outrages, and inequities which haunted contemporary society would be resolved by transcendent love [*emphasis in original*]."[40] But the issues all return to identity, which is the issue that Senator Sunraider wrestles with in his call-and-response with Reverend Hickman.

As his name implies, McIntyre is wellborn and has the sense of privilege and social belonging, including a genealogical precedent complete with a coat of arms, that the senator wants. Although McIntyre fancies himself a progressive, the reality is that his liberalism is idealistic and superficial, at best. Perhaps it is McIntyre's vision of progress that is faulty, based as it is on a vision of integration that is ahistorical and ultimately unsustainable. Like Ellison, McIntyre is a firm believer in democracy and even goes so far as to adopt a personal slogan—"Democracy is love, love is democracy"—reflecting a belief that social conflict is as much a part of internal reconciliation as it is of public discourse. While this is a personal choice that McIntyre has made, his choice has public implications. In a reference to *Heart of Darkness,* his love for Laura is ultimately compromised by his anxieties about being able to reconcile what that love would mean for how he thought of himself and how he was thought of by others: "But now the questions of who I was, and who and what my parents and relatives were and had been, tore me apart. History, both past and future, haunted my mind.... Now, for the first time since childhood, I felt need for the security symbolized by that thin chain of being personified by my parents, that lifeline of kinship which extended through time and space, from England and France to America, that I hoped would sustain me in my adventure into the dark interior of society."[41] McIntyre's relationship with Laura, made ambiguous by his own insecurities, invokes Jessie Rockmore's own lost hope in democracy and its possibilities for Black uplift.

McIntyre is as much concerned with the loss of meaning of his own past as he is with the realization that Laura herself may know relatively little about hers. In a moment of contemplation that echoes the obsession in *Invisible Man* that Mr. Norton shares with the invisible narrator about his murky belief that the narrator somehow represents Mr. Norton's destiny, McIntyre wonders "Who and what stood back there in the dark behind her? How would they assume form, become repersonalized, now that they were linked with my future destiny?"[42] Ellison's concern, reflected in McIntyre's racial anxieties about the manifestation of the past in the present, is for a precarious present unable to reconcile what might be hiding in the darkness of the past. This is a brief romantic episode of an educated progressive who *thinks* he wants to be at the vanguard of cultural change until he recognizes the uncertainty of what his beliefs mean. In presenting it, Ellison encapsulates an allegorical representation of America's past, present, and future.

The episode is narrated through Welborn McIntyre's recollection. But after he arrives at Laura's apartment to tell her parents that Laura is pregnant with his child and that they are planning marriage, the narration reflects the kind of call-and-response between the Reverend Alonzo Hickman and the dying senator that dominates book II. Laura's mother recognizes the burden of race that Welborn himself cannot yet comprehend. Ellison had expressed anxieties about what *Brown v. the Board of Education of Topeka, Kansas,* would mean to Americans intent on living in a present unencumbered by the burdens of a racialized past. This, perhaps, is why Laura's mother is angry enough at Welborn's obvious hypocrisy that she ends their conversation by chasing him out of the apartment with a shotgun and with the instruction to forget Laura and their relationship. McIntyre is perhaps disillusioned by the confrontation. He is certainly confused by the reality that he and Laura's mother hold radically different visions of American life. Hers is certainly not the democracy that McIntyre idealistically envisions. McIntyre's feelings of rejection and defeat echo Jessie Rockmore's.

This is a complicated social drama that McIntyre cannot understand, particularly in the larger social drama unfolding around Senator Sunraider's assassination. Given the circumstances he has experienced, it is completely understandable why McIntyre is as disillusioned as he seems to be. At a professional level, he has reported on a Black man so angered and disillusioned at being a citizen in a country based on inequality and white supremacy that he burns his car on the senator's lawn in a response that is as much public as it is private. At a personal level, McIntyre has been forced to acknowledge and respond to a view of American life that he never knew existed in his experiences with Laura's mother. With the end of his relationship to Laura, he has experienced and lost a meaningful relationship in his life. He has witnessed the absurd, existential consequences of Jesse Rockmore's profound disappointment. And in a broader moment of recognition and disillusionment, he has experienced the shooting of a US senator on the floor of the Senate.[43] The disillusionment into which McIntyre and Rockmore fall represents a more fundamental crisis of faith in the possibilities of integration. If the improvisational form of the novel represents for Ellison the possibilities of integration, the impasse that confronts McIntyre and Rockmore (and perhaps even Ellison himself) is the impossibility of coming to terms with all the references to Black American sermons, blues, jazz, folktales, and cultural traditions that Ellison invokes perhaps not being the tools of integration that he envisioned.

What McIntyre describes in his flashbacks to LeeWillie Minifrees, Laura, and Jessie Rockmore is a process in which he comes to terms with his experiences of race. His process represents the broader reconsideration that the nation was undergoing as it faced the meaning and implications of integration after six decades of Jim Crow segregation. As McIntyre observes, a senator known for his racism reminisces about the past as he lies dying in the companionship of a Black minister. The relationship between these two men is the true heart of the novel but, as Albert Murray observes, McIntyre is "the most fascinating character in the novel."[44] Part II of *Three Days before the Shooting...* includes a revision of the McIntyre section, indicating that Ellison continued to see McIntyre's presence in the novel as an important thread somehow connecting his experiences to Reverend Hickman and the senator. The editors of the volume note that this is likely the final episode that Ellison revised before his death. McIntyre's presence indicates a commentary on the limitations of integration and racial assumptions. McIntyre may or may not get beyond the sense of guilt and responsibility that he feels. After all, McIntyre continues to maintain his relationship to his own complicated identity. While he knows that he participates in the experiences of Black people in America that his section of the novel draws upon, he continues to resist the reality of what integration means for him as an individual and for America as a collective, democratic entity. He sees the past, but he can neither reconcile the past with the present nor move beyond his impulse to repress the past.

What is clear in the shooting of the senator is that something culturally significant has occurred. But given Ellison's expansive comments on his thoughts about the role of the novelist and the form of the novel itself, his very conscious desire to write an epic novel that represented the summation of what it means for both Black people and white people to be American would inevitably be interrupted by the ways "life was stepping in and imposing itself" on his composition.[45] The imposition of life to which Ellison refers comprised the assassinations that took place during the 1960s—he specifically cites the Kennedys and the Reverend Dr. Martin Luther King Jr.—that changed the mood of the novel from comic to tragic. The realities of contemporary American culture were merging seamlessly with the novel's compositional present and making it difficult for Ellison to determine what cultural understanding could reasonably be assumed and what cultural markers required some clarification. The McIntyre section of the novel confirms Ellison's thoughts about the ways race conceals all manner of social values and cultural assumptions.

There is a certain restlessness to the Hickman section that speaks to the Black America about which he reminisces in book II of the novel. The senator's shooting is the central action of the novel, but it is the Reverend Hickman's presence that defines the relationship he renews with the senator. From the beginning, it was Ellison's plan to write a novel that used the democratic equality of multiple narrators to communicate on the lower frequencies to which his invisible narrator alluded in the final sentence of *Invisible Man*. But, early in its composition, Ellison recognized Reverend Hickman's expanding presence. In a letter to his friend Albert Murray from April 2, 1960, Ellison wrote:

> The work with old Hickman, Bliss and Severn goes on, with Hickman moving more and more into the role of hero and the old guy is so large that I've just about given in to him, some other crazy sonsabitches have been boiling up

out of the pot, one who sacrifices a fishtailed caddy on the Senator lawn, and another who discovers that a coffin he'd been saving for 30 years or so had rotted away and decided then and there that the whole American government had fucked up and orders a case of Jack Daniels and a white cooch dancer to come to his house and flip her g-string.[46]

Hickman takes over because, much like Jim in Twain's *Huckleberry Finn*, he is the moral center of the novel. The Reverend Alonzo Hickman provides continuity for a novel perched at the indeterminate intersection of the Korean Conflict and the civil rights movement. Hickman looks backward to a segregated world, defined by vernacular religious and musical expressions.

In some ways, the Reverend Hickman takes over the novel because, although the shooting of the senator initiates a crisis, the senator is too protean for the reader to know entirely clearly who he really is. Conversely, the Reverend Hickman, who is firmly rooted in Black America, represents a democratic optimism of what the country can be. Ellison wanted to distill the expansiveness of time into discernible units that he could reassemble in a way that provided some sense of meaning and perspective: "Literature is a form of art wherein time can be reduced to manageable proportions; and the diversity of experience can be assembled to show an immediate pattern: to conserve memory, focus energies, ideals and to give us some idea of the cost and glories of those ideals."[47] In his reminisces with the senator, Hickman engages in that exact process of reducing time to a pattern of events. The Reverend Hickman's power in the novel is that he exemplifies a transmission of culture characterized by communication and exchange rather than by racial affiliation.

Culture, rather than familial association, forms the individual and, as such, could be actively chosen and constructed rather than unilaterally inherited. If anything, familial bonds represent for Ellison a limitation that must be escaped by individuals in order to reach something much more closely resembling cultural affiliation. This is certainly what Huckleberry Finn did in his decision to "light out for the Territory." Huckleberry Finn actively sought to escape the constrictions of middle-class approval in favor of a far broader geographical space for self-definition. Democracy is uniquely able to provide individuals the opportunity to create and recreate themselves beyond the influences of their family. The same can also be said of Ellison's view of

Black authors in America. Race imposes a cultural lineage that artificially binds Black American authors together solely based on race and regardless of aesthetics.

The Reverend Hickman spends a great deal of time in his conversation with the senator idealizing the cultural geography of their shared experiences and then transposing that past into a culturally continuous present. Without a functioning culture, none of this is meaningful and can only lead to the kinds of cultural chaos reflected in LeeWillie Minifree's decision to burn his Cadillac on the senator's lawn, Jessie Rockmore's disillusionment, and the senator's shooting on the floor of the US Senate. What Ellison saw during his extended composition of the novel were insufficient attempts to create a narrative of ancestry that was robust enough to reconcile the nation's contemporary incarnation with its stated ideals at the nation's founding, during its reconstructions after the Civil War, and during the nation's second Reconstruction, after *Brown v. the Board of Education of Topeka, Kansas.* Ellison saw the form of the novel and his role as novelist as reducing the chaos of what he described to a manageable proportion. The competing ideologies were present in a nation torn asunder by World War II, the Cold War, civil rights, anti-colonial politics, and Black identity politics that challenged the relationship of Black people to America itself and to people around the globe who had been colonized. These competing ideologies may have brought more disorientation than clarity. This is particularly true relative to competing understandings of race, culture, and the influences of the past.

Ellison consciously, through Hickman, constructed a response to the chaos of American culture by replacing racial affiliation with a cultural affiliation that he regarded as being quintessentially American and unambiguously integrated. What Hickman describes to the senator are cultural production and the importance of recognizing and remembering that culture: "Do we still [celebrate Juneteenth]? Why I should say we do. [...] Because we haven't forgot what it means. Even if sometimes folks try to make us believe it never happened or that it was a mistake that it ever did...."[48] The Reverend Hickman's response to the kinds of contemporary crises of identity are represented in the senator's transformation. The senator had rejected the racially ambiguous origins that characterized him when he was known as Bliss by the Black community that embraced him. He had transformed himself into Senator Adam Sunraider, who espoused virulently racist attitudes toward Black people and toward the chaos those attitudes created. The Reverend Hickman's presence returns the senator to those aspects of Black culture that are indisputably American. The boomerang of history that Ellison first articulated in *Invisible Man* suggests a vision of history that is both circular rather than linear and episodic rather than progressive. By taking over the novel in the way he does, the Reverend Hickman simultaneously demonstrates the ways in which contemporary and future representations of cultural production bear a responsibility to recognize the weight of the past.

The complexities of the conversation shared by the Reverend Hickman and the dying senator did not simply reflect the meaning contained in the nation's chaos. Those complexities were the very elements that constituted democracy. What defined America was its very conscious break with what Ellison saw as an overly reductive view of the responsibilities individuals had to history and the past. The presence of slavery and enslaved people dating back even before the nation's origins meant for Ellison that culture was one of the few areas that Black people in America could influence. By extension, this influence of cultural and artistic agency fell to novels and the novelists who produced them. While the Reverend Hickman can choose neither his ancestors nor his past, he can choose as an individual to seize and maintain a meaningful understanding of the past. In a collective context, the Reverend Hickman provides cultural meaning through the call-and-response cultural rituals of the blues, sermons, jazz, and Juneteenth celebrations.

The Reverend Hickman may be the clearest example of Ellison's belief that Americans in general, and particularly Black people in America, must have access to their history to assert their agency in the present and to avoid the kind of disillusionment that plagues Jessie Rockmore. The Reverend Hickman took the novel over because Ellison, perhaps unknowingly, attached to the Reverend Hickman, the former jazz musician turned minister, many of the qualities of the artist. Democracy allows individuals to claim some of the ideals of American exceptionalism as they reconcile individual, social, and cultural disparities into a shared cultural experience. The Reverend Hickman's description to the senator of the Black American culture that the senator has erased symbolically accentuates the process of erasure that was present at the founding of American democracy. This is very much in alignment with

Ellison's views of the responsibilities of the novelist. By engaging in a process like the Reverend Hickman's, the novelist's art preserves the meaning of shared cultural experience.

During the speech he gives just before being shot, the senator echoes some of this when he says that

> Where we have been is where we shall go. We move from the realm of dreams through the valley of the practical and back to the realm of rectified dreams. Yes, but how we arrive there is *our* decision, *our* challenge, and *our* anguish. And in the going and in the arriving our task is to tirelessly transform the past and create and re-create the future. In this grand enterprise we dance to our inner music, we negotiate the unknown and untamed terrain by the soundings of our own inner ear.... Indeed, we *shall* reshape the universe—to the forms of our own inner vision [*emphasis in original*].[49]

By describing cultural plurality in the context of the unavoidability of fate, Ellison describes the individual and collective process that most fully exemplifies his thoughts about democracy. The "grand enterprise" the senator describes is the presence of individual choice. That choice is simultaneously grounded in the promise of democracy and the individual's decision to identify with the available alternatives. Without the authority of democracy and the inspiration of individualism, culture was reduced from a complex series of interactions to a homogeneous mass culture devoid of individual subjectivity and historical awareness.

Ellison's outlook was fundamentally shaped by his thoughts about preserving the continuity of Black culture in America and recognizing its influences amid the chaos of a contemporary culture intent on re-creating itself. In many ways, Ellison's theory of culture was his attempt to defend democracy in the face of the fast-moving complexities that *Brown v. the Board of Education of Topeka, Kansas,* brought to American modernity. *Three Days before the Shooting...,* particularly in its original conceptualization, served as a curative intervention to the assaults on democracy and American identity—individual and collective—that Ellison saw unfolding throughout the public sphere. This is what the Reverend Hickman's conversation with the senator attempts to do. Because of the depth of their long, shared past, Hickman and the senator represent precisely the kind of work in which individuals must engage. Because of the symbolic action in which they are engaged, Ellison's characters in both *Invisible Man* and *Three Days before the Shooting…* often display two-dimensional, archetypal qualities rather than the qualities of growth, interiority, and change that are often associated with three-dimensional character development. This is not to suggest that these qualities are somehow mutually exclusive. Rather, the incompatibility of the two suggests the very point of cultural friction to which so much of Ellison's work returns.

Book II of *Three Days before the Shooting…* is basically an extended deathbed rumination on the complex relationship between the Reverend Hickman and the senator as the senator clings to life after the shooting. It is also the space that allows Ellison to provide glimpses into the ambiguity of the senator's parentage. In the section entitled "Bliss's Birth," Ellison invokes the sense of frustration that the Reverend Hickman has about his inability to confirm the senator's parentage when Hickman thinks to himself, "Poor Bliss, the terrible thing is that even if I told you all this, I still couldn't tell you who your daddy was, or even if you have any of our blood in your veins."[50] Bliss may be Black. Or maybe not. The senator is unable to live within that ambiguity. He is undeniably Black by culture. The senator's deprivation of any certainty regarding his parentage is the basis of his racial antagonism.

In a compositional note, Ellison reminds himself that the senator "[g]oes seeking for life among whites, using the agency of racism to punish Negroes for being weak, and to achieve power of his own. As with many politicians politics is a drama in which he plays a role that doesn't necessarily jibe with his own feelings. Nevertheless, he feels humiliated by a fate that threw him among Negroes and deprived him of the satisfaction of knowing whether he is a Negro by blood or only by culture and upbringing. He tells himself that he hates Negroes but can't deny his love for Hickman. Resents this too. // He is a man who sees the weakness in the way societal hierarchy has dealt with race and it is through the chink that he enters white society and exploits it."[51] The senator's anxiety with and hostile response to racial ambiguity is, for Ellison, analogous to America's.

The irony is that, while the senator and the nation desperately want to evade the implications of ambiguity, the reality is that identity, as the Reverend Hickman's conversation with the senator about culture implies, cannot simply be reduced to race, bloodlines, and parentage. In raising Bliss from his origins as a foundling, the Reverend Hickman wants Bliss to transcend America's racial impasse. As Albert Murray correctly recognized, Ellison wanted to write an American epic novel using a broad palette of allegorical reference firmly rooted in America's past. Hickman realizes that the senator's repudiation of his past and his subsequent betrayal of Black Americana is more than simply an individual or a political act.

According to the editors of *Three Days before the Shooting...*, in 1993 Ellison substantially revised and expanded the portion of the manuscript containing the prologue from book I, as well as the episode that occurs at the Lincoln Memorial and at Jessie Rockmore's house. As they note, Ellison's computer revisions during the 1990s largely return to areas of the novel that he had completed as early as the 1950s. In some ways, these revised sequences, gathered in a section the editors entitled "Hickman in Washington, D.C.," represent some of Ellison's final thinking about the novel on which he had worked for so long. In an extended essayistic aside about the senator, Hickman ruminates on the ways the Black congregation saw in Bliss the embodiment of transcendence over the past: "[W]ith our little boy preacher as symbol and spokesman we set out to overcome the limitations imposed by our history and this country's ongoing contentions. And by embracing that child as the unique symbol of a unity to come we hoped that the combined promises of Scripture and this land's Constitution would be at last fulfilled and made manifest."[52] The senator's betrayal to the Black people who raised him as their own is epic in its consequences and heartbreaking in its realities. Since the Reverend Hickman's conception of the world is based on race, as are the conceptions of others in the novel like LeeWillie Minifrees, Welborne McIntyre, Jessie Rockmore, and even Severen, the senator's unacknowledged estranged son-turned-assassin, the world they share will only be reduced to chaos and disillusionment. True freedom—individual and cultural—can only be achieved when identity is no longer achieved solely through the ambiguities of racial identification.

In two computer-composed sequences that the editors give the name "Hickman in Georgia & Oklahoma," the Reverend Hickman has gone home to Waycross, Georgia, before going to Oklahoma City, Oklahoma, where, among other people, Hickman talks to a shamanistic man of Black and Native American heritage named Love New. The inclusion of these Oklahoma passages is not surprising, especially given the impact of the region on Ellison's early life and on his vision of America. Early in the novel's conception, Ellison seemed to see Oklahoma as a central aspect of his novel's epic sweep. Notes cited by the editors indicate that, for Ellison, "The first book is that of the frontier. / / The middle book that of the city. / / The third book that of the nation."[53] It is not clear how or where the sections of the novel set in Georgia and Oklahoma were to be incorporated into the novel. Given Love New's hybrid identity, Ellison may have envisioned him representing the most American view of America contained in the novel, particularly since Love New argues for an amalgamation of race, identity, and nation. He relates to the Reverend Hickman his belief that "The privilege of freedom comes at a price even for a man who's no longer shackled by all the color confusion that haunts this country. Because if you accept the fact that you're neither black nor white, Gentile nor Jew, Rebel-bred nor Yankee-born, you have the freedom to be *truly* free.... Take the risks of identity that go with true freedom and you can be your own man. Then when your value, your manhood, is measured by the whiteness of your skin you can laugh whenever they decide to stand back and measure themselves and their ways against the myopic standards of others [*emphasis in original*]."[54]

Ellison's focus on freedom in the computer-generated sequences that he worked on late in the novel's composition reveals his attempt to devise an experimental form that could link individual cultural obligations to the past and to the shared aspirations of American culture. The computer-generated sequences of *Three Days before the Shooting...* speak to Ellison's attempts to enclose his literary forebears in a geographical space that would allow him to locate his own voice as he improvised on the influences of the experiences from which he drew. Ellison's study of music had taught him the value of recognizing and expanding the boundaries of limitation. Freedom—even the freedom of individual identity—was neither absolute nor without restraint. Individuals are affected by circumstance. But individual experience is not entirely determined by circumstance. Circumstance elicits both sadness and the resilience to laugh despite the pain.

Culture shapes the artists representing it as much as artists shape the culture their work chronicles. Ellison, going back to his earliest interactions with Kenneth Burke, had said that the novel, by its very definition, is fundamentally a symbolic process of ritual because the form provides wholeness in the face of chaos and complexity. Love New echoes the restorative pastoral role that the Reverend Alonzo Hickman occupies for so many of the novel's episodes. One sees in Love New's appearance in the novel a sense of coherence and possibility. Both lie unseen below the fragmentary surface of human experience in the intertwined relationship between visibility and invisibility, between what is tragic and what is comic, and between what is shadow and what is act.

Masking characterizes Ellison's invisible narrator as completely as it describes Rinehart and Bliss / Senator Sunraider. The tragicomic mask is Ellison's strategy for expressing and altering the reality so much of his work describes. For Ellison, it may be the only way for the nation to acknowledge its past and move toward a more sustainable future. As Love New suggests, race, nation, and identity function around the tension between individual and collective qualities that have been given and the qualities toward which individuals and groups actively aspire. The interplay of the tragic and the comic on these factors is what distinguished Ellison's writing from the work of many of his contemporaries and was, for Ellison, the true emblem of humanity and the human condition.

NOTES

PREFACE AND ACKNOWLEDGMENTS

1. Ellison, *Three Days before the Shooting...*, 239.

2. Ellison, "The World and the Jug," 178.

3. Keats, Letter to George and Tom Keats, 21, 27 (?) December 1817, *Selected Letters of John Keats*, 60.

4. Keats, Letter to Richard Woodhouse, 27 October 1818, *Selected Letters of John Keats*, 195.

INTRODUCTION

1. Tuttleton, "The Achievement of Ralph Ellison," 5.

2. Denby, "Justice for Ralph Ellison."

3. Parrish, *Ralph Ellison and the Genius of America*, 2.

4. Wright, *Shadowing Ralph Ellison*, 11.

5. Ellison, "'A Very Stern Discipline,'" 757.

6. Morel, ed., *Ralph Ellison and the Raft of Hope*, 8.

7. Watts, *Heroism and the Black Intellectual*, 12.

8. Watts, *Heroism and the Black Intellectual*, 13.

9. Watts, *Heroism and the Black Intellectual*, 119.

10. Watts, *Heroism and the Black Intellectual*, 113.

11. Watts, *Heroism and the Black Intellectual*, 28.

12. Watts, *Heroism and the Black Intellectual*, 144n44.

13. Foley, *Wrestling with the Left*, 20.

14. Quoted in Rice, *Ralph Ellison and the Politics of the Novel*, 64. It is contained in the Ralph Ellison Papers, Manuscripts, Library of Congress, box 105, folder 2.

15. Ellison, "What America Would Be Like Without Blacks," 584. Qtd. in Dickstein, "Ralph Ellison, Race, and American Culture," 35.

16. Posnock, ed., *The Cambridge Companion to Ralph Ellison*, 2–3.

17. Morel, "'In a Strange Country,'" 252.

18. Allen, *Talking to Strangers*, 53.

19. Ellison, "Twentieth-Century Fiction and the Black Mask of Humanity," 81.

20. Turner, "Awakening to Race," 657.

21. Ellison, "The Way It Is," 319. For a discussion of this episode of Ellison's wartime journalism, see Foley, *Wrestling with the Left*, 39–42.

22. Quoted in Foley, *Wrestling with the Left*, 43, 360n31.

23. Ellison, *Invisible Man*, 201–2.

24. Foley, *Wrestling with the Left*, 229.

25. Bradley, *Ralph Ellison in Progress*, 5.

26. Ellison, "Introduction" to *Shadow and Act*, 56.

27. This is paraphrased from a presentation delivered by Audre Lorde on a panel entitled "The Personal and the Political Panel" at a conference on the Second Sex that was sponsored by New York University Institute for the Humanities on September 29, 1979. In commenting on papers addressing difference within the lives of American women, Lorde notes: "For the master's tools will never dismantle the master's house. They may allow us temporarily to beat him at his own game, but they will never enable us to bring about genuine change. And this fact is only threatening to those women who still define the master's house as their only source of support." See Lorde, "The Master's Tools Will Never Dismantle the Master's House," 110.

28. Smethurst, *The Black Arts Movement*, 48.

29. Rampersad, *Ralph Ellison*, 470–72.

30. Rampersad, *Ralph Ellison*, 513.

31. Ellison, "Society, Morality and the Novel," 698. See also Rice, *Ralph Ellison and the Politics of the Novel*, 69.

32. Tuttleton, "The Achievement of Ralph Ellison," 5.

1. INVISIBLE TO WHOM?

1. Cruse, *The Crisis of the Negro Intellectual*, 147.

2. Cruse, *The Crisis of the Negro Intellectual*, 509.

3. Cruse, *The Crisis of the Negro Intellectual*, 565. For further discussions of the influences of radicalism on American literature during the period, see Wald, *Writing from the Left*, especially 67–122, 171–232, and *Trinity of Passion*, 1–15, 108–45; Nelson, *Revolutionary Memory*, 11–85; Maxwell, *New Negro, Old Left*, 13–61, 153–78; as well as Denning's *The Cultural Front*, 1–50, 200–229; Foley, *Radical Representations*, especially 44–85, 86–128, 249–441; Dickstein, *Dancing in the Dark*, 92–153, 173–211; Schrecker, *Many Are the Crimes*, especially 3–41, 119–53; Storch, *Red Chicago*, 42, 43, 52, 53; 214–16, 222–27; Kelley, *Freedom Dreams*, 36–59, 60–109; Cruse, *The Crisis of the Negro Intellectual*, 147.

4. Ellison, "The Little Man at Chehaw Station," 503.

5. For discussions of the influences of the cultural front, see Denning, *The Cultural Front*, especially 1–50, 200–229; Dolinar, *The Black Cultural Front*, 3–20, 21–70.

6. Foley, *Wrestling with the Left*, 53, 17–18.

7. Ellison, "Recent Negro Fiction," 26.

8. Ellison, "Roscoe Dunjee and the American Language," 458.

9. Ellison, "In a Strange Country," 145, 146.

10. Jackson, *Ralph Ellison,* 295. For a broader discussion of Ellison's work during the period, see especially Jackson's chapter 10, "Labor of Love: 1943–1944," 282–303.

11. Ellison, "Introduction to the Thirtieth-Anniversary Edition of *Invisible Man,*" 480.

12. See Jackson, *Ralph Ellison,* 294–96, for a discussion of the circumstances surrounding Ellison's composition of "Flying Home," and "Ralph Ellison, Sharpies, Rinehart, and Politics," especially 71–81, for a discussion of the evolution of Ellison's political and cultural thought during the period.

13. Ellison, "Flying Home," 150.

14. Ellison, "Introduction to the Thirtieth-Anniversary Edition of *Invisible Man,*" 481.

15. Ellison, "Flying Home," 150.

16. Ellison, "Flying Home," 151, 152, 153.

17. Ellison, "Flying Home," 155.

18. Ellison, "Flying Home," 159.

19. Ellison, "Flying Home," 172.

20. Ellison, "The Great Migration," 23–24.

21. Ellison, "Harlem Is Nowhere," 324.

22. Ellison, "Editorial Comment" (1942), i, iii.

23. Ellison, "*An American Dilemma:* A Review," 340.

24. Wright, *Shadowing Ralph Ellison,* 87.

25. Rampersad, *Ralph Ellison,* 140.

26. Ellison, "Harlem Is Nowhere," 321.

27. Ellison, "Harlem Is Nowhere," 323–24.

28. Schryer, *Fantasies of the New Class,* 2–3, 205n14; Pease, *Visionary Compacts,* 14.

29. Lepenies, *Between Literature and Science,* 13.

30. Rampersad, *Ralph Ellison,* 77; Jackson, *Ralph Ellison,* 141–47.

31. Park, "Racial Assimilation in Secondary Groups with Particular Reference to the Negro," 620. See also Lal, "Black and Blue in Chicago," 546–66.

32. Locke, ed., *The New Negro,* 7. For a discussion of the ways Robert E. Park's theories of race and sociology influenced Alain Locke and Charles S. Johnson and, by extension, their conception of the New Negro movement, see Lal, "Black and Blue in Chicago," 552–54.

33. Quoted in Lal, "Black and Blue in Chicago," 553.

34. Ellison, "*An American Dilemma:* A Review," 332.

35. Frazier, "The Negro Middle Class and Desegregation," 291–301.

36. Jackson, *Ralph Ellison,* 303; Rampersad, *Ralph Ellison,* 181.

37. Qtd. in Ellison, "*An American Dilemma:* A Review," 339.

38. Ellison, "*An American Dilemma:* A Review," 339.

39. For discussions of folk authenticity in vernacular theory, see Nicholls, *Conjuring the Folk,* 4–7; Baker, *Modernism and the Harlem Renaissance,* 68; Fuss, *Essentially Speaking,* 90; and Kelley, *Race Rebels,* chapters 1–3. For postcolonial critiques of modernity and the vernacular, see Chakrabarty, "Postcoloniality and the Artifice of History," 20–21; Spivak, "Can the Subaltern Speak," 271–313; Scott, *Weapons of the Weak,* 1–27.

40. Kelley, "Notes on Deconstructing 'The Folk,'" 1400–1408, quotation on 1402.

41. Ellison, "Editorial Comment" (1942), i.

42. Wright, *12 Million Black Voices,* 147.

43. Lucy, "'Flying Home,'" 257–77; Nicholls, *Conjuring the Folk,* 2–19; Reilly, "Richard Wright Preaches the Nation," 116–19.

44. For a discussion the influence of these policies on Ellison, see Henderson, "Transforming Action," 103–20; Jackson, *Ralph Ellison,* 304–25.

45. Ellison, "Editorial Comment," *Negro Quarterly* (1943), 301. See also Lucy, "'Flying Home,'" 258–75.

46. Ellison, "An American Dilemma: A Review," 337.

47. Schryer, *Fantasies of the New Class,* 57–58.

48. Warren, *So Black and Blue,* 70.

49. Foley, "Ralph Ellison as Proletarian Journalist," 552.

50. Crable, *Kenneth Burke and Ralph Ellison,* 98.

51. Ellison, "On Initiation Rites and Power," 524–25.

52. Ellison, "Ellison: Exploring the Life of a Not So Visible Man," 247.

53. Ellison, "An Interview with Ralph Ellison," 91.

54. Ellison, "Five Writers and Their African Ancestors," 67.

55. Ellison, "The Art of Fiction," 9–10.

56. Ellison, Letter to Albert Murray (June 2, 1957), *Trading Twelves,* 166.

57. Ellison, "Indivisible Man," 377.

58. Ellison, "Indivisible Man," 527.

59. Ellison, "Ellison: Exploring the Life of a Not So Visible Man," 249.

60. Ellison, "The Art of Fiction," 11.

61. See Maier, "Tell It Like It Is, Baby," 24–42.

62. Jackson, *Ralph Ellison,* 180–81. For a discussion of the complications inscribed in Ellison's longstanding intellectual engagement with Hemingway, see Hochman, "Ellison's Hemingways," especially 513–27.

63. Ellison, "The Essential Ellison," 363. See also Henderson, "Transforming Action," 136.

64. Parker and Herenden, "KB and MC," 97; Skodnick, "CounterGridlock," 16. For a more expansive discussion focusing on Kenneth Burke's thinking during this time, see George and Selzer, *Kenneth Burke in the 1930s,* 1–57, 141–80.

65. Ellison, "The Essential Ellison," 364. See also Maier, "Tell It Like It Is, Baby," 52–55. For assessments of the intellectual influences and relationship between Ellison and Burke, see Parrish, "Ralph Ellison, Kenneth Burke, and the Form of Democracy," 117–30; Eddy, *The Rites of Identity* 95–113; Albrecht, "Saying Yes and Saying No," 50–60; O'Meally, *The Craft of Ralph Ellison* 73, 78, 161; Genter, "Toward a Theory of Rhetoric," 193–200; Pease, "Ralph Ellison and Kenneth Burke," 65–74; Arac, "Toward a Critical Genealogy of the U.S. Discourse of Identity," 200–211; Crable, *Ralph Ellison and Kenneth Burke at the Roots of the Racial Divide,* 79–111.

66. Ellison, Letter to Richard Wright, August 24, 1946, *The Selected Letters of Ralph Ellison,* 222.

67. Ellison, "Remembering Richard Wright," 670.

68. Ellison, Letter to Kenneth Burke, November 23, 1945, *The Selected Letters of Ralph Ellison,* 204.

69. Ellison, "The Essential Ellison," 373. See also Henderson, "Transforming Action," 93–100.

70. Henderson, "Transforming Action," 93–97; Denning, *The Cultural Front,* 1–50, 96–114, 200–229.

71. Qtd. in George and Selzer, *Kenneth Burke in the 1930s,* 202.

72. Rampersad, *Ralph Ellison,* 90; Thompson qtd. in Naison, *Communists in Harlem during the Depression,* 218; Jackson, *Ralph Ellison,* 367–68.

73. Ellison, "An Interview with Ralph Ellison," 97.

74. Qtd. in Deutsch, "Ellison's Early Fiction," 53.

75. George and Selzer, *Kenneth Burke in the 1930s,* 5.

76. Burke, *Attitudes toward History,* 263.

77. Ellison, *Flying Home and Other Stories,* xxxviii. See also Henderson, *Transforming Action,* 120–25, for a discussion of Ellison's early stories in the broader context of social action.

2. THE GOLDEN AGE, TIME PAST

1. Yaffe, *Fascinating Rhythm,* 73.

2. Yaffe, *Fascinating Rhythm,* 68.

3. Weeks, "Sound and Meaning," 163–65.

4. Bell, "The Embrace of Entropy," 23.

5. Brody, "Why Did Ralph Ellison Despise Modern Jazz"; Rampersad, *Ralph Ellison,* 419–20.

6. Ellison, "'My Strength Comes from Louis Armstrong,'" 275.

7. O'Meally, *The Craft of Ralph Ellison,* 169.

8. Ellison's musical opinions have been seen from numerous perspectives, though much of the attention addresses in some way the relationship between Black modernism and literary aesthetics to what Ellison so often says about chaos and complexity. See, for example, Moten, *In the Break,* 63–73; Bell, "The Embrace of Entropy, 21–45; and Anderson, "Ralph Ellison's Music Lessons," 85–101.

9. Ellison, *The Selected Letters of Ralph Ellison,* 531; Rampersad, *Ralph Ellison,* 355–56.

10. Ellison, *The Selected Letters of Ralph Ellison,"* 530, 531. See also Pinkerton, "Ralph Ellison's Righteous Riffs," 195–200.

11. Ellison, "Harlem Is Nowhere," 325.

12. Ellison, "On Bird, Bird-Watching and Jazz," 259.

13. Ellison, "On Bird, Bird-Watching and Jazz," 259.

14. Ellison, "On Bird, Bird-Watching and Jazz," 259.

15. Ellison, "On Bird, Bird-Watching and Jazz," 264.

16. Ostendorf, "Ralph Waldo Ellison," 113.

17. Ellison, *The Selected Letters of Ralph Ellison,* 491.

18. Yaffe, *Fascinating Rhythm,* 65–81.

19. Ellison, "Interview with Ralph Ellison," 261.

20. Pinkerton, "Ralph Ellison's Righteous Riffs," 187.

21. Ellison, "The Charlie Christian Story," 270.

22. For a discussion of performance, bebop as a response to modernity, migration, and cultural dislocation, and Ellison's critique of the music that supplanted the music of his youth, see Maier, "'Tell It Like It Is, Baby,'" 93–127. See also Pinkerton, "Ralph Ellison's Righteous Riffs," 195–200; Anderson, "Ralph Ellison's Music Lessons," 94–101; and Habig, "Politicizing Poetics, Narrative Syncopations, and Jazz Aesthetics," 99–100, 224–26.

23. Anderson, "Ralph Ellison's Music Lessons," 87.

24. Anderson, "Ralph Ellison's Music Lessons," 99.

25. Ellison, "Blues People," 286–87.

26. Ellison, "Blues People," 285.

27. O'Meally, ed., "Introduction to 'Blues People,'" *Living with Music,* 120.

28. Von Eschen, *Satchmo Blows Up the World,* 61–62.

29. Riccardi, *What a Wonderful World,* 194; Von Eschen, *Satchmo Blows Up the World,* 68–71; Nocera, "Louis Armstrong, the Real Ambassador."

30. Ellison, "Homage to Duke Ellington on His Birthday," 81.

31. Ellison, "The World and the Jug," 160.

32. Ellison, *Three Days before the Shooting…,* 717.

33. See Pinkerton, "Ralph Ellison's Righteous Riffs," 198; Bell, "The Embrace of Entropy," 21–45.

34. Pinkerton, "Ralph Ellison's Righteous Riffs," 187.

35. Neal, "Ralph Ellison's Zoot Suit," 116.

36. Pinkerton, "Ralph Ellison's Righteous Riffs," 189.

37. Bradley, *Ralph Ellison in Progress,* 34.

38. Ellison, "Hidden Name and Complex Fate," 203.

39. Ellison, "That Same Pain," 73–74.

40. Ellison, "A Completion of Personality," 295. See also Jackson, *Ralph Ellison,* 178–81, 186–87, 188; and Hochman, "Ellison's Hemingways," 517.

41. Hochman, "Ellison's Hemingways," 516.

42. Ellison, "Society, Morality and the Novel," 716; Jackson, *Ralph Ellison,* 146–47. See also Hochman, "Ellison's Hemingways," 513.

43. Ellison, *Invisible Man,* 577.

44. Ellison, "Recent Negro Fiction," 25.

45. Ellison, "The Golden Age, Time Past," 245. See also Hochman, "Ellison's Hemingways," 513–21.

46. Ellison, "Hidden Name and Complex Fate," 205.

47. Ellison, "Hidden Name and Complex Fate," 205.

48. Ellison, "Change the Joke and Slip the Yoke," 107.

49. Ellison, "The World and the Jug," 160.

50. Ellison, "Indivisible Man," 360.

51. Ellison, "The Charlie Christian Story," 267.

52. Ellison, "Homage to William L. Dawson," 442.

53. Ellison, "The World and the Jug," 185.

54. Baker, "Failed Prophet and Falling Stock."

55. Ellison, "Living with Music," 230.

56. Murray, "Improvisation and the Creative Process," 112.

57. Ellison, "Richard Wright's Blues," 129.

58. Douglass, *Narrative of the Life of Frederick Douglass,* 20.

59. Douglass, *Narrative of the Life of Frederick Douglass,* 20.

60. Douglass, *Narrative of the Life of Frederick Douglass,* 20–21.

61. Ellison, *Invisible Man,* 381.

62. Messmer, "Trumpets, Horns, and Typewriters," 589.

63. Ellison, "The Art of Fiction," 10.

64. Du Bois, *The Souls of Black Folk,* 7.

65. Du Bois, *The Souls of Black Folk,* 128.

66. Cruz, *Culture on the Margins,* 6. See also 19–98 for a discussion of the relationship between Black music and cultural authenticity.

67. Ellison, "Living with Music," 133–35. See Weheliye, "'I Am I Be,'" especially 99–114, for a discussion of Ellison's relationship to technological production.

3. PERSONAL VISION, LIVING CULTURE

1. Rice, *Ralph Ellison and the Politics of the Novel,* 58.

2. Rice, *Ralph Ellison and the Politics of the Novel,* 44.

3. Neal, "Ellison's Zoot Suit," 122.

4. Neal, "Ellison's Zoot Suit," 122.

5. Jackson, *Ralph Ellison,* 161–348, discusses Ellison's decade-long preparation from his arrival in New York City in 1936 through the investigation of the House Committee on Un-American Activities (HUAC) and Senator Joseph McCarthy's anti-communist activities.

6. See Foley, *Wrestling with the Left,* 27–149, and "Ralph Ellison as Proletarian Journalist," 527–46, for readings of Ellison's association with the Left during the years between 1938 and 1944; Rampersad, *Ralph Ellison,* 52–198, and Jackson, *Ralph Ellison,* 198–303, for the context of Ellison's apprentice years.

7. Neal, "The Black Arts Movement," 29.

8. Neal, "The Black Arts Movement," 30.

9. Jones and Neal, eds., *Black Fire,* 652.

10. Jones and Neal, eds., *Black Fire,* 640.

11. Jones and Neal, eds., *Black Fire,* 654.

12. Jones and Neal, eds., *Black Fire,* 656.

13. Neal, "Ellison's Zoot Suit," 105.

14. Quoted in Rampersad, *Ralph Ellison,* 549.

15. See *Black World,* December 1970 issue, devoted to "Ralph Ellison: His Literary Works and Status"; Ellison, "Indivisible Man," 357–99.

16. Corry, "An American Novelist Who Sometimes Teaches."

17. Ellison, "Haverford Statement," 436.

18. Ellison, "Haverford Statement," 436.

19. Ellison, "Haverford Statement," 433.

20. Ellison, "Transcript of the American Academy Conference on the Negro American," 414, qtd. in Sundquist, "We dreamed a dream," 108–9.

21. Ellison, "Transcript of the American Academy Conference on the Negro American," 408, 409, 437.

22. Ellison, Introduction, *Shadow and Act,* 56.

23. Ellison, "Study and Experience," 327.

24. Ellison, "Study and Experience," 326.

25. Ellison, "Study and Experience," 327.

26. Ellison, "Study and Experience," 328.

27. Ellison, "Introduction to the Thirtieth-Anniversary Edition of *Invisible Man,*" 486.

28. Ellison, "The Novel as a Function of American Democracy," 768.

29. Morel, ed., *Ralph Ellison and the Raft of Hope,* 3; Rice, *Ralph Ellison and the Politics of the Novel,* 140.

30. Ellison, "The Art of Fiction," 221; Morel, ed., *Ralph Ellison and the Raft of Hope,* 5–6.

31. Ellison, "Brave Words for a Startling Occasion," 153.

32. Ellison, "Introduction to the Thirtieth-Anniversary Edition of *Invisible Man,*" 484.

33. Ellison, "Introduction to the Thirtieth-Anniversary Edition of *Invisible Man,*" 482.

34. Parrish, *Ralph Ellison and the Genius of America,* 131n1; Posnock, *Color and Culture,* 9; Allen, *Talking to Strangers,* 27.

35. Allen, *Talking to Strangers,* 45–46; see also 18–19, 27–31; Parrish, *Ralph Ellison and the Genius of America,* 128–40, especially 130.

36. Ralph Ellison Papers, Manuscripts, Library of Congress, box 108, folder 6; box 110, folder 22; box 108, folder 5.

37. *Time,* "Black America 1970."

38. Rampersad, *Ralph Ellison,* 412–69; Conner, "Reading Ralph Ellison," 149; Parrish, "Ralph Ellison, Finished and Unfinished," 648, and *Ralph Ellison and the Genius of America,* 42–44.

39. Spillers, "Ellison's 'Usable Past,'" 147, 148.

40. Bloom, *Genius,* 808. See also Parrish, *Ralph Ellison and the Genius of America,* 66–69.

41. Parrish, *Ralph Ellison and the Genius of America,* 67–69; Rampersad, *Ralph Ellison,* 442–69, 506–10.

42. Ellison, "The World and the Jug," 185.

43. Ellison, "The World and the Jug," 184. In his introduction to the essay in *Shadow and Act,* 155, Ellison notes that the essay actually combines a piece he published in the *New Leader* on December 9, 1963, as "The World and the Jug" and a piece entitled "A Rejoinder," which he published in the *New Leader* on February 3, 1964.

44. Ellison, "Alain Locke," 446.

45. Ellison, "That Same Pain, That Same Pleasure," 63.

46. Ellison, Introductory note to "Twentieth-Century Fiction and the Black Mask of Humanity," 81.

47. Ellison, "Richard Wright's Blues," 139.

48. Ellison, "Living with Music," 236; Rampersad, *Ralph Ellison,* 386–88. Ellison, "On Bird, Bird-Watching and Jazz," 256–386, and "Blues People," 278–87.

49. Ellison, "The Way It Is," 318.

50. Ellison, "*An American Dilemma:* A Review," 340.

51. Ellison, "Remembering Jimmy," 277. See also Bone, "Ralph Ellison and the Uses of Imagination," 39–43.

52. Covo, *The Blinking Eye,* 12, 13, 14.

53. Killens, "Review of *Invisible Man.*"

54. Covo, *The Blinking Eye,* 19.

55. Neal, "The Black Writer's Role," 10.

56. Jones and Neal, eds. *Black Fire,* 652.

57. Ellison, "Study and Experience," 330.

58. Neal, "The Black Writer's Role," 11.

59. Neal, "The Black Writer's Role," 11.

60. There are several writers whose work was regularly associated with New Criticism. See Blackmur, *The Lion and the Honeycomb;* Brooks, *The Well-Wrought Urn* (especially "Gray's Storied Urn," 96–113; "Keats' Sylvan Historian: History without Footnotes," 139–52; and "The Heresy of Paraphrase," 176–96); Cleanth Brooks and Robert Penn Warren, *Understanding Fiction* (especially the section "What Theme Reveals," 286–358); and Wimsatt, *The Verbal Icon* (especially "The Intentional Fallacy," 3–18; "The Affective Fallacy," 21–39; and "Explication as Criticism," 235–51).

61. Jones, "The Myth of a 'Negro Literature,'" in *Home,* 105–15. See also Covo, *The Blinking Eye,* 27–28.

62. Jones, "The Myth of a 'Negro Literature,'" in *Home,* 113.

63. Jones, "The Myth of a 'Negro Literature,'" in *Home,* 114.

64. Jones and Neal, eds., "Afterword" in *Black Fire,* 638–47.

65. Jones and Neal, eds., "Afterword" in *Black Fire,* 652.

66. Ellison, "Five Writers and Their African Ancestors," 69.

67. Smethurst, *Brick City Vanguard,* 60.

68. Smethurst, *Brick City Vanguard,* 86.

69. Mackey, "The Changing Same," 359.

70. Jones, "Introduction," in *Blues People,* ix–x.

71. Jones, *Blues People,* 219. See also Nealton, "Refraining, Becoming-Black," 83–95.

72. Jones, *Black Music,* 38. See also Nealton, "Refraining, Becoming-Black," 88.

73. Johnson, "Hear Me Talkin' to Ya," 2, qtd. in Nealton, "Refraining, Becoming-Black," 90. For a discussion of improvisation, primitivism, and its implications as a point of comparison for African American culture, see Berliner, *Thinking in Jazz,* especially 1–20, 63–95; Gioia, "Jazz and the Primitivist Myth" in *The Imperfect Art,* 19–50.

74. Ellison, *Invisible Man,* 190; Wright, *Shadowing Ralph Ellison,* 24.

75. Ellison, "Blues People," 279.

76. Ellison, "Blues People," 279.

77. Ellison, "Blues People," 286.

78. Ellison, "Indivisible Man," 386.

79. Ellison, "Indivisible Man," 398.

80. Neal, "Ellison's Zoot Suit," 109.

81. Rowell, "An Interview with Larry Neal," 21–22.

82. Qtd. in Baker, "Critical Change and Blues Continuity," 78.

83. Ellison, "A Very Stern Discipline," 748.

84. Ellison, "A Very Stern Discipline," 748; Neal, "Ellison's Zoot Suit," 111.

85. Neal, "Ellison's Zoot Suit," 111–13.

86. Neal, "Ellison's Zoot Suit" 112.

87. Corry, "An American Novelist Who Sometimes Teaches."

88. Ellison, "A Very Stern Discipline," 733.

89. Ellison, "A Very Stern Discipline," 746; Neal, "Ellison's Zoot Suit," 110. See also Foley, *Wrestling with the Left,* especially 109–49, for an examination of Ellison's association with and subsequent repudiation of leftist politics.

90. Ellison, "Alain Locke," 441.

91. Wright, *Shadowing Ralph Ellison,* 67–77; O'Brien, *Interviews with Black Writers,* 69–75; Ellison, "Five Writers and Their African Ancestors, 86.

92. Corry, "An American Novelist Who Sometimes Teaches."

4. IN THE SHADOW OF DEMOCRACY

1. Ellison, "Hidden Name and Complex Fate," 194; see 195–97 for Ellison's extended discussion of growing up in Oklahoma with a combination of names tied "so ironically with my own experience as a writer" (194) that caused "no end of trouble" (195).

2. Morel, "In a Strange Country," 252.

3. Turner, "Awakening to Race," 657.

4. von Rautenfeld, "Thinking for Thousands," 184. For more considered examinations of Emerson's voluminous thoughts about democracy and individualism, see Cavell, *Conditions Handsome and Unhandsome,* 33–63; Gougeon, *Virtue's Hero,* especially 1–23, 24–40, 86–137, 250–336; Kateb, "Self-Reliance and the Life of the Mind," in *Emerson and Self-Reliance,* 1–36; and Lopez, *Emerson and Power,* 19–52, 163–89.

5. Emerson, "Self-Reliance," *The Complete Works of Ralph Waldo Emerson* 2: 54, 55–56; Shklar, "Emerson and the Inhibitions of Democracy," 603.

6. Emerson, "Representative Men: Uses of Great Men," *The Complete Works of Ralph Waldo Emerson* 4: 616.

7. von Rautenfeld, "Thinking for Thousands," 187; Emerson, "Representative Men: Montaigne; or, the Skeptic," *The Complete Works of Ralph Waldo Emerson* 4: 696.

8. Emerson, "Essays I: Spiritual Laws," *The Complete Works of Ralph Waldo Emerson* 2: 315.

9. Tocqueville, "Political Consequences of the Social State of the Anglo-Americans," *Democracy in America* (2012), vol. 1, pt. 1, chap. 3: 89.

10. Tocqueville, *Democracy in America* (1969), 506. Qtd. in Patel, *Emergent U.S. Literatures,* 77.

11. Tocqueville, "Of Individualism in Democratic Countries," *Democracy in America* (2012), vol. 2, pt. 2, chap. 2: 884. See also Wolin, *Tocqueville between Two Worlds,* 343–45.

12. Emerson, "Essays II: New England Reformers," *The Complete Works of Ralph Waldo Emerson* 3: 267. For discussions of the ideas that led to the evolution of Emerson's thoughts about "individuality" and "individualism," see Bercovitch, "Emerson, Individualism, and Liberal Dissent," in *The Rites of Assent*, 331–39; Patel, "Emersonian Strategies," 440–79; Sandel, *Liberalism and the Limits of Justice*, 7–11, 50–60, 95–103, 133–35; and Taylor, "Cross-Purposes: The Liberal-Communitarian Debate," 159–82.

13. Hurth, *Between Faith and Unbelief*, 143.

14. Emerson, *Emerson in His Journals*, 19, qtd. in Patel, "Emersonian Strategies," 461–62.

15. Nadel, *Invisible Criticism*, 104–23; and Lee, "Ellison's *Invisible Man*," 331–32.

16. Emerson, *The Journals and Miscellaneous Notebooks of Ralph Waldo Emerson* 2: 43; Lee, "Ellison's *Invisible Man*," 333–34.

17. West, *The American Evasion of Philosophy*, 31, 34.

18. Nadel, *Invisible Criticism*, 122.

19. Ellison, "Twentieth-Century Fiction and the Mask of Humanity," 88, qtd. in Nadel, *Invisible Criticism*, 111.

20. Ellison, *Invisible Man*, 41.

21. Ellison, "The World and the Jug," 178.

22. Watts, *Heroism and the Black Intellectual*, 49. See also Rampersad, *Ralph Ellison*, 385, 402, 444; Foley, *Wrestling with the Left*, 27–67, 281–324; Jackson, *Ralph Ellison*, 198–236.

23. Ellison, "A Special Message to Subscribers," 353–55.

24. Emerson, *The Journals and Miscellaneous Notebooks of Ralph Waldo Emerson* 2: 48; 10: 357; 11: 376; 13: 286. For a discussion of Emerson's thoughts on race, see Lee, "Reading Race In(to) the American Renaissance," 104–18.

25. West, *The American Evasion of Philosophy*, 10.

26. Ellison, "Twentieth-Century Fiction and the Black Mask of Humanity," 84.

27. Ellison, "On Initiation Rites and Power," 525.

28. Ellison, "Twentieth-Century Fiction and the Black Mask of Humanity," 90–91.

29. Ellison, *Invisible Man*, 45.

30. Ellison, *Invisible Man*, 143.

31. Ellison, "Twentieth-Century Fiction and the Mask of Humanity," 88.

32. Ellison, *Invisible Man*, 194.

33. Ellison, *Invisible Man*, 37, 41.

34. Ellison, *Invisible Man*, 41.

35. Nadel, *Invisible Criticism*, 116, 118; Albrecht, "Saying Yes and Saying No," 46–50. See also see Lee, "Reading Race In(to) the American Renaissance," 104–40.

36. Ellison, "A Very Stern Discipline," 732.

37. Ellison, "Working Notes for *Invisible Man*, 343.

38. Mumford, *The Golden Day*, 43.

39. Ellison, Letter to Alan Nadel, January 27, 1984, *The Selected Letters of Ralph Ellison*, 818.

40. Nadel, *Invisible Criticism*, 85–103; Albrecht, "Saying Yes and Saying No," 47–50.

41. Ellison, *Invisible Man*, 57.

42. Remnick, "Visible Man."

43. Warren, *So Black and Blue,* 16; qtd. in Hayman, "'Black Is . . . Black Ain't,'" 127.

44. Qtd. in Remnick, "Visible Man."

45. Ellison, "What America Would Be Like Without Blacks," 587.

46. Ellison, "What America Would Be Like Without Blacks," 584.

47. Ellison, "What America Would Be Like Without Blacks," 586.

48. Ellison, "The Little Man at Chehaw Station," 508–9.

49. Ellison, "What America Would Be Like Without Blacks," 586.

50. Ellison, "What America Would Be Like Without Blacks," 583.

51. Crenshaw, "Mapping the Margins," 1241–99; Fukuyama, *Identity,* especially 91–123. For an examination of Ellison's thoughts on race as articulating a forward-looking model of Black subjectivity, see Hayman, "Black Is . . . Black Ain't," 127–52.

52. Ellison, "Perspective of Literature," 780; Turner, "Awakening to Race," 664.

53. Ellison, "The Little Man at Chehaw Station," 504.

5. NEGRO-AMERICANIZING THE NOVEL

1. Bradley, *Ellison in Progress,* 175.

2. Ellison, *Trading Twelves,* 21; Ellison, "General Introduction," *Three Days before the Shooting . . .,* xviii.

3. See Callahan, "General Introduction," *Three Days before the Shooting . . .,* xvi–xxiii.

4. Callahan, "General Introduction," *Three Days before the Shooting . . .,* xvi.

5. Ellison, "Introduction," *Shadow and Act,* 56.

6. Ellison, "Introduction," *Shadow and Act,* 56.

7. Booth, "The Color of Memory," 686.

8. Ellison, *The Selected Letters of Ralph Ellison,* 291; Ellison, *Trading Twelves,* 21.

9. For an extensive recitation of Ellison's working style and the editorial decisions made to craft *Juneteenth* for publication, see Callahan, "The Making of Ralph Ellison's *Juneteenth,* 175–89. For a discussion of Ellison's embrace of technology and its effect on his impulse to revise, see Bradley, *Ralph Ellison in Progress,* especially 21–56.

10. Bradley, *Ralph Ellison in Progress,* 77; Parrish, "Ralph Ellison's Novel without Qualities," 105–13; Allen in *Talking to Strangers,* 26–31.

11. Parrish, "Ralph Ellison's Novel without Qualities," 92.

12. Ellison, "An Interview with Ralph Ellison," 87–88. Rampersad discusses Ellison's relation to Sprague in *Ralph Ellison,* 75–76, 298–99.

13. Ellison, "Letter to Morteza D. Sprague, May 19, 1954," *The Selected Letters of Ralph Ellison,* 360, qtd. in Rampersad, *Ralph Ellison,* 298; Warren, *So Black and Blue,* 1; and Harriss, "Race and the Religious Unconscious," 167–68.

14. Ralph Ellison was neither alone in his anxieties about *Brown v. Board of Education* nor in his reservations about its potential cultural implications. There has been no shortage of assessments from various viewpoints scrutinizing the NAACP's Legal Defense and Education Fund's focus on desegregation that culminated in *Brown v. Board of Education.* Many of these studies focus on process, implementation, and cultural implication: Daugherity and Bolton, eds.,

With All Deliberate Speed; Jackson, *Science for Segregation;* Sarat, ed., *Race, Law, and Culture;* Patterson, *Brown v. Board of Education;* Bell, *Silent Covenants;* Allen, *Talking to Strangers;* Hockett, *A Storm over This Court;* Balkin, *What* Brown v. Board of Education *Should Have Said;* Klarman, Brown v. Board of Education *and the Civil Rights Movement;* Salisbury and Lartigue, eds., *Educational Freedom in Urban America;* Day, *The Southern Manifesto;* Cobb, *The* Brown *Decision, Jim Crow, and Southern Identity;* Clotfelter, *After* Brown; and Jarausch and Klarman, eds., *From Jim Crow to Civil Rights.*

15. Ellison, "A Conversation with Ralph Ellison," 216, qtd. in Parrish, "Ralph Ellison's Novel without Qualities," 99.

16. Warren, *So Black and Blue,* 19–20.

17. Allen, *Talking to Strangers,* 25–49; Warren, *So Black and Blue,* 19–20. See also Parrish, "Ralph Ellison's Novel without Qualities," 15–18, 26; Rampersad, *Ralph Ellison,* 298–300; Bradley, *Ralph Ellison in Progress,* 89–118; and Harriss, "Race and the Religious Unconscious," 167–99.

18. McPherson, "Indivisible Man," 29. The passage quoted is from an epilogue that McPherson appended and delivered at the first Langston Hughes Festival at the City College of New York on April 11, 1984. The epilogue did not appear in the original publication of the article.

19. Bradley, *Ralph Ellison in Progress,* 91.

20. Rampersad, *Ralph Ellison,* 225–26.

21. Bradley, *Ralph Ellison in Progress,* 91.

22. Ellison, "Five Writers and Their African Ancestors," 68, qtd. in Harriss, "Race and the Religious Unconscious," 197.

23. Ellison, "An Interview with Ralph Ellison," 96.

24. Parrish, "Ralph Ellison's *Three Days,*" 197.

25. Parrish, "Ralph Ellison's *Three Days,*" 203.

26. Parrish, "Ralph Ellison's *Three Days,*" 202.

27. Ellison, "An Interview with Ralph Ellison," 97.

28. Ellison, *Three Days before the Shooting…,* 972.

29. Ellison, "A Completion of Personality," 820; Ellison, *Three Days before the Shooting…,* 973.

30. Ellison, *Juneteenth,* 356.

31. Ellison, *Three Days before the Shooting…,* 527.

32. Ellison, "A Completion of Personality," 795.

33. Ellison, *Three Days before the Shooting…,* 86.

34. Ellison, *Three Days before the Shooting…,* 140.

35. Ellison, "Haverford Statement," 429–30.

36. Ellison, *Three Days before the Shooting…,* 174.

37. Alison, "Writing Underground," 339.

38. Deleuze and Guattari, *A Thousand Plateaus,* 25.

39. Ellison, *Three Days before the Shooting…,* 100.

40. Ellison, *Three Days before the Shooting…,* 101.

41. Ellison, *Three Days before the Shooting…,* 102.

42. Ellison, *Three Days before the Shooting…,* 103.

43. Moore, "The Myth of the Writer's Block," 224.

44. Murray, "Ralph Ellison Remembered," 40.

45. Ellison, "A Completion of Personality," 792.

46. Ellison, *Trading Twelves*, 222.

47. Ellison, "A Conversation with Ralph Ellison," 216.

48. Ellison, *Three Days before the Shooting...*, 313.

49. Ellison, *Three Days before the Shooting...*, 239.

50. Ellison, *Three Days before the Shooting...*, 472.

51. Ellison, *Three Days before the Shooting...*, 975. These notes are contained in the Ellison Papers in the Library of Congress, box 140, folder 6.

52. Ellison, *Three Days before the Shooting...*, 527.

53. Ellison, *Three Days before the Shooting...*, 662.

54. Ellison, *Three Days before the Shooting...*, 850.

BIBLIOGRAPHY

Albrecht, James. "Saying Yes and Saying No: Individualist Ethics in Ellison, Burke, and Emerson." *PMLA* 114, no. 1 (January 1999): 46–63.

Alison, Cheryl. "Writing Underground: Ralph Ellison and the Novel." *Twentieth-Century Literature* 63, no. 3 (September 2017): 329–58.

Allen, Danielle S. *Talking to Strangers: Anxieties of Citizenship since* Brown v. Board of Education. Chicago: University of Chicago Press, 2004.

Anderson, Paul Allen. "Ralph Ellison's Music Lessons." In *The Cambridge Companion to Ralph Ellison,* ed. Ross Posnock, 82–103. Cambridge, U.K.: Cambridge University Press, 2005.

Arac, Jonathan. "Toward a Critical Genealogy of the U.S. Discourse of Identity: *Invisible Man* after Fifty Years." *boundary 2* 30 no. 2 (Summer 2003): 195–216.

Austin, Sarat. *Race, Law, and Culture: Reflections on* Brown v. Board of Education. New York: Oxford University Press, 1994.

Baker, Houston A., Jr. "Critical Change and Blues Continuity: An Essay on the Criticism of Larry Neal." *Callaloo* 23 (Winter 1985): 70–84.

———. "Failed Prophet and Falling Stock: Why Ralph Ellison Was Never Avant-Garde." *Stanford Humanities Review* 7, no. 1 (1999). web.stanford.edu/group/SHR/7-1/html /baker.html.

———. *Modernism and the Harlem Renaissance.* Chicago: University of Chicago Press, 1987.

Balkin, Jack. *What* Brown v. Board of Education *Should Have Said: The Nation's Top Legal Experts Rewrite America's Landmark Civil Rights Decision.* New York: New York University Press, 2001.

Bell, Derrick. *Silent Covenants:* Brown v. Board of Education *and the Unfulfilled Hopes for Racial Reform.* New York: Oxford University Press, 2004.

Bell, Kevin. "The Embrace of Entropy: Ralph Ellison and the Freedom Principle of Jazz Invisible." *boundary 2* 30 no. 2 (Summer 2003): 21–45.

Benston, Kimberly W., ed. *Speaking for You: The Vision of Ralph Ellison.* Washington, D.C.: Howard University Press, 1987.

Bercovitch, Sacvan. *The Rites of Assent: Transformations in the Symbolic Construction of America*. New York: Routledge, 1993.

Berliner, Paul F. *Thinking in Jazz: The Infinite Art of Improvisation*. Chicago: University of Chicago Press, 1994.

Black World. "Ralph Ellison: His Literary Works and Status." Vol. 20, no. 2 (December 1970).

Blackmur, R. P. *The Lion and the Honeycomb: Essays in Solicitude and Critique*. New York: Harcourt Brace, 1955.

Bloom, Harold. *Genius: A Mosaic of the Hundred Exemplary Creative Minds*. New York: Warner, 2002.

Bone, Robert. "Ralph Ellison and the Uses of Imagination." *TriQuarterly* 6 (January 1, 1966): 39–54.

Bone, Robert, and Richard A. Courage. *The Muse in Bronzeville: African American Creative Expression in Chicago, 1932–1950*. New Brunswick, N.J.: Rutgers University Press, 2011.

Booth, James W. "The Color of Memory: Reading Race with Ralph Ellison." *Political Theory* 36, no. 5 (October 2008): 683–707.

Bradley, Adam. *Ralph Ellison in Progress: The Making and Unmaking of One Writer's Great American Novel*. New Haven, Conn.: Yale University Press, 2010.

Brody, Richard. "Why Did Ralph Ellison Despise Modern Jazz." *New Yorker*, March 20, 2014. www.newyorker.com/culture/richard-brody/why-did-ralph-ellison-despise -modern-jazz.

Brooks, Cleanth. *The Well-Wrought Urn: Studies in the Structure of Poetry*. New York: Reynal and Hitchcock, 1947.

——, and Robert Penn Warren. *Understanding Fiction*. New York: F. S. Crofts & Co., 1943.

Burke, Kenneth. *Attitudes toward History*. Los Altos, Calif.: Hermes Publications, 1959.

Callahan, John F. "General Introduction to *Three Days before the Shooting...*" In *Three Days before the Shooting...*, ed. Callahan, xv–xxix. New York: Modern Library, 2010.

——. "The Making of Ralph Ellison's *Juneteenth*." *Columbia* 36 (2002): 175–89.

Cavell, Stanley. *Conditions Handsome and Unhandsome: The Constitution of Emersonian Perfectionism*. Chicago: University of Chicago Press, 1990.

Chakrabarty, Dipesh. "Postcoloniality and the Artifice of History: Who Speaks for 'Indian' Pasts." *Representations* 37 (Winter 1992): 1–26.

Clotfelter, Charles T. *After Brown: The Rise and Retreat of School Desegregation*. Princeton, N.J.: Princeton University Press, 2004.

Cobb, James C. *The Brown Decision, Jim Crow, and Southern Identity*. Athens: University of Georgia Press, 2005.

Conner, Marc C. "Reading Ralph Ellison: A Hidden Name and Complex Fate." *South Atlantic Review* 73, no. 4 (Fall 2008): 146–53.

——— and Lucas E. Morel, eds. *The New Territory: Ralph Ellison and the Twenty-First Century*. Jackson: University of Mississippi Press, 2016.

Corry, John. "An American Novelist Who Sometimes Teaches." *New York Times*, November 20, 1966. movies2.nytimes.com/books/99/06/20/specials/ellison -teaches.html.

Covo, Jacqueline. *The Blinking Eye: Ralph Waldo Ellison and His American, French, German and Italian Critics, 1952–1971*. Metuchen, N.J.: Scarecrow Press, 1974.

Crable, Bryan. *Ralph Ellison and Kenneth Burke at the Roots of the Racial Divide*. Charlottesville: University of Virginia Press, 2012.

Crenshaw, Kimberlé Williams. "Mapping the Margins: Intersectionality, Identity Politics, and Violence Against Women of Color." *Stanford Law Review* 43 (July 1991): 1241–99.

Cruse, Harold. *The Crisis of the Negro Intellectual*. New York: Morrow, 1967.

Cruz, Jon. *Culture on the Margins: The Black Spiritual and the Rise of American Cultural Interpretation*. Princeton, N.J.: Princeton University Press, 1999.

Daugherity, Brian J., and Charles C. Bolton. *With All Deliberate Speed: Implementing Brown v. Board of Education*. Fayetteville: University of Arkansas Press, 2008.

Day, John Kyle. *The Southern Manifesto: Massive Resistance and the Fight to Preserve Segregation*. Jackson: University Press of Mississippi, 2014.

Deleuze, Giles, and Félix Guattari. *A Thousand Plateaus: Capitalism and Schizophrenia*. Trans. Brian Massumi. Minneapolis: University of Minnesota Press, 1987.

Denby, David. "Justice for Ralph Ellison." *New Yorker*, April 12, 2021. www.newyorker .com/books/page-turner/justice-for-ralph-ellison.

Denning, Michael. *The Cultural Front: The Laboring of American Culture in the Twentieth Century*. London: Verso, 1996.

Deutsch, Leonard J. "Ellison's Early Fiction." *Negro American Literature Forum* 7, no. 2 (Summer 1973): 53–59.

Dickstein, Morris. *Dancing in the Dark: A Cultural History of the Great Depression*. New York: W. W. Norton, 2009.

———. "Ralph Ellison, Race, and American Culture." *Raritan: A Quarterly Review* 18, no. 4 (Spring 1999): 30–50.

Dolinar, Brian. *The Black Cultural Front: Black Writers and Artists of the Depression Generation*. Jackson: University Press of Mississippi, 2012.

Douglass, Frederick. *Narrative of the Life of Frederick Douglass, An American Slave: Written by Himself*. Ed. John R. McKivigan, Peter P. Hinks, and Heather L. Kaufman. New Haven, Conn.: Yale University Press, 2016.

Du Bois, W. E. B. *The Souls of Black Folk*. Ed. Henry Louis Gates Jr., introd. Arnold Rampersad. New York: Oxford University Press, 2007.

Eddy, Beth. *The Rites of Identity: The Religious Naturalism and Cultural Criticism of Kenneth Burke and Ralph Ellison*. Princeton, N.J.: Princeton University Press, 2003.

Eliot, T. S. *Four Quartets.* New York: Harcourt, Brace and Company, 1943.

Ellison, Ralph. "Alain Locke." In *The Collected Essays of Ralph Ellison,* ed. and introd. Callahan, 443–51.

——. "*An American Dilemma: A Review.*" In *The Collected Essays of Ralph Ellison,* ed. and introd. Callahan, 328–40.

——. "The Art of Fiction: An Interview." By Alfred Chester and Vilma Howard. In *Conversations with Ralph Ellison,* ed. Graham and Singh, 6–19.

——. "Blues People." In *The Collected Essays of Ralph Ellison,* ed. and introd. Callahan, 278–87.

——. "Brave Words for a Startling Occasion." In *The Collected Essays of Ralph Ellison,* ed. and introd. Callahan, 151–54.

——. "Change the Joke and Slip the Yoke." In *The Collected Essays of Ralph Ellison,* ed. and introd. Callahan, 100–112.

——. "The Charlie Christian Story." In *The Collected Essays of Ralph Ellison,* ed. and introd. Callahan, 266–72.

——. *The Collected Essays of Ralph Ellison,* ed. and introd. John F. Callahan. New York: Modern Library, 2003.

——. "A Completion of Personality: A Talk with Ralph Ellison." By John Hersey. In *The Collected Essays of Ralph Ellison,* ed. and introd. Callahan, 787–821.

——. "A Conversation with Ralph Ellison." By Leon Forrest. In *Conversations with Ralph Ellison,* ed. Graham and Singh, 215–21.

——. *Conversations with Ralph Ellison,* ed. Maryemma Graham and Amritjit Singh. Jackson: University Press of Mississippi, 1995.

——. "Editorial Comment." *Negro Quarterly* 1, no. 1 (Summer 1942): i–v.

——. "Editorial Comment." *Negro Quarterly* 1, no 4 (Winter–Spring 1943): 295–302.

——. "Ellison: Exploring the Life of a Not So Visible Man." By Hollie I. West. In *Conversations with Ralph Ellison,* ed. Graham and Singh, 235–58.

——. "The Essential Ellison." By Ishmael Reed, Quincy Troupe, and Steve Cannon. In *Conversations with Ralph Ellison,* ed. Graham and Singh, 342–77.

——. "Five Writers and Their African Ancestors." By Harold Isaacs. In *Conversations with Ralph Ellison,* ed. Graham and Singh, 63–69.

——. "Flying Home." In *Flying Home and Other Stories,* ed. and introd. Callahan, 147–73.

——. *Flying Home and Other Stories,* ed. and introd. John F. Callahan. New York: Vintage Books, 1998.

——. "The Golden Age, Time Past." In *The Collected Essays of Ralph Ellison,* ed. and introd. Callahan, 235–49.

——. "The Great Migration." *New Masses,* December 2, 1941, 23–24.

——. "Harlem Is Nowhere." In *The Collected Essays of Ralph Ellison*, ed. and introd. Callahan, 320–27.

——. "Haverford Statement." In *The Collected Essays of Ralph Ellison*, ed. and introd. Callahan, 431–36.

——. "Hidden Name and Complex Fate: A Writer's Experience in the United States." In *The Collected Essays of Ralph Ellison*, ed. and introd. Callahan, 189–209.

——. "Homage to Duke Ellington on His Birthday." In *The Collected Essays of Ralph Ellison*, ed. and introd. Callahan, 680–87.

——. "Homage to William L. Dawson." In *The Collected Essays of Ralph Ellison*, ed. and introd. Callahan, 437–42.

——. "In a Strange Country." In *Flying Home and Other Stories*, ed. and introd. Callahan, 137–46.

——. "Indivisible Man." In *The Collected Essays of Ralph Ellison*, ed. and introd. Callahan, 357–99.

——. "Interview with Ralph Ellison." By Arlene Crewdson and Rita Thomson. In *Conversations with Ralph Ellison*, ed. Graham and Singh, 259–71.

——. "An Interview with Ralph Ellison." By Richard Kostelanetz. In *Conversations with Ralph Ellison*, ed. Graham and Singh, 87–97.

——. "Introduction," *Shadow and Act*. In *The Collected Essays of Ralph Ellison*, ed. and introd. Callahan, 49–60.

——. "Introduction to the Thirtieth-Anniversary Edition of *Invisible Man*." In *The Collected Essays of Ralph Ellison*, ed. and introd. Callahan, 473–89.

——. *Invisible Man*. New York: Random House, 1995.

——. *Juneteenth*. Ed. John F. Callahan. New York: Random House, 1999.

——. "The Little Man at Chehaw Station." In *The Collected Essays of Ralph Ellison*, ed. and introd. Callahan, 493–523.

——. "Living with Music." In *The Collected Essays of Ralph Ellison*, ed. and introd. Callahan, 227–36.

——. "'My Strength Comes from Louis Armstrong': Interview with Robert G. O'Meally, 1976." In *Living with Music*, ed. O'Meally, 265–88.

——. "The Novel as a Function of American Democracy." In *The Collected Essays of Ralph Ellison*, ed. and introd. Callahan, 759–69.

——. "On Bird, Bird-Watching and Jazz." In *The Collected Essays of Ralph Ellison*, ed. and introd. Callahan, 256–65.

——. "On Initiation Rites and Power: A Lecture at West Point." In *The Collected Essays of Ralph Ellison*, ed. and introd. Callahan, 524–45.

——. "Perspective of Literature." In *The Collected Essays of Ralph Ellison*, ed. and introd. Callahan, 770–85.

———. "Recent Negro Fiction." *New Masses,* August 5, 1941, 22–26.

———. "Remembering Jimmy." In *The Collected Essays of Ralph Ellison,* ed. and introd. Callahan, 273–77.

———. "Remembering Richard Wright." In *The Collected Essays of Ralph Ellison,* ed. and introd. Callahan, 663–79.

———. "Richard Wright's Blues." In *The Collected Essays of Ralph Ellison,* ed. and introd. Callahan, 128–44.

———. "Roscoe Dunjee and the American Language. In *The Collected Essays of Ralph Ellison,* ed. and introd. Callahan, 453–64.

———. *The Selected Letters of Ralph Ellison.* Ed. John F. Callahan and Marc C. Conner. New York: Random House, 2019.

———. "Society, Morality and the Novel." In *The Collected Essays of Ralph Ellison,* ed. and introd. Callahan, 698–731.

———. "A Special Message to Subscribers." In *The Collected Essays of Ralph Ellison,* ed. and introd. Callahan, 351–55.

———. "Study and Experience: An Interview with Ralph Ellison." By Robert B. Stepto and Michael S. Harper. In *Conversations with Ralph Ellison,* ed. Graham and Singh, 319–41.

———. "That Same Pain, That Same Pleasure." In *The Collected Essays of Ralph Ellison,* ed. and introd. Callahan, 63–80.

———. *Three Days before the Shooting....* Ed. John F. Callahan and Adam Bradley. New York: Modern Library, 2010.

———. *Trading Twelves.* Ed. Albert Murray and John F. Callahan. New York: Vintage, 2001.

———. "Transcript of the American Academy Conference on the Negro American—May 14–15." *Daedalus* 95, no. 1 (Winter 1966): 287–441.

———. "Twentieth-Century Fiction and the Black Mask of Humanity." In *The Collected Essays of Ralph Ellison,* ed. and introd. Callahan, 81–99.

———. "'A Very Stern Discipline.'" In *The Collected Essays of Ralph Ellison,* ed. and introd. Callahan, 730–58.

———. "The Way It Is." In *The Collected Essays of Ralph Ellison,* ed. and introd. Callahan, 310–19.

———. "What America Would Be Like Without Blacks." In *The Collected Essays of Ralph Ellison,* ed. and introd. Callahan, 581–88.

———. "Working Notes for *Invisible Man.*" In *The Collected Essays of Ralph Ellison,* ed. and introd. Callahan, 341–45.

———. "The World and the Jug." In *The Collected Essays of Ralph Ellison,* ed. and introd. Callahan, 155–88.

Emerson, Ralph Waldo. *The Complete Works of Ralph Waldo Emerson*. Ed. Edward Waldo Emerson. 12 vols. Boston: Houghton Mifflin, 1903–4.

———. *Emerson in His Journals*. Ed. Joel Porte. Cambridge, Mass.: Harvard University Press, 1982.

———. *The Journals and Miscellaneous Notebooks of Ralph Waldo Emerson*. Ed. William H. Gilman et al. 16 vols. Cambridge, Mass.: Harvard University Press, 1960–82.

Foley, Barbara. *Radical Representations: Politics and Form in U.S. Proletarian Fiction*. Durham, N.C.: Duke University Press, 1993.

———. "Ralph Ellison as Proletarian Journalist." *Science & Society* 62, no. 4 (Winter 1998–99): 537–56.

———. *Wrestling with the Left: The Making of Ralph Ellison's* Invisible Man. Durham, N.C.: Duke University Press, 2010.

Frazier, E. Franklin. "The Negro Middle Class and Desegregation." *Social Problems* 4, no. 4 (April 1957): 291–301.

Fukuyama, Francis. *Identity: The Demand for Dignity and the Politics of Resentment*. New York: Farrar, Straus and Giroux, 2018.

Fuss, Diana. *Essentially Speaking: Feminism, Nature, and Difference*. New York: Routledge, 1989.

Genter, Robert. "Toward a Theory of Rhetoric: Ralph Ellison, Kenneth Burke, and the Problem of Modernism." *Twentieth Century Literature* 48, no. 2 (Summer 2002): 191–214.

George, Ann, and Jack Selzer. *Kenneth Burke in the 1930s*. Columbia: University of South Carolina Press, 2007.

Gioia, Ted. *The Imperfect Art: Reflections on Jazz and Modern Culture*. New York: Oxford University Press, 1988.

Gougeon, Len. *Virtue's Hero: Emerson, Antislavery, and Reform*. Athens: University of Georgia Press, 1990.

Habig, Stewart. "Politicizing Poetics, Narrative Syncopations, and Jazz Aesthetics in Twentieth-Century American Literary Discourse." PhD diss., University of Tulsa, 2018.

Hanlon, Christopher. "Eloquence and 'Invisible Man.'" *College Literature* 32, no. 4 (Fall 2005): 74–98.

Harriss, Mathew Cooper. "Race and the Religious Unconscious: Ralph Ellison's Invisible Theology." PhD diss., University of Chicago, 2011.

Hayman, Casey. "'Black Is . . . Black Ain't': Ralph Ellison's Meta-Black Aesthetic and the 'End' of African American Literature." *American Studies* 54, no. 3 (2015): 127–52.

Henderson, Clark L. "Transforming Action: Kenneth Burke and Ralph Ellison Out of the 1930s." PhD diss., University of Pittsburgh, 2011.

Hochman, Brian. "Ellison's Hemingways." *African American Review* 42, no. 3–4 (Fall–Winter, 2008): 513–32.

Hockett, Jeffrey D. *A Storm over This Court: Law, Politics, and Supreme Court Decision Making in* Brown v. Board of Education. Charlottesville: University of Virginia Press, 2013.

Hurth, Elisabeth. *Between Faith and Unbelief: American Transcendentalists and the Challenge of Atheism.* Leiden: Brill, 2007.

Jackson, John P. *Science for Segregation: Race, Law, and the Case against* Brown v. Board of Education. New York: New York University Press, 2005.

Jackson, Lawrence. *Ralph Ellison: Emergence of Genius.* New York: John Wiley & Sons, 2002.

———. "Ralph Ellison, Sharpies, Rinehart, and Politics in *Invisible Man.*" *Massachusetts Review* 40, no. 1 (Spring 1999): 71–85.

Jarausch, Konrad H., and Michael J. Klarman. *From Jim Crow to Civil Rights: The Supreme Court and the Struggle for Racial Equality.* New York: Oxford University Press, 2004.

Johnson, Bruce. "Hear Me Talkin' to Ya: Problems of Jazz Discourse." *Popular Music* 12, no. 1 (January 1993): 1–12.

Jones, LeRoi. *Black Music.* New York: William Morrow and Co., 1969.

———. *Blues People: Negro Music in White America.* New York: William Morrow and Co., 1963.

———. *Home: Social Essays.* New York: William Morrow and Co., 1966.

Jones, LeRoi, and Larry Neal, eds. *Black Fire: An Anthology of Afro-American Writing.* New York: William Morrow and Co., 1968.

Kateb, George. *Emerson and Self-Reliance.* Thousand Oaks, Calif.: Sage Publications, 1995.

Keats, John. *Selected Letters of John Keats.* Rev. ed. Ed. Grant F. Scott. Cambridge, Mass.: Harvard University Press, 2002.

Kelley, Robin D. G. *Freedom Dreams: The Black Radical Imagination.* Boston: Beacon Press, 2002.

———. "Notes on Deconstructing 'The Folk.'" *American Historical Review* 97, no. 5 (December 1992): 1400–1408.

———. *Race Rebels: Culture, Politics, and the Black Working Class.* New York: Free Press, 1996.

Killens, John Oliver. "Review of *Invisible Man.*" In *Freedom,* editorial director Paul Robeson, editor Louis E. Burnham, vol. 2, no. 6 (June 1952). New York: Freedom Associates. Tamiment Library and Robert F. Wagner Labor Archives. hdl.handle.net/2333.1/bnzs7n8s.

Klarman, Michael J. Brown v. Board of Education *and the Civil Rights Movement: The Supreme Court and the Struggle for Racial Equality.* New York: Oxford University Press, 2004.

Lal, Barbara Ballis. "Black and Blue in Chicago: Robert E. Park's Perspective on Race Relations in Urban America, 1914–44." *British Journal of Sociology* 38, no. 4 (December 1987): 546–66.

Lawrence, D. H. "The Spirits of Place." In *Studies in Classic American Literature*. Garden City, N.Y.: Doubleday, 1953.

Lee, Kun Jong. Ellison's *Invisible Man:* Emersonianism Revised." *PMLA* 107, no. 2 (March 1992): 331–44.

———. "Reading Race In(to) the American Renaissance: A Study of Race in Emerson, Whitman, Melville, and Ellison." PhD diss., University of Texas at Austin, 1992.

Lepenies, Wolf. *Between Literature and Science: The Rise of Sociology.* Cambridge, U.K.: Cambridge University Press, 1988.

Locke, Alain, ed. *The New Negro: An Interpretation.* 1925. New York: Simon and Schuster, 1999.

Lopez, Michael. *Emerson and Power: Creative Antagonism in the Nineteenth Century.* DeKalb: Northern Illinois University Press, 1996.

Lorde, Audre. "The Master's Tools Will Never Dismantle the Master's House." In *Sister Outsider: Essays and Speeches,* 110–13. Berkeley, Calif.: Crossing Press, 1984.

Lucy, Robin. "'Flying Home': Ralph Ellison, Richard Wright, and the Black Folk during World War II." *Journal of American Folklore* 120, no. 477 (Summer 2007): 257–83.

Mackey, Nathaniel. "The Changing Same: Black Music in the Poetry of Amiri Baraka." *boundary 2* 6, no. 2 (Winter 1978): 355–86.

Maier, Brennan McDaniel. "Tell It Like It Is, Baby": The Intersection of Culture and Democracy in Ralph Ellison." PhD diss., Yale University, 2007.

Maxwell, William J. *New Negro, Old Left: African-American Writing and Communism Between the Wars.* New York: Columbia University Press, 1999.

McPherson, James Alan. "Indivisible Man." In *Speaking for You,* ed. Benston, 15–29.

Melville, Herman. *Moby-Dick; or, The Whale.* Edited, with Historical Note, by Harrison Hayford, Hershel Parker, and G. Thomas Tanselle. Evanston, Ill.: Northwestern University Press, 1988.

Messmer, David. "Trumpets, Horns, and Typewriters: A Call and Response between Ralph Ellison and Frederick Douglass." *African American Review* 45, no. 4 (Winter 2009): 589–604.

Moore, Kevin Christopher. "The Myth of Writer's Block: Imagining American Moral Realism." PhD diss., University of California, Los Angeles, 2013.

Morel, Lucas E., "'In a Strange Country': The Challenge of American Inclusion." In *The New Territory,* ed. Conner and Morel, 245–59.

———, ed. *Ralph Ellison and the Raft of Hope: A Political Companion to Invisible Man.* Lexington: University of Kentucky Press, 2004.

Morrison, Toni. "Ghosts in the House: How Toni Morrison Fostered a Generation of Black Writers." By Hilton Als. *New Yorker,* October 27, 2003. www.newyorker.com /magazine/2003/10/27/ghosts-in-the-house.

Moten, Fred. *In the Break: The Aesthetics of the Black Radical Tradition.* Minneapolis: University of Minnesota Press, 2003.

Mumford, Lewis. *The Golden Day: A Study in American Literature and Culture.* Boston: Beacon Press, 1957.

Murray, Albert. "Improvisation and the Creative Process." In *The Jazz Cadence of American Culture,* ed. Robert G. O'Meally, 111–13. New York: Columbia University Press, 1998.

———. "Ralph Ellison Remembered: An Interview with Albert Murray." By Xavier Nicholas. *Callaloo* 35, no. 1 (Winter 2011): 31–40.

Nadel, Alan. *Invisible Criticism: Ralph Ellison and the American Canon.* Iowa City: University of Iowa Press, 1989.

Naison, Mark. *Communists in Harlem during the Depression.* Urbana: University of Illinois Press, 1983.

Neal, Larry. "The Black Arts Movement." *Drama Review* 12, no. 4 (Summer 1968): 28–39.

———. "The Black Writer's Role: Ralph Ellison." *Liberator* 6, no. 1 (January 1966): 9–11.

———. "Ellison's Zoot Suit." In *Speaking for You,* ed. Benston, 105–24.

Nealton, Jeffrey T. "Refraining, Becoming-Black: Repetition and Difference in Amiri Baraka's *Blues People. Symplokē* 6, no. 1–2 (1998): 83–95.

Nelson, Cary. *Revolutionary Memory: Recovering the Poetry of the American Left.* New York: Routledge, 2001.

Nicholls, David G. *Conjuring the Folk: Forms of Modernity in African America.* Ann Arbor: University of Michigan Press, 2000.

Nocera, Joe. "Louis Armstrong, the Real Ambassador." *New York Times,* May 1, 2015.

O'Brien, John. *Interviews with Black Writers.* New York: Liveright, 1973.

O'Meally, Robert. *The Craft of Ralph Ellison.* Cambridge, Mass.: Harvard University Press, 1980.

———, ed. *Living with Music: Ralph Ellison's Jazz Writings.* New York: Modern Library, 2001.

Ostendorf, Berndt. "Ralph Waldo Ellison: Anthropology, Modernism and Jazz." In *New Essays on* Invisible Man, ed. Robert O'Meally, 95–118. Cambridge, U.K.: Cambridge University Press, 1988.

Park, Robert E. "Racial Assimilation in Secondary Groups with Particular Reference to the Negro." *American Journal of Sociology* 19, no. 5 (March 1914): 606–23.

———. Robert Park to Emmett Scott. Park-Washington Correspondence, Booker T. Washington Papers, March 1905, Library of Congress.

Park, Robert E., and Ernest W. Burgess. *Introduction to the Science of Sociology*. Chicago: University of Chicago Press, 1921.

Parker, Donald, and Warren Herenden. "KB and MC: An Interview." *Visionary Company* 2, no. 3 (1987): 87–98.

Parrish, Timothy L. *Ralph Ellison and the Genius of America*. Amherst: University of Massachusetts Press, 2012.

———. "Ralph Ellison, Finished and Unfinished: Aesthetic Achievements and Political Legacies." *Contemporary Literature* 48, no. 4 (Winter 2007): 639–64.

———. "Ralph Ellison, Kenneth Burke, and the Form of Democracy." *Arizona Quarterly* 51, no. 3 (Autumn 1995): 117–48.

———. "Ralph Ellison's Novel without Qualities." *Raritan* 34, no. 1 (Summer 2014): 91–117.

———. "Ralph Ellison's *Three Days:* The Aesthetics of Political Change." In *The New Territory*, ed. Conner and Morel, 194–217.

Patel, Cyrus R. K. *Emergent U.S. Literatures: From Multiculturalism to Cosmopolitanism in the Late Twentieth Century*. New York: New York University Press, 2014.

———. "Emersonian Strategies: Negative Liberty, Self-Reliance, and Democratic Individuality." *Nineteenth-Century Literature* 48, no. 4 (March 1994): 440–79.

Patterson, James T. Brown v. Board of Education: *A Civil Rights Milestone and Its Troubled Legacy*. New York: Oxford University Press, 2001.

Pease, Donald E. "Ralph Ellison and Kenneth Burke: The Nonsymbolizable (Trans) Action." *boundary 2* 30, no. 2 (Summer 2003): 65–96.

———. *Visionary Compacts: American Renaissance Writing in Cultural Context*. Madison: University of Wisconsin Press, 1987.

Pinkerton, Steve. "Ralph Ellison's Righteous Riffs: Jazz, Democracy, and the Sacred." *African American Review* 44, no. 1–2 (Spring–Summer 2011): 185–206.

Posnock, Ross. *Color and Culture: Black Writers and the Making of the Modern Intellectual*. Cambridge, Mass.: Harvard University Press, 1998.

———, ed. *The Cambridge Companion to Ralph Ellison*. Cambridge, U.K.: Cambridge University Press, 2005.

Rampersad, Arnold. *Ralph Ellison: A Biography*. New York: Alfred A. Knopf, 2007.

Reilly, John M. "Richard Wright Preaches the Nation: 12 Million Black Voices." *Black American Literature Forum* 16, no. 3 (Autumn 1982): 116–19.

Remnick, David. "Visible Man." *New Yorker,* March 14, 1994. www.newyorker.com /magazine/1994/03/14/visible-man.

Riccardi, Ricky. *What a Wonderful World: The Magic of Louis Armstrong's Later Years*. New York: Pantheon Books, 2011.

Rice, Herbert William. *Ralph Ellison and the Politics of the Novel*. Lanham, Md.: Lexington Books, 2003.

Rowell, Charles H. "An Interview with Larry Neal." *Callaloo* 23 (Winter 1985): 11–35.

Salisbury, David, and Casey Lartigue Jr., eds. *Educational Freedom in Urban America: Brown v. Board of Education after Half a Century.* Washington, D.C.: Cato Institute, 2004.

Sandel, Michael J. *Liberalism and the Limits of Justice.* New York: Cambridge University Press, 1982.

Sarat, Austin, ed. *Race, Law, and Culture: Reflections on Brown v. Board of Education.* New York: Oxford University Press, 1997.

Scherman, Tony. "The Omni-American." *American Heritage* 47, no. 5 (September 1996): 68–78.

Schrecker, Ellen. *Many Are the Crimes: McCarthyism in America.* Boston: Little, Brown, 1998.

Schryer, Stephen. *Fantasies of the New Class: Ideologies of Professionalism in Post–World War II American Fiction.* New York: Columbia University Press, 2011.

Scott, James C. *Weapons of the Weak: Everyday Forms of Peasant Resistance.* New Haven, Conn.: Yale University Press, 1985.

Shklar, Judith N. "Emerson and the Inhibitions of Democracy. *Political Theory* 18, no. 4 (November 1990): 601–14.

Shreve, Grant. "Ralph Ellison's *Three Days before the Shooting. . .* and the Implicit Morality of Form." In *The New Territory,* ed. Conner and Morel, 218–42.

Skodnick, Roy. "CounterGridlock: An Interview with Kenneth Burke." *All Area* 2 (1983): 4–32.

Smethurst, James Edward. *The Black Arts Movement. Literary Nationalism in the 1960s and 1970s.* Chapel Hill: University of North Carolina Press, 2005.

———. *Brick City Vanguard: Amiri Baraka, Black Music, Black Modernity.* Amherst: University of Massachusetts Press, 2020.

Spillers, Hortense. "Ellison's 'Usable Past': Toward a Theory of Myth." In *Speaking for You,* ed. Benston, 144–58.

Spivak, Gayatri Chakravorty. "Can the Subaltern Speak?" In *Marxism and the Interpretation of Culture,* ed. and introd. Cary Nelson and Lawrence Grossberg, 271–313. Urbana: University of Illinois Press, 1988.

Storch, Randi. *Red Chicago: American Communism at Its Grassroots, 1928–35.* Urbana: University of Illinois Press, 2007.

Sundquist, Eric J. "'We dreamed a dream': Ralph Ellison, Martin Luther King, Jr. & Barack Obama." *Daedalus* 140, no. 1 (Winter 2011): 108–24.

Taylor, Charles. "Cross-Purposes: The Liberal-Communitarian Debate." In *Liberalism and the Moral Life,* ed. Nancy L. Rosenblum, 159–82. Cambridge, Mass.: Harvard University Press, 1989.

Time. "Black America 1970." Vol. 95, no. 14 (April 6, 1970).

Tocqueville, Alexis de. *Democracy in America*. Ed. J. P. Mayer. Trans. George Lawrence. Garden City, N.Y.: Anchor-Doubleday, 1969.

———. *Democracy in America*. 2 vols. Ed. Eduardo Nolla. Trans. James T. Schleifer. Indianapolis: Liberty Fund, 2012.

Turner, Jack. "Awakening to Race: Ralph Ellison and Democratic Individuality." *Political Theory* 36, no. 5 (October 2008): 655–82.

Tuttleton, James W. "The Achievement of Ralph Ellison." *New Criterion* 14, no. 4 (December 1, 1995): 5–10.

Von Eschen, Penny M. *Satchmo Blows Up the World: Jazz Ambassadors Play the Cold War*. Cambridge, Mass.: Harvard University Press, 2004.

von Rautenfeld, Hans. "Thinking for Thousands: Emerson's Theory of Political Representation in the Public Sphere." *American Journal of Political Science* 49, no. 1 (January 2005): 184–97.

Wald, Alan M. *Trinity of Passion: The Literary Left and the Antifascist Crusade*. Chapel Hill: University of North Carolina Press, 2007.

———. *Writing from the Left: New Essays on Radical Culture and Politics*. London: Verso, 1994.

Warren, Kenneth. *So Black and Blue: Ralph Ellison and the Occasion of Criticism*. Chicago: University of Chicago Press, 2003.

Watts, Jerry Gafio. *Heroism and the Black Intellectual: Ralph Ellison, Politics, and Afro-American Intellectual Life*. Chapel Hill: University of North Carolina Press, 1994.

Weeks, Todd. "Sound and Meaning: Ralph Ellison's Record Collection." *American Studies* 54, no. 3 (2015): 161–68.

Weheliye, Alexander G. "'I Am I Be': The Subject of Sonic Afro-modernity." *boundary 2* 30, no. 2 (Summer 2003): 97–114.

West, Cornel. *The American Evasion of Philosophy: A Genealogy of Pragmatism*. Madison: University of Wisconsin Press, 1989.

Wimsatt, W. K., Jr. *The Verbal Icon: Studies in the Meaning of Poetry*. Lexington: University of Kentucky Press, 1954.

Wolin, Sheldon S. *Tocqueville between Two Worlds: The Making of a Political and Theoretical Life*. Princeton, N.J.: Princeton University Press, 2001.

Wright, John S. *Shadowing Ralph Ellison*. Jackson: University Press of Mississippi, 2006.

Wright, Richard. *12 Million Black Voices: A Folk History of the Negro in the United States*. New York: Viking Press, 1941.

Yaffe, David. *Fascinating Rhythm: Reading Jazz in American Writing*. Princeton, N.J.: Princeton University Press, 2006.

INDEX

Note: Locators given here in italics refer to images in the text.

abolitionists, 117

absurdism, 4, 39–40, 95, 126. *See also* chaos and fragmentation

"Achievement of Ralph Ellison, The" (Tuttleton), 3–4, 23

acknowledgment of past, 11, 69, 135, 184, 203, 223–24, 226–36. *See also* lived experiences

activism, 45, 85, 102, 119, 146, 154, 157–58, 212. *See also* New Breed artists and activists

advancement. *See* Black social mobility

Adventures of Huckleberry Finn, The (Twain), 18, 81, 173, 175, 229

aesthetics: and Burke, 70; craft as protest, 112; cultural lineage, 158–59, 230; form of the novel, 10; leftist ideology, 79; literary modernism, 71, 89, 108; New Negro movement, 62; over politics, 27, 49, 79, 150, 156, 212; sociology, 51–52; vernacular culture, 48, 67, 112–14

"Afternoon" (Ellison), 38

agency, 24, 38, 60, 80, 84, 103, 108, 119, 160, 175, 196, 231

Alain L. Locke Symposium, 141, 162–63

Albrecht, James, 183, 188

Alison, Cheryl, 19, 224

allegorical representations, 155, 212, 223, 226, 234

Allen, Danielle S., 12, 135, 206, 210

ambiguities of race, 184, 191, 219, 233–34. *See also* chaos and fragmentation

American culture: assimilation into, 60–61; Black presence in, 73, 134; Black subjectivity, 11; collective identity, 210–11; cultural affiliation over racial affiliation, 229–31; cultural appropriation, 1, 11–12, 121, 124; cultural integration, 130–31, 151–52, 230–31; culture theory of Ellison, 70; difficulties of self-definition, 42, 72–73; Ellison's intellectual eclecticism, 141–44; formation of, 1, 3, 9, 19, 31, 40, 69, 105, 152, 165–66, 189–98, 200; informed by race, 85, 105; invisibility, 187; labor, 33–35; leftist ideology, 15–17; origins of, 97; performative quality of music, 122–23; race relations, 68–69; relationship between individual and democracy, 168–74; second novel, 199–200, 228, 235; self-identification, 119, 157, 158; sociology, 51–52; unity and radicalism, 125–27; vernacular culture, 67. *See also* Black Americans/Black American culture; jazz

American Dilemma, An (Myrdal), 50, 56–61, 67, 68, 144

"American Dilemma, The" (Ellison), 144

American Evasion of Philosophy, The (West), 173, 178

American experiment, 1, 104, 176, 192–94, 224. *See also* democracy

American history, 33, 152, 187–88, 210, 217

American Review (journal), 23

"American Scholar, The" (Emerson), 13

American society, 13, 142, 172–75, 194, 205, 223–24

American Society of African Culture, 150

American Writing (Ellison), 38

Anderson, Paul Allen, 90, 99

anti-Black racism, 60

anti-Ellison criticism, 129–32, 136, 196–97

Antioch Review (journal), 50, 58, 127, 143–44

antiwar protests, 127

Armory Hall, 170

Armstrong, Louis, 85–86, 93–103, *94*, 105

art and culture, 101, 103, 126, 156

art and politics, 75, 161–64, 176. *See also* political theory and ideology

artist, role of the, 23, 74

artistic production, 36, 67, 78, 81, 91, 93–94, 98, 115, 121

"Art of Fiction, The" (Ellison), 133

assimilation, 60–61, 115, 121, 135–36, 154, 157, 193–96

Atlantic Monthly (magazine), 157–58, 210

Attitudes toward History (Burke), 83

audiences, 4, 95, 97–99, 102–4, 173

authenticity, 98–99, 115, 123, 144–45, 193

"Awakening to Race" (Turner), 12–13, 168, 198

back-to-Africa movements, 195

Baker, Houston A. Jr., 112–13, 159

Baldwin, James, 111, 132, 136, 158

Baraka, Amiri, 99–100, 129, 150–51, 152–55

Basie, Count, 88, 91

Beaumont, TX, 45

bebop, 14, 26, 86–103, 143–44, 154–56

Bell, Kevin, 88

Berry, Abner W., 16, 146

Between Literature and Science (Lepenies), 52–53

"Birthmark, The" (Ellison), 37–38

Bixler, Paul, 58–59

Black American airmen, 39–49, *41, 44*

Black Americans/Black American culture: abstracting from American culture, 132;

agency, 80, 231; in American culture, 4–5, 9, 125; and Armstrong, 86; artistic production, 121–22; authenticity, 123–24; Black American authors, 111–13, 230; Black and White responses to *Invisible Man,* 146–48; Black Belt thesis, 64–66; Black politics and Black literary production, 134–36; Black Power movement, 20–21, 33, 112–13, 133, 138, 151, 202, 212; *Blues People,* 99–100, 153; Communist Party USA, 10, 15–18, 33–35, 46, 64–66, 75, 79–80, 159–60; contributions, 3, 5, 42, 51–53, 74, 119, 122, 138; conversation about race, 157; cultural exchange, 74; cultural identity, 11–12, 213; cultural integration, 151–52; cultural position, 205; cultural production, 4–5, 35, 60–61, 87, 99–100, 110, 115–17, 123, 230–31; democratic individuality, 175; democratic possibility, 82; identities, 209–13; implications of integration in second novel, 227–28; improvisation, 105; influenced by American culture, 134; influence of, 103; integration, 209–13; and integration, 131; invisibility, 140; leftist ideology, 15–17, 45–47; limitations, 110; migration out of the South, 14–15, 45, 50, 53–55, 61, 63–66, 73–74; Mumford's Golden Day, 188; and Myrdal, 57–61; New Breed artists and activists, 127–29, 142, 145, 151–52, 156–57, 161–62; paternalism, 69, 185–87; pathologized, 46–48, 51, 59–60, 61; pluralism, 148–49; protest literature, 4, 31, 36, 81, 89, 110–12, 117–18, 136; race and nation, 31–32, 189–98; racial difference, 139–40; radical politics, 136, 160; radical writing, 162; self-determination, 49–51; self-identification, 72–73, 122–23; social mobility, 53–56, 183, 185; in *Three Days before the Shooting...,* 224–36. *See also* folk culture/folklore; jazz; music; vernacular culture

Black Arts movement, 20–21, 81, 98, 100, 127–29, 131–32, 155–57

Black Arts Movement, The (Smethurst), 21

"Black Arts Movement, The" (Neal), 127

Black Belt thesis, 64–66

Black Boy (Wright), 48, 69, 132

"Black Boys and Native Sons" (Howe), 111

Black consciousness, 33, 63, 66, 83, 102, 133–34, 138, 196

Black Fire (Neal), 128, 151, 157–58

Black identity, 51, 130, 144, 152, 200, 209–10

Black intellectualism, 7, 9–10, 32–33, 126–34, 154, 160–62

Black nationalism: cultural integration, 135, 151–52; effects of, 15; elimination of race, 189–90, 195; Ellison's bourgeois political stance, 142, 145; Ellison's counterbalance to, 147–50; Ellison's dismissal of, 5; Ellison's intellectual eclecticism, 142; Ellison's view of democracy, 166; identity politics, 202; in "In a Strange Country," 39; intentional isolation from, 205; interdependence, 64; migration out of the south, 64

Blackness, 90, 126, 132, 135, 161, 191–93, 195, 210. *See also* Black presence

Black Power movement, 20–21, 33, 112–13, 133, 138, 151, 202, 212

Black presence: Black consciousness, 196; cultural identity, 11; culture and politics, 165, 200; in "Flying Home," 40; folk culture/folklore, 161–62; in *Invisible Man*, 13; jazz, 87, 103; in "Mister Toussan," 38; race and nation, 68, 152; ritual, 74; separation from American literature, 177–78; separatism, 21; vernacular culture, 73–74

Black readers, 147

Black Skin, White Masks (Fanon), 20

Black social mobility, 14, 53–56, 145, 161, 183, 185

Black subjectivity, 11, 121, 133, 173–74, 184

Black theater, 155

Black World (journal), 129, 148–49, 154, 157–58

"Black Writer's Role, The" (Neal), 158

Bloom, Harold, 138

"Blueprint for Negro Writing" (Wright), 64, 66–67, 83

blues, 45, 61, 99–100, 113–14, 119, 123, 153–56

Blues People (Jones), 99–100, 152–57, 160

"Blues People" (Ellison), 144

Bluest Eye, The (Morrison), 155

Bolden, Charles Joseph "Buddy," 96

Botkin, Benjamin, 47, 78

Bradley, Adam, 19, 105, 199, 204–6, 212

"Brave Words for a Startling Occasion" (Ellison), 23, 135

Brick City Vanguard (Smethurst), 152–53

Brown, Lloyd L., 146

Brown v. the Board of Education of Topeka, Kansas, 6, 133, 201–2, 204–10, 220, 226, 230, 232

Burke, Kenneth, 31–32, 70, 74–83, 111, 118, 123, 235

Callahan, John, 83, 201–4, 224

Callaloo (magazine), 158

call-and-response style, 44, 123, 137–38, 223, 225–26, 231

Cambridge Companion to Ralph Ellison, The (Posnock), 11–12

Cane (Toomer), 147

Cannon, Steve, 8

canon, American literary, and multiculturalism, 6, 35, 52, 129, 134, 207

Carnegie Corporation, 57

"Change the Joke and Slip the Yoke" (Ellison), 143

chaos and fragmentation: conception of race, 208; context of race and culture, 191; form of the novel, 209–10, 219–20; jazz, 87, 95, 97–98; literary modernism, 71; oral tradition, 73; ritual, 235; in second novel, 221; threats to democracy, 197; view of culture, 97–98, 104, 105, 146, 230–32

Christian, Charlie, 87

citizenship, 135, 145, 208

Civil Rights Act of 1964, 6

civil rights movement, 195–96; Black consciousness, 133; Black intellectualism, 154; democracy, 20; Ellison's role in, 10, 119, 140–41; integration, 130–31; Ellison's second novel and, 137, 201, 212; social implications of *Brown v. Board,* 210; and Wright, 66

Civil War, 178, 188–89, 208–9, 215. *See also* Reconstruction

class: Black social mobility, 14, 53–56, 145, 161, 183, 185; class-based elements in Ellison, 35, 44; disengaging race from, 32, 46–47, 125, 197; identity, 51, 197; and Myrdal, 60; radical politics, 160; vernacular culture, 62–63, 67; in Wright, 139

Cold War years, 10, 49, 102, 230

collective identity, 13, 62, 142, 169, 210, 213

collective mobility, 55–56

collectivism, 40, 52, 111

color line, 12, 42, 138

Common Ground, 38

Communist Party USA, 10, 15–18, 33–35, 46, 64–66, 75, 79–80, 159–60

Communists in Harlem during the Depression (Naison), 80

communities. *See* public sphere

complexity. *See* chaos and fragmentation

computer-generated sequences in second novel, 234–35

Conner, Marc, 137

continuity for Black Americans, 82, 145, 205, 232

contributions of Black American culture, 3, 5, 42, 51–53, 74, 119, 122, 138

Crable, Bryan, 70

craft, 82–83, 105–6, 112–13, 118, 140, 142, 157–58

Craft of Ralph Ellison, The (O'Meally), 90

Crenshaw, Kimberlé, 197

Crisis (magazine), 146

Crisis of the Negro Intellectual, The (Cruse), 32–33

"Critical Change and Blues Continuity" (Baker), 159

Cross Section (Ellison), 39

Cruse, Harold, 32–33, 141

Cruz, Jon, 121

cultural exchange, 60, 74, 191

cultural identity, 11, 33. *See also* New Negro movement

cultural pluralism, 90, 98, 100, 130–31, 139, 144–48, 152, 156, 163, 165–66, 184, 189–98, 205–6, 232

cultural production, 4–5, 35, 60–61, 87, 99–100, 110, 115–17, 123, 230–31

Culture on the Margins (Cruz), 121

Daedalus and Icarus myth, 44–45

Daily Worker (newspaper), 15–16, 159

Davis, Miles, 92, 98, 102, 155

Davis, Ralph, 53

democracy: acknowledgment of past, 11, 135, 223–24, 226–36; class-based elements of Ellison, 35; cultural pluralism, 131, 156, 163, 165–66, 184, 189–98, 205–6, 232; cultural production, 61, 122; democratic liberalism, 36, 52, 82, 107, 119; democratic possibility, 82, 99; Ellison's political theory, 152, 161, 206; erasure, 231; form of the novel, 11, 27, 133, 219–20, 224–30; function of the novel, 133; idealized vision, 43, 111, 136, 154, 173, 183–84, 193; individualism, 12–13, 90–91, 98, 165–72, 175–76, 193–97, 232; jazz, 85, 87; music as metaphor, 108, 114; swing-era musicians, 97; vernacular culture, 80

Democracy in America (Tocqueville), 169–70

demonstration, Communist Party USA, 207

demonstrations, 33

Denby, David, 4

Denning, Michael, 78

desegregation, 5, 209–10, 248n14

Detroit, MI, 45, 58

diasporic movements, 142, 161

difference, recognition of, 195

Direction (magazine), 37, 78, 83

disenfranchisement, 66, 184

Dixieland ensembles, 101

double consciousness, 119, 134, 151, 162, 174

Double Victory initiative, 35

Douglass, Frederick, 115–23, *116*

Du Bois, W. E. B., 119–21, *120*, 134, 174

Dutchman (Jones), 155

education, 13, 17, 59, 109, 181, 185

egalitarianism, 57, 169, 171–72, 176, 191–92

Eliot, T. S., 71–72, 74, 78, 81–82, 111–13, 118, 122–23

Ellington, Duke, 97, 103, 105, *106*

Ellison, Ralph Waldo: Alison on, 19; American culture, 4–5; antagonism toward sociology, 51–53, 57–59, 68–69, 99, 107, 155; bebop, 14, 26, 86–103, 143–44, 154–56; Black American airmen in "Flying Home," 39–45; Black Arts movement, 81; Black humanity, value of, 190; Black intellectualism, 7, 9–10, 32–33, 126–34, 154, 160–62; Bradley on, 19; and Burke, 70, 74–83; canonization, 6; class-based elements of, 35; compositional aspirations of second novel, 224–36; compositional process, 19; conception of the novel, 10–11; craft, 82–83, 105–6, 112–13, 118, 140, 142, 157–58; criticism of, 129–32, 136, 196–97; cultural characterization, 22–23; cultural identity, 11–12; democratic individualism, 12–13, 197; Denby on, 4; Depression-era work, 15; early life of, 14–17; and Emerson, 165–78; episodic writing and revision, 199–206; and Fanon, 20; Foley on, 10, 15, 18, 32, 35–36, 69; formation of national culture, 9, 19, 31, 40, 69; Golden Day revision, 188–89; and Hemingway, 74–75, 106–7; on identity and integration, 131; impact of *Invisible Man,* 18–19; intellectual and ideological transition, 48–50; Jackson on, 17; jazz, 104–5, 111; "Jazz: The Experimenters" broadcast, 88–89; leftist ideology, 5, 31–33, 39–49, 159–64; literary modernism, 70–71, 111; lived experience, 11; and Locke, 162–64; migration element in, 61–62; Morel on, 8–9; music collection, 86–87, 90; music writing, 85–94, 103–4, 143–44; and Myrdal, 57–61, 144; and Neal, 126–29, 158–62; and Park, 56; political characterization, 21–22; political theory and ideology, 126–35, 141–42, 152, 161, 163–64, 206; Posnock on, 11–12; race, 190; race and democracy, 104, 165–66, 189–98, 224; race and nation, 138–39; radical Black ideology, 125–26; response to limitations, 4, 9; Rice on, 9, 15; on role of the novelist, 215; Schweitzer Professorship, 23–24; separatism, 21, 81–82, 126, 130, 135–36, 145, 152; short stories, 36–40; social immobility, 12; transition in work and reception, 135–37; Turner on, 12–13; at Tuskegee Institute, 105–7, 139, 206–7; Tuttleton on, 3–4, 23; and Twain, 81; vernacular culture, 62–63, 66–67; view of Black self-determination, 49–51; view of society, 8; view of technique, 109; war years, 36–40; Watts on, 9–10; and white writers, 4; Works Progress Administration folklore project, 73–74; and Wright, 64–66, 108. See also *Invisible Man* (Ellison)

"Ellison's Hemingways" (Hochman), 107

"Ellison's 'Usable Past'" (Spillers), 137

"Embrace of Entropy, The" (Bell), 88

Emerson, Ralph Waldo, 13, 138, 165–78, *167*, 178–89

"Emerson and the Inhibitions of Democracy" (Shklar), 169

entertainment and expression, 98–99, 103

episodic writing and revision, 199–206
epistemology, 115
erasure, 231
Erskine, Albert, 96
Essays: Second Series (Emerson), 170
establishment theater, 159
exceptionalism, 98, 195–96, 231
exclusion, cultural, 114

"Failing Prophet and Falling Stock" (Baker),
  112–13
familial associations, 229
Fanon, Frantz, 20, 141–42
Fantasies of the New Class (Schryer), 52, 69
Fascinating Rhythm (Yaffe), 86
fascism, 16, 32, 35, 46, 75, 125
Faulkner, William, 144, 217, 222
Federal Writers' Project, 47, 127
First League of American Writers' Conference,
  77, 83
"Flying Home" (Ellison), 36, 39–45, 47, 48,
  50, 61, 63
Flying Home and Other Stories (Ellison), 83
Foley, Barbara, 10, 15, 18, 32, 35–36, 69, 206
folk culture/folklore: Black presence, 162;
  cultural exchange, 60; and Eliot, 71–72,
  78; vs. entertainment, 99; frontier-born
  evocation of, 157; New Criticism, 148;
  sociological approaches to race, 50–51, 53;
  vernacular culture, 45–46, 62–64; WPA
  project, 73–74
"Folklore and Folksay" (Partnow and Botkin),
  78
form of the novel: Ellison's conception of,
  10–11, 209–10, 214, 228, 230; engagement
  with democracy, 11, 27, 133, 219–20,
  224–30; episodic writing and revision,
  199–206; Ellison's second novel, 213–15,
  224–30; symbolic action, 77
Forrest, Leon, 190
fragmentation. *See* chaos and fragmentation
Frazier, E. Franklin, 56–57

freedom, 42, 87–89, 105, 110, 114, 146, 202,
  234–35
Freedom (newspaper), 146–47
Freud, Sigmund, 76–77
frontier-born version of Black vernacular,
  156–57
frontier opportunity, 234–35
Fukuyama, Francis, 197

Genius (Bloom), 138
geographic region and lived experiences, 196.
  See also migration out of the South
German-Soviet Nonaggression Pact, 66
Gillespie, Dizzy, 95, 98, 143–44
Go Down, Moses (Faulkner), 222
Going to the Territory (Ellison), 6, 8
Golden Day, 185, 187–89
Golden Day, The (Mumford), 188
Griffith, D. W., 144–45
group identity and experience, 53, 57, 146,
  196–97, 211

Harlem, NY: Black nationalism, 33; civil
  conflict, 46; early life of Ellison, 14–15,
  17, 159; lived experiences in, 196; New
  Negro movement, 55; in "The Way It Is,"
  144; vernacular culture in, 47. *See also*
  migration out of the South
"Harlem Is Nowhere" (Ellison), 46
Harper's Magazine, 8, 159–60, 184–85
"Haverford Statement" (Ellison), 223
Hemingway, Ernest, 74–75, 106–9, 111,
  112–13, 118
Henderson, Clark, 77–78
Heroism and the Black Intellectual (Watts),
  9–10, 175–76
"Hidden Name and Complex Fate" (Ellison),
  109, 166
historical denial, 195
history as tool for consciousness, 55–56, 83,
  137–38. *See also* Black consciousness
Hochman, Brian, 107

"Homage to Duke Ellington on His Birthday" (Ellison), 103

Horizon (journal), 39, 127

House in Washington, DC, where Lincoln died, *201*

Howe, Irving, 81, 111–12, 119, 137, 140, 142, 146

Hue and Cry (McPherson), 157–58

Huggins, Nathan, 141

Hughes, Langston, 10, 15, 78, 80, 108, 112, 147, 159

Hyman, Stanley Edgar, 39, 142–43

identities: Black American expressions of, 191–94, 209–13; collective, 142, 169, 210; distinct from white cultural space, 161; formation of, 194–98; music, 111, 114; perceptions of white Americans, 182; in the public sphere, 133; racial categories, 184; second novel's revisions, 202–3; second novel's response to contemporary crises of, 225–36; self-identity/ identification, 72–73; vernacular culture, 80–81

Identity (Fukuyama), 197

ideology: art contextualizing politics, 163–64; Black Arts movement, 132; Black music, 99; Black nationalist agenda, 147; craft over, 20, 25, 82, 158; Ellison's resistance to racialized, 81; Emerson's in *Invisible Man,* 185; identity, 142, 211; modernity, 66; over art, 154; race, 140–42; sociology, 53. *See also* leftist ideology

immigrant culture, 53

improvisation, 88–91, 101, 105, 108–11, 122, 155

"In a Strange Country" (Morel), 12, 39, 166

individual agency, 80, 108, 175

individualism/individual identity, 13, 33, 52, 98, 110, 165–72, 175–76, 182–83, 193–97, 232

"Indivisible Man" (McPherson), 210

industrialism, 50, 188

inequality, 160

integration: as aesthetic process, 223; costs and benefits of desegregation, 209; crisis of faith in the possibilities of, 225–28; cultural, 85, 129, 142; cultural and artistic, 128–31, 151–52; cultural appropriation, 12; Ellison's intellectual eclecticism, 129, 142; external cultural events, 220; radical thought, 126, 163; vs. separatist nationalism, 135

intentional fallacy, 150

interracial conflict, 56

In the Break (Moten), 89–90

"Into Nationalism, Out of Parochialism" (Neal), 159

intra-racial agency, 84

Introduction to the Science of Sociology (Park), 53

invisibility: ambiguities of race, 184; Black American presence, 208; Black and white reviewers, 146; of Black contributions, 138; expression of, 95–96; external events, 220; in "Flying Home," 40–42; relationship of Black and white racialized experience, 136; in second novel, 202–3; and social movements, 195; trope of, 151–52; Trueblood character, 187

Invisible Criticism (Nadel), 173, 183, 188

Invisible Man (Ellison), 6–13; anti-Ellison criticism, 129; and Armstrong, 86, 95–99; Black and white reviewers, 146–48; Black intellectualism, 32–33, 126–27; and Bolden, 96; boomerang of history, 231; and Burke, 78–79; democratic individualism, 165; and Douglass, 118–19; Ellison's literary stature, 142; and Emerson, 168, 173–74, 177–89; episodic writing and revision, 199–200, 202–6; improvisation, 88; integration of external events, 220; intellectual and ideological transition of Ellison, 48–50; "Introduction to the

Invisible Man (Ellison) (*continued*)
Thirtieth-Anniversary Edition of," 20, 61, 132–34; leftist ideology, 17–18; legacy of, 21–22; LeRoy passages, 18–19; literary modernism, 70–71; and Morrison, 155; and Moten, 89–90; music as metaphor, 107; narrative pattern, 224; Neal on, 104–5; New Criticism, 150; personal and cultural histories, 103; post-segregation era, 208–9; Rampersad on, 212; reframing critical interpretations of, 153; relevance of, 211; shifting ideologies, 161–62; short stories published before publication of, 36–40; sociology, 59; struggle to overcome the past, 222–23; three-dimensional character development, 233; universalism associated with epilogue of, 3, 20, 81–82; vernacular culture, 47
Iowa Review (journal), 136, 213

Jackson, Lawrence, 17, 39–40, 58, 75, 80, 107, 127
jam sessions, 104, 109–10
jazz: and Armstrong, 85–86, 93–103, *94*, 105; Black musical production, 121–22; and Hemingway, 107; influence on Ellison, 146; literary modernism, 104–13; modern jazz, 87–104; and Parker, 90–98, *92*, 100, 103, 143–44, 154–55; politicization of, 89; postwar critique of by Ellison, 85–104; and self-identification, 122–23; as transhistorical cultural expression, 154–56. *See also* bebop; swing-era music
"Jazz: The Experimenters" (television broadcast), 88–89
Jim Crow: binary view of race, 70; cultural production, 35; legacy of segregation, 152, 178; legal end of, 208–13; race and the war effort, 16, 40; "That I Had Wings" (Ellison), 38; vision of transracial democracy, 197; worldview of Ellison, 129, 138, 143

Johnson, Charles S., 55
Johnson, Lyndon B., 22, 127, 136, 212
Jones, LeRoi. *See* Baraka, Amiri
Juneteenth (Ellison), 7, 219
"Justice for Ralph Ellison" (Denby), 4

Keck, Charles, *180*
Kelley, Robin D. G., 62–63
Kenneth Burke and Ralph Ellison (Crable), 70
Killens, John Oliver, 146–47
King, Martin Luther, Jr., 22, 129–30, 138, 212, 217, 228
"King of the Bingo Game" (Ellison), 36, 38, 47

labor, 17, 33–35, 37, 68
League of American Writers, 74–75, 77–78, 83, 160
leftist ideology: aesthetics, 79; Black American culture, 15–17; Black critics, 146–47; Black self-determination, 49–51; Brotherhood section of *Invisible Man,* 178; and Burke, 76–81; democratic individualism, 195–96; Ellison's relation to, 10, 31–36, 45, 66–67, 69–70, 82, 118–19, 125–26, 159–64; in "Flying Home," 39–45; in *Invisible Man,* 17–18, 33; New Deal politics, 60; stereotyped representations of Black Americans, 5
legal segregation. *See* Jim Crow
Lepenies, Wolf, 52–53
liberal democracy, 196
Liberator (magazine), 157–58
Lifting the Veil of Ignorance (Keck), *180*
Lincoln Memorial, *216,* 234
literary form. *See* form of the novel
literary modernism: aesthetics, 71, 89, 108; art inseparable from politics, 134–35; culture reflected through, 89; Ellison's embrace of, 4, 32, 49, 118; form of the novel, 10–11; and Hemingway, 107; in *Invisible Man,* 70–71; jazz, 108–13

literary naturalism, 4, 49–50, 69, 89, 110, 136

lived experiences: commitment to radicalism, 36; cultural identity, 11; in "Flying Home," 40; form of the novel, 209–10; in *Invisible Man,* 32, 182, 202–3; modernism, 111; music, 122; and Myrdal, 58; race as, 191; related to geographic regions, 196

Living with Music (O'Meally), 100

"Living with Music" (Ellison), 111, 122

Locke, Alain, 55, 78, 147, 162–63

Lost Generation writers, 107

lyricism, 95, 98, 114

Mackey, Nathaniel, 153

"Mapping the Margins" (Crenshaw), 197

marginalization, 73, 121, 154, 192

Marxism, 5, 32, 46, 49–50, 64–67, 69, 76–78, 80, 82, 160–62

masking/performative masks, 93–94, 98, 103, 236. *See also* invisibility

Massachusetts Review (journal), 23

Masses and Mainstream (magazine), 146

McPherson, James Alan, 157–58, 211

Messmer, David, 118

middle class, 52, 55, 57, 62, 67, 151

migration out of the South, 14–15, 45, 50, 53–55, 61, 63–66, 73–74

minstrelsy, 93, 98, 187

"Mister Toussan" (Ellison), 38, 84

Mobile, AL, 45

modernity, 42, 47, 62–64, 66, 103–4, 113, 121–22, 182, 232

Montgomery bus boycott, 217

Morel, Lucas, 8–9, 12, 39, 166

Morrison, Toni, 129, 155

Moten, Fred, 89–90

multiculturalism, 134, 196

Mumford, Lewis, 187–89

Murray, Albert: Alain L. Locke Symposium, 141; and Emerson, 166; ideas of jazz and democracy, 97, 113–14, 122; Newport Jazz Festival, 90–91; second novel, 204, 227–29, 234; *Trading Twelves,* 7; vernacular culture, 72–73

music, 89, 99, 108–24, 143, 153; bebop, 14, 26, 86–103, 143–44, 154–56; *Blues People,* 153–56; Ellison's record collection, 86–87, 90; jazz and vernacular culture, 85–86; language, 122; limitation(s), 235; as metaphor, 107; modern jazz, 87–104; music writing, 85–94, 103–4, 143–44; in *Shadow and Act,* 143–44; sorrow songs, 115–21; structure in Ellison, 104–5; swing-era music, 14, 97–98, 100–101, 143–44

Myrdal, Alva, 57

Myrdal, Gunnar, 48, 50–51, 56–61, 57, 67–69, 144

"Myth of a 'Negro Literature,' The" (Jones), 150–51

myth(s), 44–45, 71, 77, 123, 129. *See also* folk culture/folklore

Nadel, Alan, 173, 183, 188

Naison, Mark, 80

Narrative of the Life of Frederick Douglass (Douglass), 115–18, 123

Nation (magazine), 146

national identity, 9, 13, 98, 197, 202

nationalist ideology. *See* Black nationalism

National Jazz Museum, 86

Nation of Islam, 196

Native Son (Wright), 15, 48, 63, 108, 111, 132, 147, 158

Neal, Larry, 104–5, 126–29, 148–49, 151, 158–62

"Negro American, The" (conference), 130–31

Negro Digest (journal), 127, 157

Negro History (magazine), 146

"Negro in Fiction, The" (Hughes and Locke), 78

Negro Quarterly (journal), 15–17, 46–47, 49, 63, 68, 161

New Breed artists and activists, 127–29, 142, 145, 151–52, 156–57, 161–62

New Challenge (journal), 15, 64, 67, 127

New Criticism, 52, 82, 148–50

New Deal era, 52, 60

"New England Reformers" (Emerson), 170

New Leader (journal), 112

New Masses (magazine), 15–16, 36–38, 46, 49, 78, 82–83, 127, 144

New Negro, The (Locke), 55, 162–63

New Negro movement, 3–4, 55, 61–67, 162–63

New Orleans, LA, 100–101

Newport Jazz Festival, 90–91

New York Age (magazine), 147

New York Herald Book Week, 148

New York Herald Tribune (newspaper), 146

New York Review of Books, 99, 153

New York Times (newspaper), 102, 127, 146

New York University, 3, 23–24

"Night Talk" (Ellison), 135–36, 213

Nixon, Richard M., 212

normative whiteness, 13, 166

"Notes on Deconstructing 'The Folk'" (Kelley), 62–63

novel. *See* form of the novel

novelist, roles of the, 10–11, 23, 49, 104, 206, 215, 228–32

"Of Individualism in Democratic Countries" (Tocqueville), 170

Oklahoma City, OK, 4, 14–15, 72, 88, 117, 121, 139, 156

Oklahoma passages in second novel, 234–35

O'Meally, Robert G., 89–90, 100

"On Bird, Bird-Watching" (Ellison), 144

"On Bird, Bird-Watching and Jazz" (Ellison), 93

"On Initiation Rites and Power" (Ellison), 71, 177

oppression and discrimination, 31, 36, 50, 56, 61, 63, 110–12, 141–42, 160

oral tradition, 73

Ostendorf, Berndt, 95

otherness, 154–56

Pan-Africanism, 5, 21, 145, 152

Park, Robert, 53–57, 64

Parker, Charlie, 90–98, 92, 100, 103, 143–44, 154–55. *See also* bebop

Parrish, Timothy, 6, 135, 137, 206, 214–15

Parsons, Talcott, 51

Partisan Review (journal), 38, 127, 143

Partnow, Hyde, 78

paternalism, 32, 69, 145, 182–83, 185–87

Pease, Donald, 52

performance, 88–98, 101–4, 109–11, 114, 121–23, 194. *See also* masking/performative masks

Phylon (magazine), 147

Pinkerton, Steve, 90, 97, 104–5

Plainfield, MA, 22, 211

"Political Consequences of the Social State of the Anglo- Americans" (Tocqueville), 169–70

political theory and ideology: art inseparable from politics, 134; culture theory, 70; of Ellison, 126–35, 141–42, 161–64; engagement with, 132–33; folk culture/ folklore, 46, 63; identity, 131; music, 89, 156; vernacular culture, 38. *See also* activism; leftist ideology

popular culture, 14, 88, 95, 101, 124, 148

Popular Front, 32–33, 36, 49, 75, 78–80

Posnock, Ross, 11–12

post-racialism, 193

postwar jazz, 90–91, 97, 104–5

Progressive era, 52

protest literature, 4, 31, 36, 81, 89, 110–12, 117–18, 136

protests, 45, 127

provincialism, 86, 130

public sphere, 52, 133, 168–69, 209–10, 232

Quarterly Review of Literature (journal), 135–36, 213

race: acknowledgment of past, 11, 69, 135, 184, 203, 223–24, 226–36; ambiguities of, 184, 191, 219, 233–34; American cultural unity, 125–27; American history, 33, 73; Black and white responses to Ellison, 146–48; Black intellectualism, 7, 9–10, 32–33, 126–34, 154, 160–62; and Burke, 76; consciousness, 23, 55, 62; cultural affiliation replacing racial affiliation, 229; cultural attitudes of racial injustice, 166, 205; cultural lineage, 230; cultural production, 60–61; culture informed by, 105; democracy in the formation of national culture, 200; disengaging class from, 32, 46–47, 125, 197; Emerson, 171–73, 183–84; identity, 126, 144, 176, 202, 205, 210–11, 213; identity anxieties, 172, 202; implications of integration in second novel, 223, 227–28; invisible presence of Black people, 18; labor, 33–37; leftist ideology, 49–51; metaphor of national aspiration, 213; and Myrdal, 57–58; and nation, 22, 31–32, 70, 85, 125, 138–39, 148; and Park, 53–57; political ideology, 140–42; protest and racial conflict, 45–46; racial difference, 139–40; relationship between race and American culture, 165–66, 189–98; separatism, 136; transracial agency, 83–84; war effort, 16

racism, 31, 35, 40, 46, 93, 102, 132

radicalism: Black self-determination, 49–51; and Burke, 76–77, 80; Ellison's association with, 10, 15–20, 31–36, 125–28, 160; reframing critical interpretations of *Invisible Man,* 33, 153; sublimation of art and politics, 162–63; and Wright, 158

Ralph Ellison (Jackson), 17, 39–40, 58, 75, 80, 107, 127

Ralph Ellison (Rampersad), 9, 22, 49, 58–59, 80, 137

Ralph Ellison and the Genius of America (Parrish), 6, 135

Ralph Ellison and the Politics of the Novel (Rice), 9, 15, 125

Ralph Ellison and the Raft of Hope (Morel), 8–9

"Ralph Ellison as Proletarian Journalist" (Foley), 69

Ralph Ellison in Progress (Bradley), 19, 199, 204

"Ralph Ellison's Music Lessons" (Anderson), 99

"Ralph Ellison's Novel without Qualities" (Parrish), 206

"Ralph Ellison's Righteous Riffs" (Pinkerton), 90, 97, 104–5

"Ralph Ellison's *Three Days*" (Parrish), 214–15

"Ralph Ellison's Zoot Suit" (Neal), 104–5, 129, 158

"Ralph Waldo Ellison" (Ostendorf), 95

Rampersad, Arnold, 9, 22, 49, 58–59, 80, 129, 137–39, 212

Raphael, Lennox, 8

"Reading Ralph Ellison" (Conner), 137

realism, 37–38

"Recent Negro Fiction" (Ellison), 36, 83, 108

Reconstruction: Black life in America, 50, 134; and canonization, 6; democratic possibility, 82, 119; dispossession of Black Americans, 178; failures and disappointments of, 47; *Invisible Man,* 182; Jacksonian democracy, 173; legal segregation, 208; protests, 45; sociology, 52, 59; vision of transracial democracy, 197

recording technology, 121–22

representative figures, 169

Representative Men (Emerson), 169

Requiem for a Nun (Faulkner), 222

revision, 105, 199–206

"Revolutionary Symbolism in America" (Burke), 77

rhetorical production, 118

"Rhetoric of Hitler's Battle, The" (Burke), 75–76, 78–79

Riccardi, Ricky, 102

Rice, Herbert William, 9, 15, 125

"Richard Wright and Negro Fiction" (Ellison), 11

"Richard Wright and Recent Negro Fiction" (Ellison), 83

"Richard Wright's Blues" (Ellison), 143

Right, political, 68. *See also* leftist ideology

Riley and Buster stories, 38

ritual(s), 31, 74, 95–97, 110, 122–23, 129, 231, 235

Rowell, Charles, 158–59

Rushing, Jimmy, 91

Satchmo Blows Up the World (Von Eschen), 102

"Saying Yes and Saying No" (Albrecht), 183, 188

Schryer, Stephen, 52, 69

Second American Writers' Congress, 74–75

second novel. See *Three Days before the Shooting…* (Ellison)

segregation, 208–12; cultural pluralism, 139–40; democratic possibility, 82; effect on cultural production, 35, 130–31, 133; Emerson's democratic ideal, 178; invisibility, 152; *Invisible Man*, 136–37; and Myrdal, 58; racial activism, 45; second novel, 217–19; self-identity/identification, 72; social immobility, 12; war effort, 16. See also *Brown v. the Board of Education of Topeka, Kansas*

self-determination, 38, 49, 66, 109, 133, 135

self-identity/identification, 38–42, 72–73, 110, 119, 122–23, 157, 161, 229

self-reliance, 13, 171, 176, 183–84, 186

"Self-Reliance" (Emerson), 168–69, 183

separatism, 21, 81–82, 126, 130, 135–36, 145, 152

Shadow and Act (Ellison), 6, 16, 19–20, 80, 131, 142–47, 154, 162, 203

"Shadow and the Act, The" (Ellison), 144

Shadowing Ralph Ellison (Wright), 6, 48

shift in literary and political partisanship, 162

Shklar, Judith, 169

slavery: Black life in America, 134; cultural and artistic agency, 231; democratic possibility, 82; and Douglass, 115–17; in "Flying Home," 42, 47; Golden Day revision, 188–89; New Negro movement, 62; paternalism, 69; reconciling with chaotic present, 222–24; vision of transracial democracy, 195–97

"Slick Gonna Learn" (Ellison), 37, 47, 84

Smethurst, James, 21, 152–53

So Black and Blue (Warren), 69, 190, 210–11

social change, 50, 68, 82, 84, 124, 128, 138

social critique, 135

social immobility, 12

social science, 51–53, 59–60, 144

social transformation, 83–84

"The Society," 170

Society and Solitude (Emerson), 168

sociology, 50–53, 55, 58–59, 68–69, 99, 107, 152–53, 155, 178

"Song of Innocence, A" (Ellison), 136, 213

sonic production, 118

sorrow songs, 115–21

Souls of Black Folk (Du Bois), 119–21, 134

"Sounds and Meaning" (Weeks), 86–87

Southern Review (journal), 149

Spillers, Hortense, 137

Sprague, Morteza Drexel, 207, 209

State Department, 102

stereotypes, 5, 51–52, 55, 93, 110, 132

"Stern Discipline, A" (Ellison), 159–60, 184–85

swing-era music, 14, 97–98, 100–101, 143–44

symbolic action, 77, 80, 82, 132–33, 233
systemic privileges, 193

Talking to Strangers (Allen), 12, 135, 206, 210
technique, artistic, 36, 105–6, 108–10
technology, 101, 121–22
territory bands, 88, 143–44
"That I Had Wings" (Ellison), 38
"That Same Pain, That Same Pleasure"
    (Ellison), 143
"The Way It Is" (Ellison), 16, 144
"Thinking for Thousands" (von Rautenfeld),
    168
Third League of American Writers'
    Conference, 75–76, 78–79
Thomas, W. I., 53
Thompson, James, 8
Three Days before the Shooting. . . (Ellison),
    232–35; ambiguities of race, 233–34;
    anticipation for, 22–24, 142; art over
    politics, 78; Black subjectivity, 11; and
    Burke, 70; Callahan's introduction to,
    201; call-and-response style in, 44,
    137–38, 223, 225–26, 231; computer-
    generated sequences, 234–35; Ellison's
    estrangement from Black intellectualism,
    135–38; episodic writing and revision,
    105, 199–206; experimentation during
    war years, 36–37; form of novel as
    democratic, 224–33; ideas present in short
    fiction, 42; invisibility, 202, 220–21; jazz,
    103–4; masking, 236; McPherson on, 210;
    migration element in, 61; modernism, 71;
    narrative form, 215–20, 224; Parrish on,
    214–15; posthumous release of, 7; post-
    segregation era, 211–13; progress of, 213–
    15; race and class, 47; Rockmore episode,
    223–24; role of the novelist, 214–15;
    Watts's critique of, 9
Time magazine, 136, 191
Tocqueville, Alexis de, 169–70

Tomorrow (journal), 38–39, 127
Trading Twelves (Ellison), 7
Transcendentalism, 171–75
"Transforming Action" (Henderson), 77–78
"Trumpets, Horns, and Typewriters"
    (Messmer), 118
Turner, Jack, 12–13, 168, 198
Tuskegee Airmen, 40–42, *41, 44*
Tuskegee Institute, 14, 53–55, 59, 71, 75,
    105–7, 139, 206–7
Tuttleton, James, 3–4, 23
Twain, Mark, 18, 74, 81, 173, 175, 229
12 Million Black Voices (Wright), 63–64, 66
"Twentieth-Century Fiction and the Black
    Mask of Humanity" (Ellison), 143, 188

unity, 37, 43, 111, 125, 171, 198. *See also* chaos
    and fragmentation
universalism: of Black vernacular, 74;
    conception of self-reliance, 176, 186;
    Emerson, 173, 176; in epilogue of *Invisible
    Man,* 3, 20, 81–82; of *Invisible Man,* 138,
    146; New Criticism, 150; universalist
    aesthetics, 36, 79, 140
urban America: chaos reflected in, 98;
    cultural advancement, 55–56; migration
    out of the South, 14–15, 45, 50, 53–55, 61,
    63–66, 73–74; vernacular culture, 64, 67,
    74
"Uses of Great Men" (Emerson), 169

vernacular culture, 156; aesthetics, 48, 67,
    112–14; and Armstrong, 85, 93, 103; and
    Burke, 80; cultural reconciliation, 108; and
    Douglass, 118; in "Flying Home," 44–45; as
    framework for artistic expression, 77–78;
    in Harlem, 47; modernity, 62–63; music,
    119, 121–22, 156; and national culture,
    85, 152; over political ideology, 38; self-
    identity/identification, 72–73; sociology,
    51–53; universality of, 74

Visionary Compacts (Pease), 52
Von Eshcen, Penny, 102
von Rautenfeld, Hans, 168
Voting Rights Act of 1965, 6, 136

Warren, Kenneth, 69, 190, 210–11
Washington, Booker T., 14, 53–55, *54*, 59, 139, *180*, 181
"Waste Land, The" (Eliot), 71
Watts, Jerry Gafio, 9–10, 175–76
Weeks, Todd, 86–87
West, Cornel, 173, 178
"What America Would Be Like Without Blacks" (Ellison), 191, 194, 196
"(What Did I Do To Be So) Black and Blue," 87, 96
white Americans: American identity, 189–98; audience, 96, 98–99, 102, 117, 137, 148–50, 196; Black contributions, 138; Black identities distorted by perceptions of, 178; Black subjectivity, 184; critics, 166; cultural identity, 11–12; cultural space, 161; democratic individuality, 166; ideologies and stereotyping, 5; influence on Black communities, 56–57; philanthropists at Tuskegee Institute, 59; segregation, 205; separatism, 126, 145; shared history, 134, 139; white supremacy, 145, 178, 197, 227; white writers, 4, 9, 108, 112–13
Worker (magazine), 146
working class, 46, 49, 51, 63–64, 67–68, 125, 195

Works Progress Administration folklore project, 73–74
"World and the Jug, The" (Ellison), 112, 119, 140, 175
World War II, 16, 35–36, 45–46, 50, 58, 61, 63–66, 84
Wrestling with the Left (Foley), 10, 15, 18, 32, 206
Wretched of the Earth, The (Fanon), 141
Wright, John, 6, 48
Wright, Richard: *Black Boy,* 48, 69, 132; Black radicalism, 158; "Blueprint for Negro Writing," 64, 83; canonization, 6; Communist Party USA, 66; craft, 105–6, 112–13; Ellison's apprentice period, 15, 48; Ellison's break with, 81, 111–13, 119; folk culture, 63–64; and Hemingway, 74–75; ideological influence, 132, 157–58; leftist ideology, 5, 49, 80, 159; literary naturalism, 69; Marxist ideology, 66–67; *Native Son,* 15, 48, 63, 108, 111, 132, 147, 158; naturalistic representations of race, 50, 53; New Negro movement, 62, 64; photo, *65;* self-determination, 66–67; *Shadowing Ralph Ellison,* 6, 48; *12 Million Black Voices,* 63–64, 66; vernacular culture, 44–45, 63, 67–68; white writers, 108; Writers' Congress, 78
"Writer and Politics, The," 78–79
"Writing Underground" (Alison), 19, 224

Yaffe, David, 86